CIRCUITOUS JOURNEYS

Circuitous Journeys

Modern Spiritual Autobiography

by

DAVID J. LEIGH

FORDHAM UNIVERSITY PRESS
New York
2000

CONTENTS

ACKNOWLEDGMENTS

I would like to express my gratitude to colleagues and friends who have helped with various versions of the manuscript: Philip Boroughs, Hamida Bosmajian, Jeffrey Cain, Peter Ely, John Hawley, Tibor Horvath, Patrick Howell, Justin Kelly, Janet Blumberg, Mike MacDonald, Elizabeth Morelli, and Andrew Tadie. It goes without saying that John Mahoney of Boston College and Mary Beatrice Schulte of Fordham University Press have been invaluable in the final editing process. Finally, I cannot be thankful enough for the responses by hundreds of students in my classes on autobiography at Gonzaga University and Seattle University.

Earlier versions of chapters three and five respectively have appeared in *The Riddle of Joy: G. K. Chesteron and C. S. Lewis*, ed. Michael H. McDonald and Andrew A. Tadie (Grand Rapids, MI: Eerdmans, 1989) 290–304, and in *Ultimate Reality and Meaning: Interdisciplinary Studies* 13 (March 1990) 33–49. Permission to reprint has been granted by Wm. B. Eerdmans Publishing Company for the Lewis chapter, and by the Institute for the Study of Ultimate Reality and Meaning for the Malcolm X chapter.

Several sentences from the chapter on Menchú also appeared in a chapter in *Historicizing Christian Encounters with the Others*, ed. John Hawley (London and New York: Macmillan and New York UP, 1998) 182–93. Permission to reprint has been granted by both Macmillan and New York University Press.

Excerpts from "Little Gidding" in *Four Quartets*, copyright 1942 by T. S. Eliot and renewed 1970 by Esme Valerie Eliot, reprinted by permission of Harcourt Brace & Company.

Excerpts from "Burnt Norton" in *Four Quartets*, copyright 1936 by Harcourt Brace & Company and renewed 1964 by T. S. Eliot, reprinted by permission of the publisher.

Excerpts from "East Coker" in *Four Quarters*, copyright 1940 by T. S. Eliot and renewed 1968 by Esme Valerie Eliot, reprinted by permission of Harcourt Brace & Company.

PREFACE

My own story of meeting these ten major religious autobiographers of our century—Thomas Merton, Dorothy Day, Gandhi, C. S. Lewis, Malcolm X, Black Elk, Paul Cowan, Rigoberta Menchú, Dan Wakefield, and Nelson Mandela—is no mere ghost story. They have haunted my imagination for thirty years. In 1961, I was studying Augustine's *Confessions* in Latin as a daily exercise between classes to keep up my reading ability in classical languages for graduate school. In the middle of this exercise, I came across Merton's *The Seven Storey Mountain* and immediately plunged into its detailed story of Merton's spiritual journey from France to Cambridge to Columbia University and eventually to a Trappist monastery in Kentucky. Although I disputed the starkness of some of his distinctions, I became a lifelong devotee of his vision.

My memory of my first encounter with Dorothy Day's *The Long Loneliness* is now a bit hazy, but it was probably in the late 1960s while I was studying theology in Toronto and working in an urban parish to help build a community organization. It was just a month before my ordination as a Jesuit priest in 1968 that I read the second installment of Merton's life story, *The Sign of Jonas*, the journal of his years of entrance into the Catholic priesthood in the monastery. The balance he maintained amid the tensions of being both a monk and a writer ("traveling in the belly of a paradox," he called it) supported me during that turbulent spring and summer.

Although I had once sworn to myself that I would never get trapped in late eighteenth-century British literature, I fell into that period in writing my dissertation in English at Yale from 1970 to 1972. It was in the middle of my thesis on the relationship between autobiographical writings in pre-romantic writers like William Cowper and in Wordsworth that I first read a new book by M. H. Abrams entitled *Natural Supernaturalism*. In this controversial book, Abrams claimed that autobiography and the circuitous journey are the central forms of romantic and modern literature. This was precisely what I was trying to show about the shift in poetic form between the eighteenth and the nineteenth centuries.

In 1975, I decided to teach a separate course in autobiography for students in either English or Religious Studies. This course—"Religious Experience Through Autobiography"—gradually took shape, first as an historical study based on John S. Dunne's categories derived from the life stories of St. Paul, Augustine, Dante, Cellini, Bunyan, Rousseau, Wordsworth, Kierkegaard, Newman, Jung, and Sartre. Over the next fifteen years, I slowly shifted the course to a study of Augustine's *Confessions* and a half-dozen twentieth-century spiritual autobiographies. In teaching the lives of my spiritual heroes of the first half of the century—Day, Merton, Gandhi, C. S. Lewis, Chesterton, Eliot—I discovered literary and psychological patterns that were quite different from Dunne's more philosophical or theological categories. Then, as I added on more recent books by Malcolm X, Black Elk, Paul Cowan, Dan Wakefield, Rigoberta Menchú, and Nelson Mandela, I tried to help students recognize these patterns as they reflect or counteract patterns in the surrounding culture. Here I was helped by Michael Novak's notion of "religion as autobiography" in his introductory text for students of religion, *Ascent of the Mountain, Flight of the Dove*. Later I was aided by developmental patterns synthesized by Walter Conn in his *Christian Conversion* from the work of thinkers like Erik Erikson, Lawrence Kohlberg, James Fowler, and Carol Gilligan. All these will appear in my present study.

In writing the articles that became the seed for this book, I was puzzled by three questions that my students in classes on autobiography often asked: First, what makes a book a religious or spiritual autobiography? Second, what is distinctive about twentieth-century religious autobiographies? Third, why should we read these particular autobiographies?

The full definition of a religious autobiography will emerge only gradually as I describe the patterns of the ten modern life stories in the light of Augustine's *Confessions*. For only in that classic text was an entirely different literary form first created, one that would provide an approach to religious experience from within the developing subjective standpoint of the individual person. According to Roy Pascal, the first theorist of autobiography in English, autobiography in its pure form is the reconstruction of the unified movement of one life from a coherent viewpoint. In this movement, the past and present interpenetrate in such a way that outer events reveal the inner spirit of the person, and inner growth is reflected in symbolic outer events. In philosophical or religious autobiographies, the story of the development of the character of the writer becomes simultaneously the formation of a philosophy. In the words of Nietzsche in *Beyond Good and Evil*, "Gradually it has become clear to me that every great philosophy has been the personal confession of its author, as it were his involuntary and unconscious memoir" (13). In such a developing philosophy, the search for an adequate image and shape of the life search for ultimate meaning becomes central. When this lifelong search for an ultimate reality that gives meaning to one's life in the face of evil, suffering, and death becomes the theme of the book, then the writer has created a "spiritual autobiography."

But what makes twentieth-century autobiographies different? The answer to this question is also very complex and will emerge more clearly in the first chapter of this study. Although John Dunne has shown how the shape of the individual life story changes form as the cultural context changes, he devotes most of his *A Search for God in Time and Memory* to examining the philosophical and religious patterns of pre–twentieth-century authors. Those he focuses on in the current century, Yeats, Jung, and Sartre, for instance, did not undergo a major personal transformation in relation to any of the major world religions. Thus, as I struggled to find the literary and psychological patterns peculiar to twentieth-century spiritual autobiographers, it was only through such patterns that I could discern their religious significance. The ten autobiographies in the present study span the Catholic, Protestant, Muslim, and Hindu traditions in England, India, Latin America, South Africa, and the United States, yet the stories exhibit a remarkable similarity in their narrative form and literary patterns. There is a similarity, too, in their portrait of the modern seeker for the "self" in relation to an obscure vision of ultimate meaning.

While some of these patterns are vaguely reminiscent of those in Augustine's *Confessions*, most are different. Most noticeable, of course, is that the context or world of these modern stories is radically other. Their search for ultimate meaning takes place in a world marked by four traits not found in traditional societies. The presence of these four traits (three of which I have derived from Dunne's study) frames the narrative form and symbolic patterns of the modern religious autobiographer, whether in Catholic, Protestant, or Eastern traditions. These four traits are alienation, autonomy, appropriation, and inauthenticity.

The first trait, religious alienation, expresses the decline of religious mediation through a visible church, with its community, leadership, sacraments, and religious art. Increasingly since the Reformation, religious seekers have struggled for faith without the assistance of any institutional human mediation between themselves and the ultimate. Like Luther crying out for assurances of salvation and John Bunyan agonizing over the possibility of divine rejection, the modern seeker has found little help from official mediators. The religious challenge of the modern era for the person not born into a vital community of faith is, as Jung said, "the exposure of human consciousness to the undefined and indefinable" (*Psychology* 105). Thus, the religiously alienated person in the typical modern autobiography is constantly searching for a new type of mediator. But this search has not been a silent or anonymous one, as the outburst of spiritual journals since 1650 testifies. For the alienated seeker becomes a sort of mediator for others by telling the story of his or her frantic search for the ultimate. As we shall see, the very writing of the autobiography by previously unmediated seekers paradoxically provides a sort of mediation of its own.

The second modern trait, autonomy, derives from the breakdown of a traditional hierarchical society in which personal identity was affirmed by the gender, family, village, occupation, and class into which a person was born. Before the great political and industrial upheavals of the eighteenth century, Western seekers did not have to struggle so vigorously to author their own existence, for it had been authorized by their given place in the hierarchical society. In an effort to affirm his identity in a time when he found no such place, Rousseau, for example, begins his *Confes-*

sions by boldly celebrating his uniqueness: "I am like no one in the whole world. I may be no better; at least I am different." As the socially autonomous man, he goes on to prove his uniqueness by telling in great detail and with considerable exaggeration all the events, nasty and notorious, by which he was continually reasserting himself.

When they recognized the artificiality of their society, many seekers for the ultimate after the time of Rousseau escaped to their individual experiences of nature as the way to personal identity. The classic of this romantic autobiography is Wordsworth's *Prelude*, which attempts to create an epic of the growth of the poet's mind in relation to nature. Ever since, modern seekers have found in nature (or the imaginative world) as related to the sincere religious self a substitute for both religious and societal mediation of their identity. The autonomous seeker is thus often one who uses the very act of self-expression, especially in lyric or novel (disguised autobiography), as a way to the ultimate.

The third trait, appropriation, comes from the modern lack of a sense of common human nature and an identifiable self. In an effort to overcome the loneliness characteristic of modern technological society, the seeker for the ultimate must create both a "self" and a relationship to other selves. For an extreme existentialist like the early Sartre, this creation of the self is "out of nothing"; for a less radical existentialist like Kierkegaard, the creation of the self is more like an assimilation process. As Dunne says, " 'Becoming who you are' would then be the modern man's maxim. . . . Instead of stages like those of the ancient man running a gamut of experience or those of the medieval man climbing a ladder of experience, the modern man has subordinate personalities or identities or points of view" (61–62). Thus, the challenge for the seeker in the modern faceless society is to try on various faces or masks in the sense of a series of roles or "selves." The ideal is to be true to the deepest Self. As we shall see, various modern religious thinkers call for fidelity to this deep Self as the common way of seeking the ultimate. This search becomes for some a search within the unconscious (Jung, Wakefield, Black Elk); for others, a search within social and religious roles (Day, Merton, Eliot, Lewis). In either case, the driving force is loneliness coming from the lack of a solid sense of the self within a common humanity or community. The goal is the appropriation of one's truest self in a fragile bond with others in relationship to the ultimate Self.

The fourth trait, inauthenticity, refers to the loss of a sense of inner freedom in the modern world. Paradoxically, the isolated seeker who clings to the autonomy of self-creation eventually cries out for freedom from the deterministic forces of modern civilizations as described by the social sciences. The paradox is perhaps embodied most strikingly in Sartre's movement from his earlier emphasis on absolute existentialist freedom to his later embracing of the determinisms of Mao. Whatever the source of these determinisms in nineteenth-century thought (in Darwin, Freud, Marx, Durkheim), the modern seeker for meaning feels trapped by the power of psychological influences, biological urges, or societal structures. In response to this entrapment, he or she searches for an ultimate that will also be personally and socially liberating. Thus, the modern religious autobiographer will struggle to free the self from an other-directed society and a totalized existence. Authentic transformation of the self will call for commitment to the transformation of the social order to make room for both justice and freedom.

What marks the modern context of spiritual autobiography? To summarize: the modern autobiographer is an alienated seeker struggling with unmediated existence, an autonomous searcher struggling with an unauthorized identity, a self-appropriating thinker struggling with the lack of a stable sense of the self, and an authentic proponent of social change struggling with a paralyzing environment.

But why these ten autobiographies? Why not others? Part of my answer is literary; part is personal. The literary answer is that these ten are almost all (Black Elk and Menchú being exceptions) consciously written by authors working in the tradition begun by Augustine, nearly all of whom had read the *Confessions* sometime during their lives. Most were written during the author's midlife period; all give a complete life story from childhood images through adolescent wanderings to several stages of religious conversion. All are written by authors with sufficient creativity to provide the reader with a complex pattern of narrative and symbol that rewards a close study in order to reveal their full meaning and gaps in meaning. In brief, all these spiritual journeys are told by true storytellers.

These ten are not, of course, the only spiritual autobiographies of the century. I have frequently taught others in my courses, such as those by Jung, Joyce, Weil, Thérèse of Lisieux, Kazantzakis, Schweitzer, Daniel Berrigan, or Ruth Burrows, for example. But these ten have touched me at times of significance in my own journey. Just as several of them were helped on their journey by reading the others, so my own journey as a teacher of autobiography has been transformed by the very texts I attempt to interpret. I have emulated the contemplative Merton as a stabilizing model in my life as an active priest and teacher. I have been spurred on by Day and Gandhi in my intermittent involvement with non-violent social change. I have learned to seek the religious spark in literature by reading the imaginative journey of C. S. Lewis. I have been awakened to a respect for what some Native Americans call the "old ways" (expressing what Vatican II called a "profound religious sense") through meeting Black Elk. I have come to see our urban world in painful new colors through the eyes of Malcolm X. I have realized my spiritual kinship with and difference from the history of Paul Cowan. I have felt the psychic frailty of faith in the post-modern world in the life story of Dan Wakefield. I have entered into the Third World struggles for integrity and justice of Menchú and Mandela. In passing over to these lives and returning to my own, I have found myself, I trust, many twists up the circuitous journey of my own life story.

REFERENCES

Abrams, M. H. *Natural Supernaturalism: Tradition and Revolution in Romantic Literature.* New York: Norton, 1971.

Augustine, St. *Confessions.* Trans. R. S. Pine-Coffin. Middlesex: Penguin, 1961.

Black Elk. *Black Elk Speaks.* As told through John G. Neihardt. New York: Pocketbooks, 1932, 1972.

Conn, Walter. *Christian Conversion.* New York: Paulist, 1986.

Cowan, Paul. *An Orphan in History.* New York: Doubleday, 1982.

Day, Dorothy. *The Long Loneliness.* New York: Harper, 1952.

Dunne, John S. *The Search for God in Time and Memory*. New York: Macmillan, 1969.

Eliot, T. S. *The Complete Poems and Plays: 1909–1950*. New York: Harcourt, 1971.

Gandhi, Mohandas. *An Autobiography: The Story of My Experiments with Truth*. Boston: Beacon, 1929, 1957.

Jung, C. G. *Memories, Dreams, Reflections*. Trans. Richard and Clara Winston. Rev. ed. Aniela Jaffe. New York: Vintage, 1965.

————. *Psychology and Religion: West and East*. Trans. R. F. C. Hull. New York: Pantheon, 1958.

Lewis, C. S. *Surprised by Joy*. New York: Harcourt, 1955.

Malcolm X. *The Autobiography of Malcolm X*. As told to Alex Haley. New York: Ballantine, 1965.

Mandela, Nelson. *Long Walk to Freedom: The Autobiography of Nelson Mandela*. Boston: Little, Brown, 1995.

Menchú, Rigoberta. *I, Rigoberta Menchú*. Trans. Ann Wright. Ed. Elizabeth Burgos Debray. London: Verso, 1984.

Merton, Thomas. *The Seven Storey Mountain*. New York: Harcourt, 1948.

————. *The Sign of Jonas*. New York: Doubleday, 1953. 1956.

Nietzsche, Friedrich. *Beyond Good and Evil*. Trans. Walter Kaufman. New York: Random House, 1966.

Novak, Michael. *Ascent of the Mountain, Flight of the Dove: An Invitation to Religious Studies*. New York: Harper & Row, 1971.

Pascal, Roy. *Design and Truth in Autobiography*. Cambridge, MA: Harvard UP, 1960.

Rousseau, Jean-Jacques. *The Confessions of Jean-Jacques Rousseau*. Trans. J. M. Cohen. Middlesex: Penguin, 1954.

Wakefield, Dan. *Returning: A Spiritual Journey*. New York: Doubleday, 1988.

INTRODUCTION

Circuitous Journeys: Modern Spiritual Autobiography

THE DIRECTIONAL IMAGE

"A man's work is nothing but a slow task to rediscover, through the detour of art, those two or three great and simple images in whose presence his heart first opened." These words of Albert Camus suggest the spark that ignites the narrative fire of modern religious autobiographies. In bringing their childhood to mind, each of the ten authors I will study follows a practice as old as Augustine's *Confessions*: that of re-creating an intense childhood emotional experience from which emerges an image of an ultimate goal or ideal to be pursued with passion. In Augustine's opening paragraph, he announces his theme through the image of the *cor inquietum*, the restless heart. This motif emerges from his earliest experience of hunger for his mother's milk and in his quest for language as an infant and a schoolboy. The rest of the *Confessions* flows from this motif of the "unquiet" quest for an object or person who will satisfy his hungers and his desire for dialogue. Implicit in this restlessness is the eventual goal he finds in the search for eternal rest and the eternal Word.

Similarly, modern religious autobiographies form for the reader what I call a directional image, which embodies the dynamic of their story, often associated with the motif expressed in the title or subtitle of their story. For Thomas Merton, the travels of his childhood—from France to Long Island to Bermuda to France— underlie the repeated image of his life as a journey (up the seven storey mountain of Dante's *Purgatorio*), a journey in search of a permanent "home." Dorothy Day's repeated experience of loneliness in her late Victorian childhood gives rise to her life as "the long loneliness," not merely a psychological isolation but a spiritual hunger for God in community (Coles 62). For C. S. Lewis, the early experience of the "joy" of dissatisfied desire emerges from his early fascination with a toy garden created by his brother, an image that generates a lifelong "imagination of Paradise." Gandhi traces his lifelong passion for what he calls "Truth" back to his childhood experience of his father's integrity and to his own compulsion to avoid even the smallest lie. Malcolm X spends most of his first chapter describing the "nightmare" of his childhood as a series of black/white racial conflicts. Behind those conflicts lie the tensions within Malcolm between the values of his "black" father and the values of his "half white" mother. The dynamic tension of this image of black-against-white drives Malcolm X to the extremes of each phase of his life before he reaches some resolution in a transcendent hope for racial harmony in orthodox Islam. Black Elk's entire story flows from a childhood vision, at the age of nine, which provides him with the image of circular harmony for which he struggles in vain throughout his lifetime. Similarly, Nelson Mandela's *Long Walk to Freedom* is inspired by the vision of an harmonious society modeled on the tribal unity of his childhood villages. Dan Wakefield's *Returning* suggests by its title that his life focuses on a series of places, deriving from his childhood home in Indianapolis, in particular from the place where he first experiences his body filled with "light." Finally, Paul Cowan employs the image of his lost orthodox grandfather, Jake Cohen, to lead him on his search through several lifetimes, his own and that of his parents, and his Jewish ancestors, a search in the person of what he calls "an orphan in history." Each of these autobiographers uses one basic directional image, whereas T. S. Eliot uses four images, one at the beginning of each of the *Four Quartets*, then draws them together in the ending of the final quartet.

This use of a directional image implies, of course, that the storyteller is going somewhere, even if it is, as Eliot says, "to arrive where we started / And know the place for the first time" (*Little Gidding* 241–42). The image provides the dynamic of movement and the hint of a goal to be reached. What it does not immediately indicate is what happens in all these modern stories of the wandering self (as in Augustine's *Confessions*): that, for most of the story, the direction is the wrong one. In fact, what intrigues many readers of spiritual autobiography is that the journey consists primarily in wrong turns and dead ends. As Eliot says from the viewpoint of old age in the final quartet, "From wrong to wrong the exasperated spirit / Proceeds" (*Little Gidding* 144–45). The restless heart of Augustine leads him to spend most of his story describing the deviations of adolescence in Tagaste, the practice of Manichaeanism in Carthage, his adult skepticism in Rome, and the discovery of Neoplatonism and philosophical community in Milan. Similarly, Merton's travels take him on many sidetracks and into many false roles as he climbs the purgatorial mountain toward Gethsemani. Day's long loneliness causes her to seek out infamous and merely "natural" companionship in Greenwich Village. Lewis wanders into numerous enchanted gardens on his search for the experience of "joy," most of them literary gardens. Gandhi's dedication to "Truth" leads him into what he calls failed "experiments" in London, South Africa, and eventually India. Likewise, Black Elk spends a decade evading the responsibilities of his first vision, and then another decade trying to understand why the violence of the American West leads him into battle instead of into the harmonies of his vision. For Wakefield, a century after Black Elk, one of the turning points of his life occurs when he perceives his life as a journey instead of a battle, for most of his story consists of adolescent conflicts in various places where he is resisting the "light." Cowan explicitly describes his life as a wandering in the desert of modern history as a newly orphaned Moses in search of a homeland. Only Menchú and Mandela, both growing up in revolutionary situations, lack the luxury of prolonged wanderings from their life purposes.

This overall pattern of childhood directional images of a goal, followed by adolescent and adult wandering through illusory realizations of the directional image, and eventual achievement of the goal (often in a surprising place) fits most of these autobiographies within the Augustinian tradition. What is more surprising for a student of autobiography and narrative is that the larger structural patterns of these recent stories derive from an ancient epic narrative device first employed in autobiography by Augustine himself.

The Shape of Autobiography: The Circular Journey

What we call the beginning is often the end
And to make an end is to make a beginning.
(*Little Gidding* 214–15)

"The self reveals itself through style"—this truism, summed up by Herbert Leibowitz in his masterful book on eight famous American autobiographies from Ben Franklin to Gertrude Stein, also indicates the method of his own book. For Leibowitz shows how the sentence-level stylistics of those eight writers express dimensions of their characters, both by what they reveal and by what they conceal. Although Leibowitz occasionally mentions what he calls a "grid" or "formal plan" of each autobiography, he subordinates the larger narrative patterns to his stylistic analysis in his exploration of the selves of the authors. In my study, I propose to do the opposite: to examine first the larger narrative patterns—the chapter and section titles and divisions, the parallel and contrasting events, the major metaphors and symbolic objects—as clues to the significance of the religious search of the authors. In focusing on these larger patterns, while not neglecting "style" in the more restricted sense of the term, I hope to show how most of these modern autobiographies play off a fundamental pattern in the history of narrative, the circular journey.

In my study of Augustine's *Confessions*, I discovered that this foundational spiritual autobiography employed a general pattern of ending where it began, but on a higher level. Using a sort of chiasmic pattern within a horseshoe form (Ω), in which events of Books 1–4 raise questions to be answered in reverse order in Books 6–9 (with Book 5 serving as a transition), Augustine himself was playing off a pattern that scholars have uncovered in Homer and Virgil, the latter's *Aeneid* being Augustine's favorite childhood reading (see Whitman, Duckworth). More important than a mere convenience of plot, the circular journey pattern provided Augustine with a structural metaphor for several doctrines important to his theological understanding of his conversion story. The circular journey embodied the Neoplatonic scheme of emanation and return, but with a solid base in personal and social history. The journey also paralleled several biblical narratives with circular patterns similar to those in his own life, especially the stories of the "lost one found" such as that of the Prodigal Son from Luke 15. The autobiography also exemplified Augustine's theology of providence by showing how the events of his early life raised questions that would be answered by his later life events.[1]

Although the modern autobiographies that I will explore were almost all written by persons who had read Augustine's *Confessions* or were familiar with life stories written in the tradition begun by Augustine, none of them copied his circular structure slavishly. But all in a variety of ways used a general three-stage narrative pattern in which childhood events (stage one) raise questions that drive the author on a negative journey of wandering in a desert of illusory answers (stage two) before he or she discovers a transforming world in which the original questions can be resolved (stage three). In relation to the circular journey, then, these recent autobiographies shape themselves as what I call "spiral pilgrimages." The spiral usually moves downward away from the ultimate goal but often finds illusory objects parallel to the original directional image before recovering and reaching the authentic goal.

As we shall see in greater detail in the following chapters, several authors employ an explicitly tripartite grid for their autobiographies (Merton, Day, Wakefield), while others use simple chapter divisions that readily separate into three major structural sections with significant parallels in the persons, events, and symbolic ob-

---

[1] For a detailed reading of the *Confessions*, see my "Augustine's *Confessions* as a Circular Journey." Other sources for the symbolic use of the circle in narratives include Plato's *Timaeus*, Aristotle's *De anima*, and Dante's *Vita Nuova* and *Divina Commedia*. Mircea Eliade, in *Cosmos and History*, synthesizes many examples of circular patterns of non-historical journeys in early religions. Georges Poulet's *Les métamorphoses du cercle* traces the Renaissance transformation of the circle from a sacred to a secular symbol. John Freccero, in his erudite article ("Donne") on spatial and temporal patterns in classical and Christian thought, cites John Donne's saying, "This life is a Circle, made with a Compasse, that passes from point to point." Freccero also traces the history of the spiral image in his "Dante's Pilgrim in a Gyre." For a general bibliography on patterns in autobiography, consult Olney (*Autobiography* and *Studies*). Important works on general and religious autobiography include Bruss, Cooley, Couser, Delaney, Dunne, Eakin, Earle, Ebner, Egan, Elbacz, Fleishman, E. Griffin, Gunn, Hawkins, Heidt, Lejeune, Mehlman, Morris, Olney, Pascal, Shea, Spengemann, Starr, Weintraub, Barbour, and Conway.

jects of each section. In their illusory period of wandering, many will portray false mediators before they discover their true mentors. Dorothy Day, for instance, will follow her communist friend Rayna, her editor and fiancé, Herbert Gold, and her common-law husband, Forster Batterham, before meeting, and modeling her goal on the goals of, her final mentor and prophet, Peter Maurin. Several will try on a series of what Erik Erikson calls "negative identities" before reaching their authentic self. The young Malcolm X will become first the Harlem hustler, then the Black Muslim main minister before reaching a tentative but substantive identity as an orthodox Muslim leader of the fledgling Organization for Afro-American Unity. Many will try to live out their parents' virtues and vices before achieving some sort of resolution of these traits in their own person. Merton will live out the life of an aspiring bohemian artist/writer, like his father, and then the life of a private ascetic, like his mother, before reaching a resolution in the tension-filled vocation of a monk-writer. Many will experience the loss or death of one of their parents in the first stage, which leads them to seek a new father or new mother, first in a spiritual desert and then in a promised land. Paul Cowan will seek a "Jacob Cohen" throughout his secular wandering in the liberal movements of the 1960s and 1970s before finding him (after the death of his own father and mother) in Rabbi Singer in 1977 on the Lower East Side of Manhattan.

In examining the larger patterns of the circular journey form, we will be alert for symbolic events or objects that embody the three-level narrative structure. Similar to Augustine's obsession with the "words" or "books" of his childhood (Virgil, Cicero), his wandering (Manichaean scripture, Neoplatonic texts), and his conversion year (Lives of the Saints, the Bible) is the transforming influence of books in the lives of Merton, Day, Lewis, Malcolm X, Gandhi, and Wakefield. We will follow the patterns of sacred objects in the vision of Black Elk; the pattern of ritual in the lives of Cowan, Wakefield, Day, Menchú, and the later Merton; the repeated symbolic objects such as Malcolm X's clothes, Day's meals, or Gandhi's use of law; and the pattern of visits to his home village in the long walk of Mandela.

Finally, we will briefly examine the style of each author, focusing on the difficulty each has in renewing the language of religious experience, in finding what will suffice to convey the touch with the sacred. The concern of these writers will be to find language adequate to their conversion experience in a secularized world where religious language has become the fundamentalist's cliché or the advertiser's stock phrase. Consequently, since most of these stories are by former journalists (Merton, Day, Gandhi, Wakefield, Cowan, Lewis) or public speakers (Black Elk, Malcolm X, Menchú, Mandela), they will most often employ the straightforward, precise but less metaphorical style of the newspaper writer, while occasionally weaving in the symbolic and rhetorical style of the orator or novelist. However, Merton, Lewis, and Black Elk were also poets; Gandhi, Malcolm X, and Mandela were influential public rhetoricians; Day, Merton, Lewis, and Wakefield also wrote novels. Although none of them was completely successful in the attempt to "purify the dialect of the tribe," the conscious choice of style suggests that each knew how to use language to reach what Day calls the heart of autobiography—"giving yourself away" (10).

THE PSYCHOLOGICAL SPIRAL: BECOMING ONE'S OWN PARENT

In my beginning is my end . . .
    Home is where one starts from. As we grow older
The world becomes stranger, the pattern more complicated
Of dead and living.

(*East Coker* 1, 190–92)

Alex Haley, in the epilogue to his *Autobiography of Malcolm X*, says that he could not get Malcolm X to talk about himself until he asked him about his mother. In response to that question, Malcolm X talked until dawn, and afterward no longer hesitated to discuss his childhood experiences. Besides being what Haley calls the trigger to the explosion of self-manifestation, the portrait of the father and mother in recent religious autobiographies provides the main clue to the psychological dimension of the circular journey. Without in the least reducing the religious search to an Oedipal struggle begun in a period before memory or memoir, my study will suggest that the religious journey often takes the form of spiraling inner battles between the father-influence and the mother-influence. Besides this commonplace pattern, we will also discover the importance of both what the writer says and what the writer does not say about each parent. From these sayings and silences emerges a lifelong tension to be resolved through each phase of the circular journey. Some writers will choose one parent or reject both, but eventually all will struggle with their preconscious minds to discover some sort of harmonious tensions in what John S. Dunne calls the "search for God in time and memory."

More often than not, the search will force the autobiographer to integrate and then transcend the parents in the final stage of the journey. What Eliot calls the "pattern more complicated / Of dead and living" often begins, as it did for Augustine, with the writer describing the tensions of maternal and paternal influences in childhood. Augustine contrasts his father's pagan religion and amoral interest in his son's sexual growth with his mother's Christianity and concern for his moral responsibility, but then indicts both parents for subordinating his religious and moral growth to his education and career as a rhetorician. This tension grows as Augustine escapes from his mother (after the death and conversion of his father when Augustine is seventeen, a fact mentioned only in passing in Book 3.4 [p. 29] and again at the end of Book 9 [p. 204]). Later, Augustine describes his unmasking of the false father Faustus in order to search for a true father, Ambrose. Eventually during his upward phase, his mother follows him from Carthage to Rome to Milan, where she is consoled by Ambrose and eventually becomes Augustine's companion after his conversion to his new mother, the Church. Just as he had begun the narrative of the *Confessions* by citing his earliest memories derived from "the father who begat me and the mother who conceived" me (1.6, p. 25), so Augustine ends the autobiography by asking his readers to "remember those who were not only my parents in this light that fails, but were also my brother and sister, subject to You, our Father, in our Catholic mother the Church" (9.13. p. 204).

Although most autobiographers today do not use theology as fully as Augustine does to idealize the family psychodrama, many implicitly portray their life story as a battle to reconcile the "father" and the "mother" in themselves. One can trace early tensions between the fussy, perfectionist Quaker mother and the footloose, artistic Episcopalian father throughout the journey of

Thomas Merton—in his wandering years as both a student and an activist, and finally in his lifelong struggle to be both a monk and a writer. Dorothy Day reveals herself as living out, to some extent, the Victorian battle between the caring creator of a "home" in her mother and the aloof patriarchal professional writer in her father. Gandhi, of course, has already been described by Erikson as deeply influenced by the circumstance of his neglect of his dying father because of sexual desire for his teen-age bride, but he can be more adequately shown to have lived out a lifelong tension between the political integrity ("Truth") of his father and the religious devotion and charity ("Firmness") of his mother. Cowan explicitly announces his life search as one in which he seeks to integrate the worldly liberal passion for justice of his mother with the orthodox Jewish love of tradition latent in his father and manifest in his grandfather. Similarly, Mandela seeks to integrate his father's reconciliatory vision of cosmic harmony with his mother's practical Christianity. Finally, Menchú struggles to confront and relive her parents' martyrdom.

As each of these writers struggles to resolve these parental tensions, each reaches a stage where two fundamental obstacles—the experience of loss or death (often of a parent) and the experience of God—stand in apparent opposition. As will be clear in the next sections, these confrontations plunge the writer into the most crucial of religious struggles: that of finding an adequate notion of God ("naming the whirlwind") and that of affirming eternal life in the face of death. In psychological terms, they face the questions: who am I in the face of my death? who is my ultimate parent? In interpersonal terms, who has the words of eternal life?

LIGHT FOR THE INTELLECTUAL SPIRAL: MEDIATORS OF UNDERSTANDING

I caught the sudden look of some dead master
Whom I had known, forgotten, half recalled
Both one and many.

(*Little Gidding* 92–94)

Alone before the uncontrollable in a religiously alienated age of the autonomous individual, the modern searcher for the ultimate

must, like T. S. Eliot, seek a "master" (whether in a text, like
Dante's, or in a life, like Yeats's). For without guidance from parents or religious community and tradition, one must think last
things out for oneself. In traditional terms, this struggle leads
through many windings to a "conversion of the intellect." The
primary focus for most searchers at this stage, usually beginning
in college or the late twenties, centers on a mature notion of the
ultimate—a concept of Nature, Being, or "God." Although this
search may be prompted by the childhood emotional experience
that gave rise to the directional image, the mind seeks an enrich-
ing insight that will go beyond the limits of the imagination, engaging in a struggle for understanding of the ultimate meaning of
life that takes many years of what Emilie Griffin calls "dialectic."
For her, this term suggests an inner dialogue, sometimes with a
mentor, sometimes with an author, but ultimately within the tan-
gle of one's mind.

This search for an ultimate principle of intelligibility often begins with an awakening, as it did for Augustine when he first read
Cicero's *Hortensius* at eighteen: "All my empty dreams suddenly
lost their charm and my heart began to throb with a bewildering
passion for the wisdom of eternal truth" (3.4, pp. 58–59). From
this awakening Augustine sets out on an intellectual voyage that
visits several philosophic islands—Manichaeanism, Aristotelian-
ism, skepticism, Neoplatonism—under the tutelege of several
mentors—Manes, Faustus, Aristotle, Porphyry—before reaching
insights into the transcendence and spirituality of the Christian
God. Although Augustine's masters are "half recalled / Both one
and many" at the time of the writing of the autobiography, they
come to life not so much as parts of a logical argument for the
existence of God as enkindlers of the spark of insight within a
large intellectual scheme growing in the mind of Augustine.
Thus, these mentors serve more as symbolic figures, icons of intelligibility in the structure of the narrative, although this pattern
does include sections of argumentation and homily. For Augustine, as for most recent autobiographers, mentors and doctrines do
not automatically produce an intellectual conversion. In fact,
when the plausibility of Manichaeanism vanishes for Augustine at
the midpoint of the *Confessions*, he despairs of finding the wisdom
he has been seeking: "the more I took stock of the various theo-

ries, the more I began to think that the opinions of the majority of the philosophers were most likely to be true" (5.14, p. 108). This mental exhaustion and confusion are perhaps the greatest danger of the intellectual quest in the modern era, for they can lead to a skepticism that despairs of the entire project of understanding.

Several of the modern seekers reach such a point of intellectual cynicism (Lewis, Merton, Wakefield, Cowan), but the dynamic behind their directional images and their thirst for wisdom does not disappear. For Merton, the intellectual impulse that first came from prep-school readings of modern literature reaches an impasse in college, despite his sympathetic reading of Dante. He achieves a breakthrough by accident when he purchases Étienne Gilson's *The Spirit of Mediaeval Philosophy*. This book frees Merton from the limits of his imaginary picture of God by providing a new notion of the ultimate as "aseitas" or total self-existence. For C. S. Lewis, the imagination provides both the obstacle and the breakthrough in his search for understanding, the obstacle being the mythology of his youthful reading, and the breakthrough being the image of holiness gathered from George MacDonald's fantasy writing. Mentors for Lewis's intellectual journey include Owen Barfield (his "antiself," who keeps him intellectually honest) and Samuel Alexander (who suggests the notion that God is known not as an object to be confronted but as the implied horizon of all desires and objects). For Wakefield, although he does not describe his "returning" as primarily an intellectual transformation, many mentors appear on his journey back to his true place—J. D. Salinger, Robert Coles, Thomas Merton, and Henri Nouwen, among them—who help him stop "substituting Freud for God," as Wakefield entitles his conversion story article. The religious aspect of Wakefield's intellectual life is kept alive by Mark Van Doren, who becomes, as he became for Merton, his "guardian angel" at Columbia University and gives him a "new adult respect for Jesus." Paul Cowan's intellectual journey from liberal agnosticism to conservative Jewish faith also takes only a partially intellectual turn, for his main mentors are activists and pastors rather than intellectuals. The first, Jesuit priest Daniel Berrigan, awakens him to the need for faith to sustain a lifelong struggle for justice; the second, Rabbi Joseph Singer, teaches him the love of orthodox Jewish traditions and beliefs. Singer, however, is more than just a mentor. He becomes Cowan's new father whom Cowan finds while carrying out the final wish of his original father after the death of both his parents in an apartment fire in New York. Like Merton, Wakefield, Gandhi, Menchú, and Mandela, Cowan on his spiral pilgrimage moves beyond the light of the intellect into the darkness of death.

DARKNESS IN THE SPIRAL: ENCOUNTERING LOSS AND DEATH

> O dark dark dark. They all go into the dark . . .
> And we all go with them, into the silent funeral,
> Nobody's funeral, for there is no one to bury.
> *(East Coker* 101, 111–12)

Guided by the directional image and enlightened by insights mediated by mentors, the modern searcher inevitably confronts the darkness of loss and death. It is no accident that half the autobiographies we are exploring emphasize episodes describing the death of one or both parents during the youth of the author. Merton and Malcolm X lose both parents by the time they are sixteen; C. S. Lewis loses his mother when he is six; Gandhi, his father when he is fifteen; Mandela, his father when he is seven. Day leaves home and is cut off by her father at seventeen. Both Cowan and Wakefield place major importance in their journeys on the deaths of their parents in later life. Menchú's loss of both her parents to violent political deaths catapults her into adult responsibilities as a witness for her people. Although Black Elk attributes less significance to such events, he frames his narrative with the wounding and later with the death of his father.

Since most of these deaths occur in the childhood or wandering stage of the spiritual autobiographies, the lost parent is experienced as "gone into the dark" rather than as "gone into the world of light," as Henry Vaughan, the seventeenth-century poet, described the death of friends. Only from the final perspective does the searcher see the event of loss or death as a movement in which the child can say with Eliot: "I said to my soul, be still, and let the dark come upon you / Which shall be the darkness of God" *(East Coker* 112–13). Thus, the loss evokes in the writer a variety

INTRODUCTION 13

of immediate responses—for Lewis, the naïveté of a numbness
after prayers fail to waken his mother; for Merton, a weight of
"sadness and depression" (14) but no prayer; for Malcolm X, too
young at six to feel much at his father's death, then later feeling
only a sense of groundlessness at his mother's collapse ("as if I was
trying to walk up the side of a hill of feathers" [21]); and for
Gandhi, a profound guilt and shame for being in the "grip of
lust" for his wife when he could have been ministering to his
dying father.

All these immediate responses, however, lead the writers to
more spiritual crises. For the death of parents provokes the religious searcher to confront mortality for the first time and thus
bring about a turning point in his or her own life. For the
thoughtful seeker after an answer to what John S. Dunne calls the
most fundamental human questions—"Does my becoming end
in being or does it end in nothingness?"—the encounter with
death can be an encounter with his or her own mortality, but also
much more. In fact, for Dunne, this experience and question raise
the basic methodological issue in the study of autobiography. He
suggests that the reading of autobiography can teach the reader to
"pass over" to another person's life story for an awakening of
three degrees of concern—immediate concern, lifetime concern,
and afterlife concern.[2] Thus, for both the autobiographer and the
reader, the narration of the death of the father and mother en-
larges the context of the journey to the widest possible screen.
But since the losses occur at an early stage of the life journey, the
immediate and even existential interpretation by the writer is
often incomplete. Only later, when writing from the final standpoint of a converted person of faith, does the author realize the
full significance of the event.

---

[2] John S. Dunne sums up his search for a method of understanding autobiography: "What we need is a method of bringing to mind the time that is out of
mind. This would be a method first of bringing one's own lifetime to mind, of
passing from the 'immediate moment' in which one's concerns are confined to
the present situation to the 'existential moment' in which one's concerns are
extended to one's future and one's past. Second, it would be a method of bringing what we call one's 'deathtime' to mind, of passing from the existential moment in which one's concerns are confined to one's own lifetime to the 'historic
moment' in which one's concerns are extended to all time, both the future and
the past" (2).

For Augustine, as I have noted, the death of his father in Tagaste when Augustine was sixteen receives only a passing mention in the *Confessions* (3.4). But the loss of a close friend a few years later evokes one of the most intense crises in the autobiography:

> My heart grew sombre with grief, and wherever I looked I saw only death. My own country became a torment and my own home a grotesque abode of misery. All that we had done together was now a grim ordeal without him. My eyes searched everywhere for him, but he was not there to be seen. I hated all the places we had known together, because he was not in them and they could no longer whisper to me "Here he comes" . . . (4.4, p. 76).

This first emotional encounter with death leads Augustine to reflect later in his journey on the existential and religious dimensions of his life. He realizes that he is "sick and tired of living and yet afraid to die" (4.5, p. 77).

He regrets his love for his friend and blames himself: "I had loved him as though he would never die. Still more I wondered that he should die and I remain alive, for I was his second self" (4.6, p. 77). In effect, Augustine begins at this time to search for *permanence*. Absorbed in this search, he begins to reflect on the radical contingency and temporality in human life. Eventually his desire for a permanent love will drive him beyond the immediate, existential, and even historic moments or perspectives to what he ascribes to God at the end of Book 4: "our home is your eternity" (p. 90). This view of death as "eternal home" provides Augustine with a fully religious perspective only at the end of the autobiography. At that point, he joins his dying mother in their mutual vision of "eternal Wisdom" before she rests her unquiet heart and becomes his guide to a peaceful death: "And if [the reader] finds that I sinned by weeping for my mother, even if for a fraction of an hour, let him not mock at me. For this was the mother, now dead and hidden awhile from my sight, who had wept over me for many years so that I might live in your sight" (9.13, p. 203).

In contemporary autobiographies, most of which are written in midlife, the writer has not always come close to his or her own death. Even the vicarious death of friends or parents can provide only an imaginative encounter with one's own power to say, "I am mortal." Yet the image of oneself as dead raises the question

for many—"Who am I to be in the light (or dark) of eternity?"
This question radically changes the horizon of the autobiographer's life story. Yet the very time of writing, at midlife, usually
provokes the author into spending more time writing, not about
the afterlife itself, but about what Emily Dickinson calls "turning
toward eternity." This religious conversion process includes in
most stories more than one turn.

TWISTS IN THE SPIRAL: CONVERSION AND THE WIDENING GYRE

Although most autobiographers of the soul in the current century
include five types of conversion (affective, intellectual, imaginative, moral, and religious), they do not follow a universally predictable sequence. Yet they follow a search for the ultimate within
the levels of human consciousness. The leap from one level to the
next is a radical conversion, a transformation of the whole self and
its horizon, along with a restructuring of old and new content of
beliefs. If the patterns described by theologian Walter Conn can
be modified by adding a level of imagination, we find a pattern
of the five conversions noted above:

(1) Affective Conversion: the transformation of self-absorbed pat-
    terns of emotion ("my feelings") into loving concern for oth-
    ers' feelings (through passion and commitment);

(2) Imaginative Conversion: the discovery and transformation of
    one's directional images, which lead one beyond the self
    toward a search for ultimate meaning through a lifetime;

(3) Intellectual Conversion: the transformation of passive accep-
    tance of a given world out there into self-awareness of one's
    cognitive structures and self-appropriated sense of truth and
    value;

(4) Moral Conversion: the transformation of a pre-conventional
    pre-moral sense of pleasure or pain ("my good") into a con-
    ventional and then post-conventional awareness of values in
    themselves, both personal and social ("the good," "the com-
    mon good"); and

(5) Religious Conversion: the transformation of a partial world
    view, involving despair or merely secular concern, into com-
    mitment to total cosmic meaning and a life centered on God
    (see Conn 27).

How clearly does the classic or modern spiritual autobiography embody these five conversions? Even as Augustine's intellectual awakening upon reading Cicero's *Hortensius* on wisdom preceded his other conversions, it seems clear that this intellectual process took many years and occupied the greater part of his autobiography from Books 3 to 7. Yet his eventual religious conversion in the garden in Book 8 serves as the final catapult not so much to belief in Christianity as to belief in the power of grace to assist him in living the life of a Christian, which is precisely the content of a moral transformation. The *Confessions* do not provide insights into a distinctively affective conversion, although the pain of ending his longstanding involvement with his mistress suggests that he had moved beyond the self-absorbed lust of his adolescence to a passionate love for and partial commitment to her. Thus, one might say that the final step of his religious conversion made possible a full moral conversion and the beginning of a new form of affective conversion.

This variable pattern in the sequence of conversions is even more drastic in modern autobiographies. Merton goes through clearly marked imaginative and intellectual conversions, but, like Augustine, weaves together his moral and religious conversion, and never gives evidence in *The Seven Storey Mountain* of a satisfactory affective maturation. Day seems more predictable in the sequence of her developments—from imaginative conversion in high school to intellectual conversion in college to affective conversion in her working years. Once again, however, her moral and religious struggles weave themselves together as she approaches a religious crisis in choosing between her common-law marriage and Catholicism. For Gandhi, early moral conflicts lead to all his later conversions, although, like Merton, he never seems to reach an emotional integration. Malcolm X shows a unique pattern in that his religious conversion to the Nation of Islam precipitates all his other transformations. Cowan follows the more predictable pattern of five stages, yet never speaks much of any intellectual conversion.

If most of these modern autobiographers vary from the pattern exhibited in Augustine's classic, they also include a dimension virtually absent from the *Confessions*. In fact, what often dismays modern readers of Augustine's rejection of his mistress is not so much his break with her as his seemingly unquestioning acceptance of the societal prohibitions that made marriage with her impossible. Whether because of her slave or lower-class origins, she was, for Augustine's mother and others who were concerned primarily about his career, merely an obstacle to professional success. This lack of a social consciousness related to this issue does not mean that Augustine did not later concern himself with social evils, most particularly in his years as a bishop and in his writing of the *City of God*. But as an autobiographer in the fifth century, Augustine does not expand his religious and moral conversion to Christianity to include a social dimension, unless one were to call his rejection of his rhetorical career an implicit critique of the social structures of Roman education and law ("the insane warfare of the courts"—9.2, p. 182). In Book 8, he is converted from his worldly life to Christian commitment to God; in Book 9, he expands this conversion to include entrance through baptism into the Christian Church, and at Cassiciacum into a new form of Christian community.

What makes the conversion sequence of most modern autobiographers notably different from that of Augustine is that they explictly include a societal dimension to their moral and religious conversions. For these modern converts in an era of societal consciousness, the final twist on their spiral pilgrimages includes a turn to the least of their brothers and sisters. For Christian converts, this final step makes explicit the call of Jesus to those seeking "eternal life" as a call not merely to love God but also to love their neighbor in the person of the poor. In fact, for several of the autobiographers (Day, Gandhi, Cowan, Menchú), this turn to social awareness actually precedes and precipitates their religious conversion. For Merton, what he calls a "step to moral conversion" occurs at Columbia University when he joins the Young Communist League; a later stage of his search for a more effective expression of his conversion to Catholicism leads to work in Harlem for Friendship House with Catherine de Hueck. Again, within his life as a monk described in journals written after *The Seven Storey Mountain*, he realizes this widening gyre of concern by his movement from the personal monastic spirituality of the 1940s, through the more liturgical and communal spirituality of the 1950s, to the explicitly social spirituality of the 1960s. For

Malcolm X, conversion to the Nation of Islam necessarily calls him to work on projects for black education and economics, but the limits placed on him by this group help trigger his later conversion to the more universal faith in orthodox Islam with its broader social horizons. For Mandela, the search for justice becomes part of his youthful religious faith at the university, but later moves to the center of his journey when he confronts apartheid in Johannesburg. Only in C. S. Lewis's autobiography does one seek in vain for an explicitly societal phase of his conversions.

TENSIONS IN THE SPIRAL: RESOLUTION THROUGH WRITING

> And so each venture
> Is a new beginning, a raid on the inarticulate
> With shabby equipment always deteriorating. . . .
> (*East Coker* 178–80)

The tension just noted between personal conversion and societal awareness is only one of many experienced by modern autobiographers of the spirit. I have also mentioned the psychic tension of integrating one's paternal with one's maternal values, as between the political father and religious mother (Gandhi), or the religious father and political mother (Cowan). There are also a variety of intellectual extremes pulling the modern seeker in many directions, as in the pull on Lewis from both materialism and spiritualism. Even the experience of loss or death can plunge the writer into tensions between despair and hope, as the deaths of parents do to Malcolm X, Gandhi, and C. S. Lewis. The final movement toward religious commitment can itself produce a fierce new tension: how to live out one's faith—in action or contemplation (Merton); in social work or church and family (Day); in ministering to one's own people or in political and intercultural work (Malcolm X); in a conservative form of religious observance or in a liberal form (Cowan); in protecting a separate culture or in integrating it with a superior political power (Black Elk); in the use of violence or non-violent resistance in the quest for justice (Gandhi, Menchú, Mandela).

Like Augustine, modern autobiographers distinguish themselves from the millions of silent converts by turning to writing as a primary way to resolve these tensions. Although not called by their audience (unlike Puritan autobiographers such as the seventeenth-century John Bunyan in *Grace Abounding*) to verify the authenticity of their conversions, all the autobiographers in this study feel compelled by conscience or invited by friends to recount their story. For most of these writers, this compulsion to write proves fruitful. But not always at first. For, like Augustine, with his *Soliloquies* written in the philosophical form of a fictional dialogue with himself ten years before he attempts a narrative before God in the autobiographical form of the *Confessions*, most of these contemporary seekers make a false literary start. Four of them try to disguise their story in the form of novels—Merton in *My Argument with the Gestapo*, Day in *The Eleventh Virgin*, Lewis in *Pilgrim's Regress*, and Wakefield in *Going All the Way* and *Starting Over*. But they try these fictions either too early in their journey to gain a perspective on their conversion (Merton, Day, Wakefield), or in an unsuitable allegorical form (Lewis, following Chesterton). Later, all but Black Elk try to express the content of their conversion in essays, articles, or speeches. Only in midlife and usually a decade after their religious conversion do they turn to the narrative of the self, to direct autobiography. As I shall show in my study of the structures of the circular journey in each story, all prove to be generally successful, with a few reaching classic status.

One clue to the success of these autobiographies is their style. For the less successful, the failure to resolve the tensions of their life will show itself in the failures of their style. This stylistic breakdown may appear, for instance, in passages of powerfully detailed prose followed by abstract moralizing (as in *The Seven Storey Mountain*); in a journalistic flatness of sentences lacking in metaphor or symbol (as in parts of Day, Gandhi, Cowan, and Mandela); in a tendency to pile up details, allusions, and borrowed structural devices (as in Wakefield); or in religious jargon or dead metaphors used to explain doctrines (as in parts of Malcolm X or Merton). But, for the most part, the writers of these life stories find what Milton called an "answerable style" to the questions lived out in their journeys. Just as Augustine could embody the chiasmic and paradoxical form of his life story in his stylistic use of chiasmus and paradox, so Merton can sum up his discovery of the integration through faith of "nature" and "grace" in the style of the first two sentences of his story:

> On the last day of January 1915, under the sign of the Water Bearer, in a year of a great war, and down in the shadow of some French mountains on the borders of Spain, I came into the world.
> Free by nature, in the image of God, I was nevertheless the prisoner of my own violence and my own selfishness, in the image of the world into which I was born. (3)

The realistic details of the periodic first sentence express his birth as an empirical fact on the level of human history on a wide temporal, astrological, and geographic screen ("nature"). The second sentence interprets these facts from his later theological standpoint as a Catholic convert and monk—as one created free and good in the divine image but prone to sin in the image of the fallen world ("grace"). Like Augustine in the first book of the *Confessions*, which embodies the same Christian doctrine of creation in the events of the author's youth, so Merton uses the chiasmic structure of these two opening sentences, with the reversal of the place of the main subject ("I came into the world . . . I was nevertheless a prisoner"), to convey his interpretation as an autobiographer of the spirit on pilgrimage as a captive traveler.

Similarly, the opening of *Black Elk Speaks* includes a summary sentence that embodies in its structure of three nouns followed by three clauses the three central points of its narrative:

> But now that I can see it all as from a lonely hilltop, I know it was the story of a mighty vision given to a man too weak to use it; of a holy tree that should have flourished in a people's heart with flowers and singing birds, and now is withered; and of a people's dream that died in bloody snow. (2)

The sentence first establishes the perspective of the entire book in a separate, opening dependent clause that controls the direction of the sentence ("now that I can see . . ."). Next the writer indicates the definite pastness of the book in his main clause ("I know it was the story"), and then concludes with the three main elements of the autobiography ("a mighty vision," "a holy tree," and "a people's dream"). Each of these elements is in turn cut away by the forces in the story that betray them. But the next sentence immediately answers this loss depicted in the story by distinguishing what may yet save the narrative: "But if the vision was true and mighty, as I know, it is true and mighty yet; for such things are of the spirit, and it is in the darkness of their eyes that men get lost" (2). The tension between the power and truth of the vision and the "darkness in men's eyes" remains, but the re-counting of the vision in the words of autobiography re-creates its power and rearticulates its truth for the future. Such a tension between the autobiographer's *vision* and the readers' *darkness of perception* provide one reason for the continued power of spiritual autobiographies.

The Unfinished Spiral: Reading the Gaps and Silences

> And all is always now. Words strain,
> Crack and sometimes break, under the burden. . . .
> *(Burnt Norton* 149–50)

Finding language for the spiritual journey of the self has always been problematic. Augustine begins his *Confessions* with four paragraphs of speculation and prayer about the difficulty of shaping any finite language to express experience of the Infinite: "Can any man say enough when he speaks of you? Yet woe betide those who are silent about you! For even those who are most gifted with speech cannot find words to describe you" (1.4, p. 23). He then begins the story of his infancy as a time of learning to speak and write—but a time dependent on memory, his own and that of his parents. After a lifetime of learning to be a rhetorician—a master of words as signs—Augustine ends Book 9 by describing in words a mystical experience of God as Word, an experience that he simultaneously admits was beyond the reach of words:

> And while we [my mother and I] spoke of the eternal Wisdom, longing for it and straining for it with all the strength of our hearts, for one fleeting instant we reached out and touched it. Then with

a sigh, leaving *our spiritual harvest* [Rom 8:23] bound to it, we returned to the sound of our own speech, in which each word has a
beginning and an ending—far, far different from your Word, our
Lord, who abides in himself for ever, yet never grows old and gives
new life to all things. (9.10, pp. 197–98)

This inevitable gap between the human signifier and the divine
signified, which has been a perennial problem for both the theologian (for example, Aquinas on "divine names") and the spiritual
autobiographer, has become a series of fissures for contemporary
readers. As I have already noted, the modern context of religious
alienation has produced a gap between the seeker and the mediation of traditional religion, a gap causing years of search by a
Christian like Lewis or a Jew like Cowan to cross over with the
help of private mediators. The context of democratic autonomy
since the eighteenth century has also left the seeker with a gap
between the self and any social authorization of the search, as in
the case of Day or Merton having to leave their families, cities,
and class to find for themselves any ultimate meaning. The context of the individual search for a true sense of the deep self,
which I have called with Dunne the problem of self-appropriation, has driven many searchers to try on a number of masks or
identities, thus causing gaps within the unity of the psyche—for
instance, in the inconsistencies among the short-lived negative
identities of the young Malcolm X or Dan Wakefield. Finally,
the social and psychic pressure toward inauthenticity creates gaps
between what the searcher consciously desires and what may be
unconsciously driving him or her on, as Cowan, Merton, and
others discover in the process of writing their autobiographies. As
Merton says in *The Sign of Jonas*, the second autobiographical attempt of his life, "The complaints about the world in the *Mountain* and in some poems are perhaps a weakness. . . . The world I
am sore at on paper is perhaps a figment of my own imagination.
The business is a psychological game I have been playing since I
was ten. And yet there is plenty to be disgusted with in the
world" (163). Thus, the writing of autobiography may be one
bridge across the fissures of inauthenticity, one way to learn to
play fairly one's "psychological game."

Some deliberate omissions or disguising of names occurs for

reasons of sensitive concern for the privacy or reputation of living persons, as Day, Merton, and others acknowledge. Other gaps occur because the author sees no reasons to include details of secular events in a spiritual autobiography, such as Lewis's Oxford teaching and writing, Cowan's journalism, and Black Elk's family life. More troublesome gaps appear in episodes that include painful emotional experiences which the author cannot or will not confront, at least in public. Thus, even though Day tells us she is not going "to leave out all the sins" as she did in her earlier version of her autobiography, she fails in *The Long Loneliness* to mention some liaisons, and even an abortion, which her biographer uncovers (Miller ch. 5). Similarly, Merton idealizes his father's life as a painter and his influence on Merton, a move that leads to a variety of new interpretations of his life (see Mott, Cooper). Ideological influences can lead to misreadings of stages of one's life story, as Malcolm X admits to Haley while recounting his Black Muslim period from his later perspective as an orthodox Muslim. Ideology can also lead to historical omission, inaccuracies, or coalescences, as David Stoll has shown with regard to Menchú. Bizarre emotional patterns can be glossed over in vague phrases, as in Lewis's finessing of his relationship with Mrs. Janie Moore, a gap that biographers interpret in very different ways (see Green and Hooper, W. Griffin, and Wilson).

These fissures, moreover, have been widened in recent years by literary and philosophical theories that see all writing as a linguistic, psychological, or psychic game that cannot be won. For deconstructionists like Derrida or DeMan, autobiography is necessarily incoherent because of unbridgeable gaps between the inner concept and the outer image, between the present writer and the past life story, between the thinking self and the writing self, all such gaps expressed in the use of ambiguous figures of speech within the life story. This ambiguity is multiplied when one tries to cross the cultural gap to read an autobiography from another religion, as a caucasian Westerner does when taking up the life of Gandhi or Malcolm X.

The ten autobiographies of this study not only embody many of these gaps but show an awareness of them. On their title pages, *Black Elk Speaks* and *The Autobiography of Malcolm X* exhibit the most obvious gaps—those between the one who lived or spoke

the life story and the one who writes it, between the oral author
(Black Elk, Malcolm X, Menchú) and the manuscript author ("as
told through John G. Neihardt" or "with the assistance of Alex
Haley"). Haley's epilogue brings out even more clearly the circumstances of the writing of the autobiography—the shifting situation of Malcolm X's life during the midnight meetings with
Haley, the breakthrough achieved by talking about his mother,
the final days of Malcolm X's life and their parallels that Haley
finds with the opening events of Malcolm's childhood. Neihardt's
preface and postscript give Black Elk's story a frame that (along
with his changes in the chronology, his omission of details, and
his exclusion of Black Elk's later life and conversion to Catholicism) alters the significance of the story.

Paul Cowan's journalistic research into his ancestors' motives
and lives leads him to admit that "much of a book like this must
be largely speculative, and the guesswork is mine" (viii). Merton
is only one of several autobiographers who express a variety of
self-interpretations as they review their original texts. For instance, Gandhi admits in the preface to his autobiography that he
was warned by a friend: "Supposing you reject tomorrow the
things you hold in principle today?" (xi). Several other writers
acknowledge the gaps between what Lewis calls "general" autobiography and a "spiritual" autobiography, the latter focusing ex-
clusively on the personal journey toward a religious conversion.
Even the latter, as Wakefield says, "could be viewed as a spiritual
journey as well as a series of secular adventures of accomplishment
and disappointment, personal and professional triumphs and defeat" (xi). Thus, he, like others, is aware of the many "frameworks" within which an autobiography can be read. Even the
circumstances of living as an ongoing "self" in the present limit
the completeness of the written story of one's life.

Despite these gaps, we still read these autobiographies. All are
still popular and available ten to seventy years after their first appearance. They touch our lives with the authenticity and challenge of their human expression of the search for the ultimate.
Why? Are they merely parables of the life journey, helpful "fictions" to bolster our imaginations in the struggle for faith in an
age of unbelief? They do use "fiction," in the sense of creative
selections of narrative devices common to both novels and

journalistic stories. But as autobiography, they include enough externally verifiable details—specific events, persons, conversations—to distinguish them from novels and to appeal to the reader's desire for a different type of truth or objectivity. Certainly, they do not exhibit the detached objectivity of scientific experiments that eliminate the subjectivity of the writer as much as possible. Rather, these autobiographies are, in Lewis's words, "suffocatingly subjective" in their concentration on the inner personal experience of the writer. They are also not a complete account of all important family and personal details, as given from the outside in their biographies, for example in Brown on Gandhi, Miller on Day, Mott on Merton, or Griffin or Wilson on Lewis. Neither are they intermittent collections of moments of their lives, as found in their letters or diaries.

Instead of using the frequently parodied and obviously inadequate analogy of the "mirror" as a figure of objective truth (as if all knowing were merely "taking a look" at an object, a person, an idea, or a process), let us examine the process of coming to know another person in ordinary life. For this daily human process seems a more helpful analogy for reading an autobiography than the analogy of looking at an object or of watching a scientific experiment. In coming to know another person, we notice at least the following components or steps:

We come into the other person's presence and focus our attention on perceiving and understanding that person through the expressions on his or her face, words, gestures, and so forth. As we attend to the person, we are peripherally aware of ourselves as we converse with him or her. Afterward, we often think over what the person said or did, sometimes summing up that individual's personality in such phrases as, "What a friendly guy," or "She's a perceptive woman," or "Quite a talkative old man." Perhaps we go on to ask ourselves questions about the person's motives or character—"Why did she say that?" or "What was the meaning of that strange gesture?" or "What sort of a person would respond that way to a simple remark?" In this process of seeking for insight into the person, we usually compare the various times we have met him or her to see if we find patterns in the words or actions. In all these reflections, of course, we are certain that we are talking with and about the same person, just as we are the same one doing the perceiving, questioning, and reflecting. In fact, we can go further and compare all our other personal friendships in order to help us find patterns in this particular person's character. In addition, supplementing all these personal reflections, we can bring to bear what we have learned of the larger social patterns that are relevant to this new person—for instance, the nationality, job and social situation, political opinions, and so on. In the complex but conscious process of talking with this new person, we usually take time to tell him or her some important events in our own life and listen to the response.[3]

In brief, we regularly experience ourselves in conversation with other persons in which we are simultaneously aware of ourselves, our cognitive process, and the other; from this basic triple consciousness we are able to reflect on ourselves in relationship to others and to the context of our world; and from this reflection we are able to narrate ourselves as living a life story. Autobiography, to sum up, is a narrative that embodies the life story of an author as self-conscious subject present to itself but also reflectively exploring and affirming the interrelationships of his or her interior, interpersonal, and social world. While lacking the clarity and necessity of other types of knowledge—scientific, mathematical, or metaphysical—the story told by the autobiographer can be heard and interpreted by the astute reader with the reasonable

---

[3] If one were to sum up this interpersonal knowledge in more formal language, the process might go something like this: (1) we are present to ourselves as *conscious subjects* of a series of acts of questioning, seeing, listening, guessing, coming to insight, examining the insight for its coherence and correspondence with the experience; (2) we have the ability to *reflect* and actually do reflect (in a later moment) on these acts, even bringing to explicit attention what was only unnoticed or peripherally present to our awareness; (3) we have the ability as conscious selves to *explore* not only the present moment but also through memory the past as related to the present and as projecting into the future; (4) we have the ability to *affirm* the previous three stages of consciousness as acts of our personal unified selves developing in time; (5) we have the ability to relate all these acts to the interpersonal world and the social world within which they occur and which influence these acts as well as provide objects to be experienced, understood, and judged; (6) we have the ability to recognize and organize our lives as *narratives* in time, with a beginning–middle–end, with connections of various types (causal, incidental, etc.) and expressed in the devices of narration.

For a more speculative treatment of the knowledge of the self in relation to other persons, the reader might consult Ricoeur, Levinas, Lonergan (chs. 1 and 3), Polanyi, and Buber.

degree of probability and reliance given to any other example of interpersonal knowledge. Of course, one must bring into play all the interpretative powers used in any literary work—a sense of language, metaphor, structure, signs of presence and absence, silences, gaps, and glimmers. The use of such powers, however, leads to greater reflective awareness and more accurate understanding of the person revealed in and between the lines of the autobiography. One must also bring to the interpretation of an autobiography whatever one learns from other sources— biography, social history, psychology, and the like.

With all these aspects grasped as true of oneself and of others as self-revealers, the reader can recognize the benefit that Dunne finds in the process of "passing over" to another's life story through the reading of autobiographies:

> The process of passing over by sympathetic understanding to others and coming back to a new understanding of ourselves may itself be the hint of an answer to the questions we raise. . . . Passing over is the way a man discovers the shape of the life story in other ages, the story of deeds, the story of experience, and coming back from this to his own time is how he discovers by contrast its current shape, the story of appropriation. (ix)

In an age of religious alienation from a common community of faith and mediation, or in an age of social individualism and autonomy, one can find mediators in the lives of those who have found spiritual meaning *in their life story* and have embodied that meaning in an autobiography. In fact, the act of writing, rather than being an alienating experience of the loss of self, can become a moment of insight into the fullness of the self, moving the writer from what Merton calls the merely "empirical self" to the level of the "deep self" open to the Ultimate (or what Dunne, following Yeats, calls the "soul"). The writing of one's life journey seems to have been for these ten central religious autobiographers of our century the creation in symbolic form of the self-affirmation of the person as transformed from lost to found, from seeker to discoverer, from alienated to reunited with a higher and deeper One. The autobiography as narrative provides, not a "mirror" for the naïve observer, but an analogous form, using all the devices of narrative, for the shape of the life story.

The human self does not exist in mere spiritual isolation, but is essentially a symbolizing and narrating being. As a person, he or she must express or embody the question that is at the core of its self in time and space through choices, events, relationships, and institutions of daily life with other selves. So, too, the autobiographer of that questing self must find in narrative the plot, frame, character, setting, and style which prove "answerable" symbols to the question raised by the life story. The reader, while always alert for the inadequacy of the symbol, can intelligently entrust himself or herself to the experience of the other's life story insofar as he or she is willing to trust any personal relationship. To know the other as other is always a risk, but without the risk, one loses one's very self and one's way. For only in passing over can one return to the fullness of one's own journey. Even in an age of the whirlwind, one can listen in on others' lives for the still small voice. Without entering the consciousness of others by sharing their narrated life stories, the reader remains locked in the prison of the present self, and, as Eliot says at the beginning of *Burnt Norton*, "If all time is eternally present / All time is unredeemable" (4–5). But to enter the "time past and time future" of others' life stories is to "allow but a little consciousness," enough perhaps to redeem and have the time of one's life, for "only through time time is conquered" (83–85, 90). The use of language and story to "pass over" may be precarious, but, for the careful reader, as for Eliot confronting the lives of Dante or Yeats in *Little Gidding*, "the words sufficed / To compel the recognition" (99–100). The act of writing and the act of reading an autobiography of someone who has redeemed the lifetime from mere factual time by discovering the pattern of its conversions—its images, feelings, insights, commitments, twists, tensions, losses, gaps, and symbolic form—are to be called to explore the spiral of one's own exploring:

> We shall not cease from exploration
> And the end of all our exploring
> Will be to arrive where we started
> And know the place for the first time.
> (*Little Gidding* 239–42)

REFERENCES

Augustine, St. *Confessions*. Trans. R. S. Pine-Coffin. Middlesex: Penguin, 1961.

Barbour, J. D. *The Conscience of the Autobiographer*. New York: St. Martin's, 1992.

Brown, Judith M. *Gandhi: Prisoner of Hope*. New Haven: Yale UP, 1989.

———. *Gandhi's Rise to Power: Indian Politics, 1915–1922*. Cambridge: Cambridge UP, 1972.

Bruss, Elizabeth W. *Autobiographical Acts*. Baltimore: Johns Hopkins UP, 1976.

Buber, Martin. *I and Thou*. New York: Scribner's, 1970.

Coles, Robert. *Dorothy Day: A Radical Devotion*. Reading, MA: Addison-Wesley, 1987.

Conn, Walter. *Christian Conversion*. New York: Paulist, 1986.

Conway, Jill Ker. *When Memory Speaks: Reflections on Autobiography*. New York: Knopf, 1998.

Cooley, Thomas. *Educated Lives: The Rise of Modern Autobiography in America*. Columbus: Ohio State UP, 1976.

Cooper, David D. *Thomas Merton and the Art of Denial*. Athens: U of Georgia P, 1989.

Couser, G. Thomas. *American Autobiography: The Prophetic Mode*. Amherst: U of Massachusetts P, 1979.

Delaney, Paul. *British Autobiography in the Seventeenth Century*. London: Routledge & Kegan Paul, 1969.

Duckworth, George E. *Structural Patterns and Proportions in "The Aeneid."* Ann Arbor: U of Michigan P, 1962.

Dunne, John S. *The Search for God in Time and Memory*. New York: Macmillan, 1969.

Eakin, Paul John. *Fictions in Autobiography*. Princeton, NJ: Princeton UP, 1985.

Earle, William. *The Autobiographical Consciousness: A Philosophical Inquiry into Existence*. Chicago: Quadrangle, 1972.

Ebner, Dean. *Autobiography in Seventeenth-Century England: Theology and the Self*. The Hague: Mouton, 1971.

Egan, Susanne. *Patterns of Experience in Autobiography*. Chapel Hill: U of North Carolina P, 1984.

30   CIRCUITOUS JOURNEYS

Elbacz, Robert. *The Changing Nature of the Self: A Critical Study of the Autobiographic Discourse.* Iowa City: U of Iowa P, 1987.

Eliade, Mircea. *Cosmos and History: The Myth of the Eternal Return.* New York: Harper, 1959.

Eliot, T. S. *The Complete Poems and Plays of T. S. Eliot: 1909–1950.* New York: Harcourt, 1971.

Fleishman, Avron. *Figures of Autobiography.* Berkeley: U of California P, 1983.

Freccero, John. "Dante's Pilgrim in a Gyre," *PMLA* 76 (June 1961): 168–81.

———. "Donne's 'Valediction Forbidding Mourning,' " *English Literary History* 30 (1963): 335–76.

Green, Roger, and Walter Hooper. *C. S. Lewis: A Biography.* New York: Harcourt, 1974.

Griffin, Emilie. *Turning: Reflections on the Experience of Conversion.* New York: Doubleday, 1980.

Griffin, William. *Clive Staples Lewis: A Dramatic Life.* New York: Harper, 1986.

Gunn, Janet. *Autobiography: Toward a Poetics of Experience.* Philadelphia: U of Pennsylvania P, 1982.

Hawkins, Anne. *Archetypes of Conversion.* Lewisburg, PA: Bucknell UP, 1985.

Heidt, Edward. *Vision Voiced: Narrative Viewpoint in Autobiographical Writing.* New York: Peter Lang, 1991.

Leibowitz, Herbert. *Fabricating Lives: Explorations in American Autobiography.* New York: Knopf, 1989.

Leigh, David J. "Augustine's *Confessions* as a Circular Journey," *Thought* 40 (Mar. 1985): 73–88.

Lejeune, Philippe. *On Autobiography*. Trans. Katherine Leary. Ed. Paul John Eakin. Minneapolis: U of Minnesota P, 1989.

Levinas, Emmanuel. *The Levinas Reader.* Trans. Sean Hand. Cambridge, MA: Blackwell, 1989.

Lonergan, Bernard. *Method in Theology.* New York: Herder, 1972.

Mandela, Nelson. *Long Walk to Freedom: The Autobiography of Nelson Mandela.* Boston: Little, Brown, 1994.

Mehlman, Jeffrey. *A Structural Study of Autobiography.* Ithaca, NY: Cornell UP, 1974.

Merton, Thomas. *The Seven Storey Mountain.* New York: Harcourt, 1948.

————. *The Sign of Jonas*. New York: Doubleday, 1953, 1956.

Miller, William. *Dorothy Day: A Biography*. San Francisco: Harper, 1982.

Morris, John N. *Versions of the Self: Studies in English Autobiography from John Bunyan to John Stuart Mill*. New York: Basic Books, 1966.

Mott, Michael. *The Seven Mountains of Thomas Merton*. Boston: Houghton, 1984.

Olney, James, ed. *Autobiography: Essays Theoretical and Critical*. Princeton, NJ: Princeton UP, 1980.

————. *Metaphors of Self: The Meaning of Autobiography*. Princeton, NJ: Princeton UP, 1972.

————. *Studies in Autobiography*. New York: Oxford UP, 1988.

Pascal, Roy. *Design and Truth in Autobiography*. Cambridge, MA: Harvard UP, 1960.

Polanyi, Michael. *Personal Knowledge*. Chicago: U of Chicago P, 1958.

Poulet, Georges. *Les métamorphoses du cercle*. Paris: Plon, 1961.

Ricoeur, Paul. *Oneself as Another*. Chicago: U of Chicago P, 1992.

Shea, Daniel B., Jr. *Spiritual Autobiography in Early America*. Princeton, NJ: Princeton UP, 1968.

Shumaker, Wayne. *English Autobiography: Its Emergence, Materials, and Forms*. Berkeley: U of California P, 1954.

Spengemann, W. C. *The Forms of Autobiography*. New Haven, CT: Yale UP, 1980.

Starr, George A. *Defoe and Spiritual Autobiography*. Princeton, NJ: Princeton UP, 1965.

Stoll, David. *Rigoberta Menchú and the Story of All Poor Guatemalans*. Boulder, CO: Westview, 1999.

Stone, Albert E. *Autobiographical Occasions and Original Acts*. Philadelphia: U of Pennsylvania P, 1982.

Weintraub, Karl J. *The Value of the Individual: Self and Circumstance in Autobiography*. Chicago: U of Chicago P, 1978.

Whitman, Cedric. *Homer and the Heroic Tradition*. Cambridge, MA: Harvard UP, 1970.

Wilson, A. N. *C. S. Lewis: A Biography*. New York: Norton, 1990.

1

Thomas Merton's
The Seven Storey Mountain

A HALF-CENTURY after its publication, *The Seven Storey Mountain* remains the most popular of Merton's fifty books. Why is this life story, with all its youthful exaggerations, stylistic lapses, and revealing omissions, so readable?[1] I would suggest that Merton's practice as a young novelist and poet helps to explain the power and popularity of his autobiography. The autobiography embodies in a rudimentary but sophisticated narrative Merton's resolution of a profound personal crisis. In a later book, *Conjectures of a Guilty Bystander*, he explains that ". . . a personal crisis is creative and salutory if one can accept the conflict and restore unity on a higher level, incorporating the opposed elements in a higher unity" (189). This literary structure of "incorporating the opposed elements in a higher unity" describes Merton's version of the circular journey of his life. This picture of a circular journey of "opposed elements" moving up the "seven storey mountain" of his purgatorial life holds the central plot of the autobiography together. It also holds the imagination of the readers as they follow the journey and discover that it contains the major traits of modern spiritual autobiographies—Merton's directional image, his narrative sections, his parental conflicts, his insights through mediators, his confrontations with death, the sequence of his conversions, and his use of writing.

Unlike the other, middle-aged autobiographers in this study, Merton began writing his life story when he was only in his late

---

[1] Recent studies of Merton's *The Seven Storey Mountain* have tried to reread his life story by focusing on what he omits from the final text. Cooper, Kountz, Mott, Padavano, Shannon, and others have provided many insights into Merton's unhappy childhood, his idealization of his father, his one-sided portrait of his godfather, his exaggerated view of life at Cambridge, and his lack of details about his contemplative prayer and his sexual life. But we still have much to learn from the structures and patterns of the autobiography itself.

twenties. Yet he chose as a title a circular journey form—the spiral seven-storey mountain of the *Purgatorio*, which describes the middle portion of Dante's journey. Ironically, or perhaps prophetically, Merton's age of twenty-nine when he begins his story in 1944 turns out to be just past the midpoint of his life (1915–68). The twenty-seven years of his pre-monastic life narrated in *The Seven Storey Mountain* make up the first half of his life story. Yet his relative prematurity, both as an autobiographer and as a monk, suggests why many of the "opposed elements" of the narrative are eventually resolved in a "higher unity" that itself will undergo further circling in his subsequent autobiographical writings. In brief, Merton's early encounters with death precipitate many premature conflicts that lead to a lifelong series of unexpected spirals on his journey.

MERTON'S DIRECTIONAL IMAGE: THE CAPTIVE TRAVELER

Merton's fundamental childhood experience was one of abandonment to captivity. These feelings derived from the death of his mother when Tom was six, and the frequent travels of his father, leading up to the latter's death when Tom was sixteen. But the imagery of exile and captivity flowing from the experience of abandonment begins with the opening paragraph. Here Merton describes his birth in the middle of "a great war" where he is a "prisoner of my own violence and my own selfishness, in the image of the world into which I was born," a world that is "the picture of Hell" full of "self-contradictory hungers." Thus, he is born not into a purgatory but into a hell, the one place that has abandoned God and feels itself abandoned in turn. This description is followed by a sentence describing soldiers abandoned in trenches of the First World War. This section, in turn, leads into the pages portraying his father and mother, both of whom are simultaneously "captives" of the infernal world and "lifted above" it by their vocation as artists (3). This image of simultaneous captivity and freedom leads into the primary dynamic self-image of Merton himself throughout the autobiography—*a traveling prisoner in search of freedom and home*. Like his mother, who had journeyed from America, and his father, from New Zealand to

Prades in southern France where Tom was born, Merton in the story "began a somewhat long journey" (4). His journey is a variant of Augustine's running the gamut of experience, for Merton wants "to grab everything and see everything and investigate every experience and then talk about it" (4).

There is no need to recount Merton's numerous travels in his autobiography, especially in Part One. What is important to note is the tension—"self-contradictory hungers"—in Merton's feelings and images of himself: an incessant traveler seeking a permanent home, a searcher for freedom always envisioning a permanent relationship. These tensions appear in his earliest drawings. At one time, he draws "a picture of the house, and everybody sitting under the pine trees, on a blanket, on the grass." But most of the time, he draws "pictures of boats" (9). Later, in describing his reading, Merton tells of playing "prisoner's base all over those maps" in his geography books and then concludes, "I wanted to become a sailor" (10–11). After listening to stories of Greek mythology, he dreams of traveling with Jason or Theseus "towards the freedom of my own ever-changing horizon" (11). He sums up the tensions of his earliest sense of vocation in a comment on his fascination with an anchor in a stained-glass window in the local Episcopal church: "Strange interpretation of a religious symbol ordinarily taken to signify stability in Hope. . . . To me it suggested just the opposite. Travel, adventure, the wide sea, and unlimited possibilities of human heroism, with myself as the hero" (13).

After the death of his mother, Tom's sense of abandonment and his desire for both travel and home become jumbled together by what he calls the "continual rearrangement of our lives and our plans from month to month" (18). He describes the boat and train trip from Long Island to Provincetown (16–17), where he revels in the fishing boats and listens to his father reading out of a John Masefield book "full of pictures of sailing ships" (17). After returning to Long Island, Tom learns "how to draw pictures of schooners and barks and clippers and brigs" (17). From there, when his father returns by boat to Bermuda, Tom is taken along to the island, where he is shuffled from place to place as his father's painting demands. Finally, his father returns to New York for an exhibition, calls for Tom, but then leaves him and his brother with their grandparents for two years on Long Island. The exits and journeys of this section of the autobiography become paradigms of the overall movement of Merton's life story: a short-term home, then abandonment, and, finally, reunion, often on a series of islands—Long Island, Bermuda, England, Isle of Wight, Manhattan, Cuba. Eventually Gethsemani monastery itself becomes a sort of spiritual island.

Even during the relative permanence of the years in southern France described in "Our Lady of the Museums," Merton begins another journey, at age ten, with the arrival at Calais and a long train trip with his father to the Midi, where he says, "I felt at home" (32). In fact, his main desire here is for a "home" with his father and brother (33). Yet in the Lycée where he boards during the week, he writes adventure stories based on travel novels like *Westward Ho!* (52). After describing the relatively stable three years in St. Antonin, where he is once again separated from his father in the detested boarding school, Merton ends this chapter with his father's announcement that his son is going to England, an event that makes his whole world resound with what Merton calls "liberty, liberty, liberty" (60). Just as his father had completed building their house (composed of fragments of local religious architecture in France), Tom is uprooted from the Midi and sent to live with his Aunt Maud in Ealing near London. In brief, the directional imagery of the first two chapters—the account of his childhood—suggests the inner tension of Merton's entire life: when he travels, he wants a home; when he finds a home, his father has to move, and so Tom, too, longs to travel. Thus, Tom becomes the captive of his contradictory hungers for both freedom and stability.

Surrounding or supporting this directional image is the major elemental metaphor in the first part of *The Seven Storey Mountain*—water. It is no coincidence that Merton tells us in the first sentence of the book that he was born under the sign of the Water Bearer, for he mentions water in nearly every episode of his childhood: his father's birth "beyond many oceans" (4); the return to New York by a "crossing of the sea" (6); his own drawing of ocean liners (9); his desire to be a sailor and "go to sea" (13); the Provincetown trip, when the "waters spoke loudly" (16); life in Bermuda, where "the sun shone on the blue waters of the sea, and on the islands in the bay" (19). Even when he reaches France, the country becomes the "spring of natural waters, . . . cleansed by grace" (30), where he learns to "drink from fountains of the Middles Ages" (32).

The water metaphor, however, is ambiguous—at times associated with cleansing, at others, with falling into an abyss. These two traditional symbolic meanings of water in literature are not insignificant in Merton's autobiography. For in each of the three parts of the text, Merton identifies in himself a desire for *cleansing* and also a fear of the *abyss*. The word "clean," for example, is used to describe his father's painting on the first page of the autobiography and appears dozens of times throughout the text. Similarly, his desire for freedom leads him in Part One across waters of abandonment to various abysses of sin or near madness; in Part Two, he passes through the "Red Sea" of baptism to the abyss of anticlimax in his life of minimal Catholic practice but ends with a description of himself reaching "the edge of an abyss" in his desire for a vocation to the priesthood: "the abyss was an abyss of love and peace, the abyss was God" (255). In Part Three, when he enters the monastery to make a retreat at Gethsemani, he finds the place beneath the sign "God alone" to be "frighteningly clean" (321), and as he arrives, he says, "I stepped into the cloister as if into an abyss" (323). There he sees monks in the liturgy bowing "like white seas" and describes a new monk taking his white habit: "The waters had closed over his head, and he was submerged in the community" (325). During the retreat, Merton experiences "graces that overwhelmed me like a tidal wave, truths that drowned me with the force of their impact" (323). Finally, he addresses, on the last page of the narrative, a poem to his dead brother, "buried at sea" (403). Even the epilogue renews the water imagery by describing Merton's other self—the writer—as "the old man of the sea" (411).

In effect, the directional image of the "captive traveler" expands through its contradictory associations with both cleansing water and the original abyss to include the conflicts of an upward circular movement in his life story. As sailor and hero, he desires both travel and home, seeks cleansing and experiences the abyss in the same objects, reaches land which often turns out to be an island, and concludes with these contradictory hungers only tentatively resolved. He recapitulates the travel imagery in the epilogue: "We cannot arrive at the perfect possession of God in this life, and that is why we are travelling and in darkness. But we already possess Him by grace, and therefore in that sense we have arrived and are dwelling in the light" (419).

In brief, he ends his story by transferring to God the contradictions of his circular journey (and simultaneously reminding us of the paradoxical limits of language about God):

> I cannot bring any other man on this earth into the cloud where I dwell in Your light, that is, Your darkness, where I am lost and abashed. I cannot explain to any other man the anguish which is Your joy nor the loss which is the Possession of You, nor the distance from all things which is the arrival in You, nor the death which is the birth in You because I do not know anything about it myself and all I know is that I wish it were over—I wish it were begun.
> You have contradicted everything. (419–20)

Thus, Merton, following his directional image, ends his journey where Augustine begins his: with the paradoxes of language about the beginning and end of all words.

MERTON'S NARRATIVE STRUCTURE: THE CIRCULAR JOURNEY UPWARD THROUGH CONFLICTS

Even this brief study of the directional imagery of *The Seven Storey Mountain* suggests that the story combines uneasily the traditional narrative patterns of the journey and the battle. This tension reflects the pattern of the two archetypal religious autobiographies in the West: Augustine's *Confessions*, a quest story, and John Bunyan's *Grace Abounding*, a psychomachia or "soul struggle." The tension between these two patterns reflects itself in the very titles of the chapters. In Part One, "Prisoner's Base" suggests the captivity of the players in this children's game and their desire for travel. "Our Lady of the Museums" and "The Children in the Market Place" picture the static situation in which the hero is battling with various voices or temptations. "The Harrowing of Hell" recaptures the image of movement again, but a movement that is painful and reluctant on the part of the hero. The last, of course, in tradition recalls the freeing by Christ of ancient captives in the underworld, primarily from purgatory. Thus, the titles of Part One coincide with the circular journey, moving from the hell of the opening scene up the spirals of the mountain of Dante's *Purgatorio* in subsequent chapters.

In Part Two, the title of the first chapter, "With a Great Price," suggests the tension of the sufferings of Christ; the other, "The Waters of Contradiction," indicates the Exodus movement of the Israelites through the Red Sea into their desert wanderings. Once again, the combination of battle and journey appears in the imagery of the first two titles in Part Three, "Magnetic North" and "True North"; whereas the last two titles point to places of tension and its release: "The Sleeping Volcano" of Harlem and "The Sweet Savor of Liberty" of Gethsemani (the latter a place of inner battle for Christ on his journey to death and resurrection).

What the chapter titles do not indicate, however, is the complexity of narrative patterns in the overall autobiography. A closer analysis of the main events of each of the three parts uncovers a repeated threefold pattern of movement: (1) journey movement forward (upward and centripetal); (2) battle movement back and forth between extremes (sideways and centrifugal); (3) negative journey movements backward or into dead ends (downward and centrifugal). In several parts of the narrative, we discover parallels between the specific events or persons in each of these three movements, thus making it another variant of the circular journey found in other modern spiritual autobiographies. As a realistic writer giving detailed accounts of his journey, with interspersed theological commentaries, Merton uses the symbolic parallels only intermittently, but with enough regularity to remind the reader of Malcolm X or Dorothy Day.

No critic so far has convincingly shown the structural key to *The Seven Storey Mountain* to be any seven "storeys" or "stories" within the autobiography. But if we focus on the external *journey* only in Parts One and Three, leaving aside Part Two for analysis later as primarily an internal *battle* leading to a double conversion, we find a clearer narrative pattern. In the journeys of Parts One and Three, the following seven "stories" emerge, all narratives of the gradual loss of family, home, and identity; then a gradual search through Catholicism for a new family, home, and identity.

Part One is a story of descent ending in the subways of New York City; Part Three is a story of ascent ending in the gardens of Gethsemani monastery.

(1) Merton leaves his childhood home with his parents in Douglastown, after the loss of his mother, to wander in Bermuda (I, 1).

(2) Merton settles in his youthful home with his father in St. Antonin, only to travel to stay with his aunt in Ealing near London (I, 2).

(3) Merton lives as an adolescent in Oakham and Cambridge, during which period he loses his father, gains worldly godparents, and begins his moral wandering (I, 3).

(4) Merton moves back to New York and finds an intellectual home at Columbia University, only to lose his grandparents and continue his spiritual wandering (I, 4).

After his conversion experiences of Part Two, Merton settles in three new places.

(5) Merton searches for priesthood in Greenwich Village (III, 1).

(6) Merton creates a monastery in the world in Olean (III, 2).

(7) Merton experiments with social involvement at Friendship House in Harlem (III, 3).

However helpful this charting of the seven places of his purgatorial journey might appear, it does not suggest the many parallels between the events of Part One and the events of Part Three. For instance, we find surprising similarities on the train journeys of each of these parts. Both the opening and the closing parts begin with a train journey. Part One opens with his trip across France to a temporary home in New York; Part Three begins with a train trip from New York to the Franciscan seminary where he becomes "vaguely aware of my homelessness" just before he is rejected from any home, parents, or identity with the Franciscans (296–97). The middle of Parts One and Three includes important train trips as well. In fact, the train trips form something of a triangle, in Part One between Paris, southern France, and Rome; in Part Three between New York City, Olean, and Gethsemani. Both sections also include ocean voyages: Part One between England and New York, Part Three between New York and Cuba.

The trip to Rome in I, 3 suddenly becomes an accidental pilgrimage, where Merton visits churches, forms his first image of

Christ in the ancient Catholic culture, and experiences a vision of
his deceased father that impels him to prayer for the first time in
his life (109). The trip to Cuba in III, 1 is also a pilgrimage, this
time a deliberate one, where he also visits churches, forms his first
image of the Virgin (as Our Lady of Solitude) in a contemporary
Catholic culture, and has a "manifestation of God's presence"
during the Mass, an event that impels him to contemplation for
the first time (279–85). The former event precedes the first mention of a passing desire "to become a Trappist monk" (114); the
latter event leads into his rejection as a Franciscan candidate and
eventual desire to become a Trappist. In fact, the first pilgrimage
parallels both the Cuban pilgrimage and the pilgrmage to Gethsemani for his first retreat (320ff.).

Both Parts One and Three also end with a train trip. Part One
ends with a train taking Merton down into the "tunnel under the
river" toward Long Island, the low point of his homeless wanderings when he is suffering a nervous breakdown after the death of
his grandparents (161). He calls this experience "the death of the
hero" in the "blind alley" of despair which he had reached on his
purgatorial descent through Part One. Part Three likewise ends
with a train trip (III, 3) which carries him across the river on a
bridge to Kentucky, the end of his search for a spiritual home in
Gethsemani where, after "a civil, moral death" to the past, he
experiences an exultation of joy at entering "the four walls of my
new freedom" (369, 372).

Thus, as we have noted, the first part of Merton's captive travels
moves from total family home on an island (Douglastown) to a
one-parent home first on an island (Bermuda) and then amid monasteries in France (St. Antonin), then to a parentless series of
schools in the country (the Lycée, Oakham, Cambridge), and, finally, across an ocean to the city where his grandparents die, leaving him in a radical identity crisis (New York City). Similarly, Part
Three moves outward (after his inner two-stage conversion to Catholicism and desire for priesthood in Part Two) through a series
of temporary schools and homes (Perry Street, St. Bonaventure,
Harlem) to a final home on a spiritual island in the Kentucky
countryside. Just as he calls St. Antonin a center of past Catholic
culture in France, and New York City the center of the "world"
(with all the negative theological connotations of this term from

St. John's Gospel), so he finds in the monastic island of Gethsemani the true spiritual center of the country: "This is the center of all the vitality that is in America" (325). Many of the details associated in Merton's mind with the values of his early homes—the birds singing on Sunday in Douglastown (10), the "sacrament of her land" in France (32), the building of a home from religious artifacts (39), the fascinating books filled with pictures of cathedrals and abbeys (43)—all these reappear in different forms in the portrait of his final monastic home in the chapters on Gethsemani (III, 4).

This broad parallelism between the travel and places of Parts One and Three is reinforced by the remarkable parallels between the persons who influence Merton on his journey. It is no coincidence that Part One reads like a series of losses or deaths of those closest to Tom (his mother, his father, his aunt, his godfather, his friends, his grandparents, and, finally, his old self as "hero" of his story). What seems more surprising is that Part Three reads like series of parallel attempts to regain a father (Dan Walsh, Abbot Dunne), an aunt-figure (Catherine de Hueck), a godfather (his confessor), friends (Lax, Gibney, etc.), even grandparents (the older monks), and a new self as "saint" to be. Perhaps the most consistent parallel lies between the gradual separation from his brother of Part One and the gradual reunion with him in Part Three. In the six appearances of John Paul in Part One, he first appears as an ideal baby having a "serener nature" than Tom's, and "singing a little tune" to which the family listens (8). Next his brother provides Tom with a model of unselfish love by his dedicated following of his rejecting older brother and friends (23). After their separation in childhood when Tom goes to live with his father, leaving John Paul with his grandparents, Tom sees him only on the family visits to France (45) or England (76). Reunited in Douglastown when Tom goes to Columbia, they play music and go to movies together before John Paul goes off to a year of "inner confusion" at Cornell (148–51). The movement of physical separation leads, ironically, to a similar ending, when Tom describes his brother's first year at Cornell as a "long sordid riot" similar to his own at Cambridge. If the two brothers move apart and then together in their moral journey downward in Part One, they move upward together, with Tom again leading the way, throughout the six appearances of John Paul in Part Three. John

Paul first joins Tom at Mass during a visit to Cornell (287), then goes into and out of the Naval Reserve, following his "restlessness" to Mexico (309). All the while, John Paul is considering Catholicism, a fact he finally admits to his brother on visit to Olean (335). After Tom learns of John Paul's decision to join the Canadian Air Force, he commends him to the care of St. Thérèse (355). Finally, the two brothers unite during John Paul's visit to Gethsemani, where he takes instructions from Tom and is baptized (393). The narrative ends with the death of the younger brother, commemorated in Tom's best poem at that point of his life as a writer and a monk.

Although perhaps motivated in part by a desire to make amends for his mistreatment of John Paul as a child, Merton's extensive parallels of himself and his brother serve a more important religious and literary purpose. They provide an embedded story reinforcing the validity of Merton's own upward circular journey. In both brothers, one notices a parallel between the negative identities taken on during adolescence and a later positive identity emerging during moral and religious conversion. At Ealing, Tom goes through a "religious phase"; at Oakham, he takes on the identity of a student of literature; at Cambridge, he becomes an aesthetic sensualist; at Columbia, he shifts from communist to journalist to "big man on campus." Nearly all these negative or partial identities, which he takes on during his downward spiral as he struggles after the death of his mother and father, are transformed in Part Three into parallels in the form of positive identities by which he is preparing himself for his ultimate life commitment. The merely superficial religious phase of his early adolescence becomes an intense period when he tries to live as a monk in the world. The student of literature at Oakham becomes the young instructor of English at St. Bonaventure's College in Olean. The aesthetic sensualist of Cambridge and Columbia becomes the serious pursuer of asceticism through a private version of the Jesuit *Spiritual Exercises* and through retreats in monasteries. The three-month communist rebel of his first semester at Columbia becomes the social worker with Catherine de Hueck in Harlem. The Columbia University journalist becomes the obsessive Olean novelist who turns out a novel every six months. The "big man on campus" who had to leave campus because of nervous exhaustion becomes the obscure teacher who chooses to leave campus at mid-term to follow his call to be a Trappist. In fact, the negative self-portrait as a failed captive of the world (I, 4; p. 164), which concludes Part One, parallels in reverse the positive self-portrait of himself as he enters the monastery (III, 3; p. 370): "I found that it was I who was emptied and robbed and gutted. What a strange thing! In filling myself, I had emptied myself. In grasping things, I had lost everything. In devouring pleasures and joys, I had found distress and anguish and fear" (164).

These traits are reversed as he describes himself entering the monastery in Part Three: "I was free. I had recovered liberty. I belonged to God, not to myself: and to belong to Him is to be free, free of all anxieties and worries and sorrows that belong to this earth, and the love of the things that are in it" (370).

What Merton does not mention explicitly until the epilogue is that he also brings into the cloister a "shadow" or "double" who creates new and lifelong problems of identity. As he himself admits:

> By this time I should have been delivered of any problems about my true identity. . . .
> But then there was this shadow, this double, this writer who had followed me into the cloister.
> He is still on my track. He rides my shoulders, sometimes, like the old man of the sea. I cannot lose him." (410)

The young man who had exhibited a double identity when he wrote novels as a child, essays on Blake and Dante as a teenager, and articles and reviews as a college student (Part One) continues to develop a double identity as a poet and novelist in Part Three. The lifelong tension of Merton's double identity derives, as we shall now see, from the double identity that he inherited from his two talented but intensely different parents.

MERTON'S BATTLE FOR INTEGRATION OF A PARENTAL DOUBLE IMAGE

Recent critics have explored many aspects of the influence of Merton's parents on his life.[2] What might shed new light on the

---

[2] The influence of Merton's parents has been well illuminated by Mott, Hawkins, Cooper, and others. They have shown, for example, how Merton's portrait

influence of his mother and father is the precise *age* of Tom when he experiences loss of and abandonment by each of them. His mother's sickness, which made her appear "thin and pale and rather severe" to Tom (14), begins when he is five years old and separates her from him when he is six, with her death in October 1921, just three months before Tom turns seven. This year is regarded by developmental psychologists as the end of the stage in which a child develops a sense of "initiative" along with a primitive form of conscience. The failure to develop either initiative or a conscience brings about aberrant forms of guilt. Furthermore, if traumas occur at this point, Erikson says, "the superego of the child can be primitive, cruel, and uncompromising," so that one effect might be "deep regression and lasting resentments because the parents themselves do not seem to live up to the new conscience" (255–57). For Tom, his mother at this stage helped develop his strong drives of initiative and a severe desire for perfection and control, but she then abandoned him when she died suddenly. This loss traumatizes him in the middle of a crucial life transition. His inner conflict at the division between his desires and his control helps explain why he can find no way to express the "tremendous weight of sadness and depression" (14) he feels after reading her letter to him about her fatal illness. In fact, many of Merton's extreme swings from self-criticism (or projected criticism of the "world") to extroverted play or self-publicity can be seen as the effects of extremes of repression and showing off, both signs of the truncated stage of initiative-*vs.*-guilt in Erikson's schema of human growth. Also lacking in Merton is the virtue to be achieved during this stage—a clear purpose in one's life.

One can see in much of Merton's life story a search for the "sense of purpose" he failed to achieve because of the timing of the death of his mother. However, he had achieved the virtues of

---

of his father omits some of the painter's weaknesses and deemphasizes the emotional effects of his affairs and intermittent desertions of Tom during childhood. Conversely, Merton's memory of his mother as a worried perfectionist is very one-sided, reflecting more his experience of sharing her with his brother and then losing her to stomach cancer when Tom was six. Hawkins's diagnosis of this memory as an "idealization of a weak father" and the "negation of a strong mother" is not unfounded.

the previous stages of childhood development—a basic trust and hope (I) and an autonomous power of will (II). Thus, he searches as a lifelong traveler for a purpose that eventually includes the field where truth/hope is most important (religion) and autonomous power of will is vital (art). But it takes him a lifetime to integrate these two fields in his psyche, precisely because of the fissure between initiative and guilt occasioned by the death of his mother when he is almost seven. Of course, along with this tension, she bequeathed to him several character traits that develop in unexpected ways—perfectionism, independence of character, and a Quakerlike respect for inferiority (Hawkins). "Mother wanted me to be independent, and not to run with the herd. I was to be original, individual, I was to have a definite character and ideals of my own. . . . [My life as a monk is] the thing for which I most thank and praise God, and which is of all things the ultimate paradoxical fulfilment of my mother's ideas for me" (11).

If his mother's influence proves paradoxical because of the timing of her death, his father's influence proves even more complicated. The idealized portrait of Owen Merton—emphasizing his religious sensitivity, his desire for a home, his respect for creation, his contemplative sense, and his "clean" aesthetic power—omits some of the painful aspects that must have affected Tom: his abandonment of the two boys for his painting, his inability to support the family, and his dalliance with a friend's wife before Tom's eyes in Bermuda. These painful traits lead Merton to an exaggeration, perhaps, of his father's artistic achievements and to some of his own inner conflicts over his ability as an artist-writer (Cooper). What is obviously influential is the timing of his father's death in January 1931—just days before Tom's sixteenth birthday. Whatever may have been the effects of earlier fluctuations in his father's presence in Tom's life, the total loss of a father at this crucial time of what Erikson calls "identity development" proved to be devastating to the young Merton. It occasioned the role confusion, susceptibility to infatuations, identification with literary heroes, temporary enthusiasm for ideologies, and negative identities that mark his journey from ages sixteen to twenty-one. In fact, one can see these negative identities forming and shifting all through what he later calls "The Harrowing of Hell" at Oakham and Cambridge, and among "The Children in the Market Place" at Columbia. The death of his father also led Tom to search for models and mediators who could provide the "fathering" he misses, a need he feels ever more painfully with the rejections by his godparents and the death of his grandparents—all recorded in the first part of his autobiography. As many critics have remarked, this abandonment by so many parent figures before he is twenty-one made Merton both fearful of and vulnerable to rejection throughout his life.

The timing of his father's death also helps explain why the young Merton, despite his popularity and outgoing personality, never achieved a satisfactory, long-term friendship with a woman. Even his censored account in *The Seven Storey Mountain* of his college years allows glimpses of his furtive romances and infatuations, as does a passing reference to the notorious affair that led to his permanent exile from England (Mott 84). If, as Erikson contends, the inability to settle one's identity also exacerbates the struggle for satisfaction in the next stage of personal development (intimacy), these emotional wanderings are more understandable. Merton's lack of an experience of positive intimacy made him desirous for the sublimated forms of religious love after his conversion, but also made him vulnerable to a midlife crisis over a brief but intense romantic involvement twenty years after he completed his autobiography (Mott 438ff.).

These experiences of loss of both parents created in Merton the tensions expressed in his chosen directional image—the captive traveler. The tensional image leads into a series of opposing ideas and values that transform the journey motif of Part One into the battle motif of Part Two. Here he reaches the midpoint of his autobiography, which he describes as crossing through the "Waters of Contradiction" (II, 2) because of divine grace earned "At a Great Price" (II, 1).

MERTON'S MEDIATORS ON HIS CIRCULAR JOURNEY

As we mentioned in our brief overview of the journey patterns of Parts One and Three, the structure of Part Two shifts from external journeys to an internal battle, a psychomachia. Through the stages of that early journey, Merton had gained a series of insights and values with the help of various mediators (163–65). But each of these insights or values had been matched by secular countervalues, producing the numerous tensions we found in his imagery and narrative patterns. The image of unselfish love provided by his brother in childhood (23–24) conflicts with the experience of selfish love he discovers in his infatuations. The sacramentality he discovered in France during his years at St. Antonin comes into conflict with the secular wasteland he finds in the insipid religious training at Oakham, the modern literature of his reading at Oakham, and the dissipated social life at Cambridge. The care for others he learns from his father or aunt conflicts with his self-hatred and with the aestheticism he learns from his guardian (80ff.). The early fascination with the Christ-figures of art in Rome and in the New Testament conflicts with the gentlemanly-class Christianity he sees in the Anglican church.

Thus, when Merton comes to narrate his central conversion story in Part Two, he shifts from a travel narrative to a description of the inner battle between the forces of "nature" and "grace" in his experience. Interestingly, he begins this section with a short treatise on grace and nature. He describes the situation of human "nature" as a series of conflictual and selfish problems that can be resolved only by divine help. As Merton puts it: "[I]n the concrete order of things God gave man a nature that was ordered to a supernatural life. . . . Our nature, which is a free gift of God, was given to us to be perfected and enhanced by another free gift that is not due it. This free gift is 'sanctifying grace' " (169).

He concludes this section by telling the reader that God draws people from the conflicts of nature to the transformations of divine grace "through the action of our fellow men" (170). This last phrase indicates the narrative thread that holds together the episodes of Part Two—the mediators who help Merton gain the insights and appreciate the values that will resolve the conflicts within the blind alley of his college life story.

> God brought me and a half a dozen others together at Columbia, and made us friends, in such a way that our friendship would work powerfully to rescue us from the confusion and the misery in which we had come to find ourselves. . . . All our salvation begins on the level of common and natural and ordinary things. . . . Books and ideas and poems and stories, pictures and music, buildings, cities,

places, philosophies were to be the materials on which grace would
work. (177–78)

Although the period covered by II, 1 is approximately the two
years of 1937 and 1938, Merton does not structure his conversion
battle in a chronological order. An outline of the main conflicts,
mediators, and resolutions indicates two main stages—first, in II,
1, i–iv, he describes an intellectual stage in which six groups
of people help him with what he calls the theoretical "groundwork of conversion" (204). Once these "internal contradictions
were resolving themselves out" (205), he still has to face the problem of will-to-action. Just as his conscience had previously gone
through tensions between repressive denial and extroverted
showing off, so now he realizes the tension cannot be resolved
merely in his mind. Thus, in II, 1, v–vi, Merton resolves the
irresolutions of his will by three dramatic actions—first by going
to Mass, then by going to see a priest, and finally by accepting
baptism.

Although this series of conflicts and resolutions seems somewhat arbitrary, they accord with the general "faculty psychology"
which Merton picked up in his reading of scholastic philosophy.
His first step, mediated by the Thomistic philosopher Gilson, is
to move beyond the "faculty" of the imagination to an intellectual notion of God. The next step, mediated by Mark Van Doren,
is to move from merely academic knowledge to the intellectual
seriousness of "real" knowledge of life. Third, assisted by Robert
Lax and other friends, Merton begins to take religion, especially
its contemplative dimension, seriously. Fourth, from reading
Blake and Huxley, he gains a respect for the "supernatural" life
of active contact with God through prayer, both ascetical and
mystical. Fifth, assisted by Bramachari, he regains respect for
Western religion, particularly St. Augustine and *The Imitation of
Christ*. Finally, by reading Jacques Maritain, he clarifies his thinking through the use of categories from Aristotelian and scholastic
philosophy, particularly the notion of the "virtues," as well as
the distinction between art and morality, including the difference
between intellectual and moral virtues. This latter distinction
gives Merton a language in which to express the major turning
point in the chapter—the movement from mere "theory" about

how to resolve his internal contradictions to the "practice" of living out the resolution.

As Hawkins has noted, this resolution, although mediated first by his reading of Catholic literature and apologetics, is then further mediated by a combination of inner experiences (which Hawkins traces to his Quaker mother) and ritual experiences (traced to his Episcopalian father). Just as, lacking ritual, Merton could not express his inner childhood griefs over the loss of his mother and father, so now, with ritual, he can express his desire for union with Christ, first through attending Mass (210) and later through his baptism (222–24). Just as in Part One he had experienced Christ in Rome through an encounter with Christian art, so now in Part Two he learns about Christ as God incarnate through an encounter with doctrine in a parish sermon. Both the image and the doctrine will come alive in his contemplative and active life in Part Three when he meditates on the life of Jesus during his attempt to make the Jesuit *Spiritual Exercises*. He finds in Catholicism the resolution to the conflict between his earlier love of communal, public sacramentality and his teenage love of personal autonomous experience.

If chapter II, 1 structures Merton's two-year struggle for a religious conversion around a series of conflicts resolved by mediators, chapter II, 2 structures his year-long wandering after his baptism around several random experiences—generally lacking mediators. These random experiences include his move to Greenwich Village, his attempt to become a writer, and his eventual realization of a desire deeper than merely living a minimal Catholic life. If II, 1 was almost step by step in its logical resolution of intellectual and then moral "internal contradictions" with the help of friends, II, 2 begins with an image of the directionless wanderer falling into "the abyss of anticlimax" (227). The first movement is embodied by Merton in the image of the Exodus passage that he cites at the beginning of II, 2; the second, in the post-Exodus passage describing the wandering in the desert (226). He spends several pages explaining, in terms derived from his later experience, why he wasted that year. He blames his wandering on lack of spiritual direction and prayer, on inadequate religious goals, on habits of moral laxity, on unfamiliarity with Catholic devotional life, and on his domination by merely worldly ambi-

tions "to be a writer, a poet, a critic, a professor" (231). Only
later does he realize that mere ritual and inner change of heart are
not enough to transform a person to live beyond borderline religion. "What a strange thing that I did not see how much that
meant, and come at last to the realization that it was God alone I
was supposed to live for, God that was supposed to be the center
of my life and of all that I did" (233).

His lack of a "center" reflects itself in the very lack of narrative
structure in this chapter. He simply describes his random moves—
into a Greenwich Village apartment, on to an aimless round of
parties, through all-night discussions and flurries of writing poems
and reviews, and, finally, into a halfhearted effort at starting a
Ph.D. program in English at Columbia. In the midst of this random activity, still seeking to satisfy contradictory hungers, Merton
is suddenly confronted in the spring by a challenge from his best
friend, Lax, who poses the question: " 'What do you want to be,
anyway?' " (237). This question leads Lax to challenge him further by presenting him with the "weird" ideal of Christianity—
" 'to become a saint' " (238). This desire startles Merton enough
to make him read some writings of John of the Cross, but he
finds himself burdened by the "duplicity and compromise" of his
complex motivations. He discovers that this "complexity" of
mind turns everything into a merely intellectual game, a sort of
aesthetic version of Christianity that calls for minimal ritual and
moral practice amid a maximum of worldly ambitions. Even the
reading of Augustine's *Confessions* at this time does not jar Merton
from his drifting (242). However, Augustine's insight into his
own conversion as both an acceptance of grace ("Give me chastity") and an act of personal commitment in the present moment
("now") began to ferment in Merton.

What jolts Merton out of this aimless desert of wandering is
difficult for him to describe. It is not merely the pressure from
the threat of World War II, or the painful loss of his wisdom
teeth, or even his struggle to find a peaceful response to the war.
His transformation comes the morning after an all-night party,
when, as he says: "Somewhere in the midst of all this, an idea had
come to me, an idea that was startling enough and momentous
enough by itself, but much more astonishing in the context. Perhaps many people will not believe what I am saying. While we

were sitting there on the floor playing records and eating this breakfast the idea came to me: 'I am going to be a priest' " (253).

He comes out at dusk after reading a book on the Jesuits, walks along the Sixteenth Street sidewalk near the Jesuit church, then feels a sudden "prompting" to go in. He finds a benediction service of Eucharistic worship in progress. Here he kneels and, as Augustine did, *wills to accept grace*: " 'Yes, I want to be a priest, with all my heart I want it. If it is Your will, make me a priest—make me a priest' " (255). The dialectic of a divided and merely "natural" will is resolved. Now he can resume the journeys of his youth on a higher level as he seeks direction toward the center.

DID MERTON EXPERIENCE CHRISTIAN CONVERSION?

What sort of a conversion sequence do we discover in these patterns that Merton outlines in his circular journey? Some critics, such as Ann Hawkins, have no difficulty describing his autobiography as a three-level fully Christian conversion, with a peculiarly "sacramental" flavor. In contrast to this descriptive analysis, Walter Conn finds in *The Seven Storey Mountian* no full and complete "religious conversion," a term Conn reserves for the "relatively rare occurrence" of persons who reach the top stage of the developmental psychologists' scale (Conn ch. 6).[3]

My reading of Merton's conversion sequence is somewhat different from that of either Hawkins or Conn. With the former, I insist that Merton's conversion is fundamentally religious in the central part of his autobiography. With the latter, I acknowledge

---

[3] Hawkins describes *The Seven Storey Mountain* as a three-part private/public process. Part One is a pre-conversion stage centered on a private vision of his dead father followed by a public, "sacramental" visit to Roman churches. Part Two is a corporate conversion to Catholicism, again centered on two experiences, each involving a private "call" and a public ritual (his baptism and his decision to become a priest). Part Three is a communal conversion to monastic life, in which he experiences privately being chosen and then "sacramentalized" to enter the Trappist order. Walter Conn acknowledges that Merton underwent several changes—cognitive, affective, and moral conversions—with a Christian dimension added at his baptism. Although Conn admits that the final part of the autobiography shows the characteristics of "religious conversion" described by William James, Conn finds Merton's identity not sufficiently solidified to be ready for a fully religious conversion in 1939.

that this religious conversion is still rudimentary, thus showing significant need for growth, a growth he actually achieves in the twenty years recorded in his later journals and letters. Unlike either, I also find an imaginative conversion essentially linked to the intellectual, affective, and moral transformations of his college years. Beginning with his early experiences of monasteries and churches, and fostered by his reading of Blake and Dante in England, the directional image of himself as captive traveler takes on a potentiality for a religious self-image. This potentiality comes to life briefly in his religious phase at Ealing and more seriously at Rome after the vision of his father. But it is never fully actualized as a conversion of the imagination until, at Columbia, he studies the poetry of Blake, Hopkins, Joyce, Crashaw, and others. This imaginative self-image sparks his movement through the intellectual struggles to resolve the contradictions he sees as the "groundwork" of his moral decision to go to church in 1937–38.

Conn is willing to use the term "moral conversion" to describe all the stages we have noted in Merton's growth in responsibility at Columbia—from his early commitment to communist ideas, through his struggles with a position on war, and, of course, including his personal moral battles with a secular hedonist lifestyle. This moral development occurs both before and after his baptism and his decision to seek the priesthood. It seems only consistent to acknowledge the fundamentally religious character of his transformation of his identity and movement toward belief in God found in the latter half of *The Seven Storey Mountain*. For this transformation includes as essential elements what are usually considered religious activities: the prayer experience leading up to Merton's baptism (II, 1); the shallow but searching sacramental life leading up to his desire for sanctity and priesthood (II, 2); his testing of his vocation to Franciscan life (II, 1); his attempts to live as a monk in the world (III, 3); his discernment of a choice between life as a novelist, a social worker, or a monk (III, 4); and his eventual entry into the monastery (III, 4). Although he ends with an epilogue that reveals serious gaps in his identity, Merton plants in his autobiography most of the seeds of the later growth (and lapses) that Conn considers essential for "religious conversion." The final Merton of *The Seven Storey Mountain* is very much, as he admits, a paradox, a man in tension, a divided searcher—a captive traveler who has reached his destination of "freedom within four walls," only to find that "place" does not matter, because his fundamental journey is interior and lifelong. But the rest of the journey has been hinted at in his earlier experiences. Merton has already planted the seed of "universality" in his college interests in mysticism and Eastern thought, the seed of social compassion in his work with Catherine de Hueck in Harlem, and the seed of "totality" in his monastic vows. What he has also planted is the seed of doubleness that he accepts only later as part of the paradox of his entire life—the double of Merton the writer. Perhaps Conn is partially correct—this "double" does still require a religious conversion.

RESOLVING THE CONFLICTED JOURNEY THROUGH WRITING

As with other twentieth-century religious autobiographers, Merton's tensions are both intensified and resolved through his writing. When he was a child, his mother kept his every word and mood in a diary. He overcame some of the frustrations of boarding at the Lycée in France by writing adventure stories and travel novels. At Ealing, he told his aunt that he wanted to be a novelist and journalist. At Oakham, he learned to write well enough to earn a scholarship to Cambridge. At Columbia, he joined a group of writers and journalists for work on student publications, edited the student yearbook, and wrote a master's thesis on Blake. All these occurred in the midst of and as responses to the tensions we have described in his journey.

Merton's growth as a writer, however, seems to become more reflective *after* his baptism. For, as we have seen, this event occurs in the middle of his story, leaving him in the middle of the tensions between being a Christian and being a novelist. In his religious search, he immediately follows up his baptism by spending the year of drifting in writing articles, reviews, and a novel. But his most satisfying writing occurs as a result of the religious struggles to discover what Hawkins calls his "communal" vocation. On his pilgrimage to Cuba, he writes his first satisfactory poem. Yet he immediately discovers that deeper religious experience is beyond words: "[A]nother overwhelming thing about this awareness was that it disarmed all images, all metaphors. . . . The strange thing about this light was that although it seemed so 'ordinary' in the sense I have mentioned, and so accessible, there was no way of recapturing it" (285). This struggle for words will continue through a lifelong tension—between his wordless religious experience as a contemplative, and his prophetic and poetic vocation. Even as he writes three novels during his two-year search for a vocation, he throws two of them away. After losing his sense of place in New York City, he begins "to drink poems out of the hills" around Olean in the same period. Later as a monk, he begins to write poems but soon fears that his writing will compete with his monastic duties. Even when he is permitted, and later ordered, as a monk to write, he finds this activity creating a new division in the self that he believed had been healed and unified and transformed by the grace of his conversion and vocation.

In fact, even the act of writing about his conversion and vocation brings out in him a new tension. Like others—Day, Lewis, Wakefield—he begins his autobiography at Olean in the form of a novel, continues it in essays and poems, only then trying to recreate his life story in a fully autobiographical genre. The very act of writing that had helped resolve the tensions of his journey as a captive traveler now precipitates a new conflict and becomes the occasion of a new paradox. As he describes himself in an Augustinian apostrophe to God at the end of *The Seven Storey Mountain*, he uses his old travel imagery but adds the new element of fire:

> We cannot arrive at the perfect possession of God in this life, and that is why we are travelling and in darkness. . . . I hear You saying to me: . . . "I will lead you by the way that you cannot possibly understand, because I want it to be the quickest way. . . . Everything that touches you shall burn you, and you will draw your hand away in pain, until you have withdrawn yourself from all things. . . . But you shall taste the true solitude of my anguish and my poverty and I shall lead you into the high places of my joy and you shall die in Me and find all things in My mercy which has created you for this end and brought you from Prades to Bermuda to St. Antonin to Oakham to London to Cambridge to Rome to New York to Columbia to Corpus Christi to St. Bonaventure to the Cistercian Abbey of the poor men who labor in Gethsemani." (419, 420, 422–23)

These very contradictory images—movement/stability, fire of cleansing/fire of pain, light/darkness, depth/height, God's land/no-man's land—will become the language of his next, and probably his best, work, *The Sign of Jonas*. Even as he resolves his earlier conflicts by finding a "higher unity" in the circular journey of his autobiography, he finds himself moving onward to a new series of conflicts. In the prologue of this next journal, Merton announces: "I find myself traveling toward my destiny in the belly of a paradox."

REFERENCES

Conn, Walter. *Christian Conversion*. New York: Paulist, 1986.
Cooper, David D. *Thomas Merton and the Art of Denial*. Athens: U of Georgia P, 1989.
Erikson, Erik. *Childhood and Society*, 2nd ed. New York: Norton, 1963.
Hawkins, Anne. *Archetypes of Conversion*. Lewisburg, PA: Bucknell UP, 1985.
Kountz, Peter. *Thomas Merton as Writer and Monk: A Cultural Study, 1915–1951*. Chicago: Carlson, 1991.
Malits, Elena. *The Solitary Explorer: Thomas Merton's Transforming Journey*. New York: Harper, 1980.
Merton, Thomas. *Conjectures of a Guilty Bystander*. Garden City, NY: Doubleday, 1966.
———. *Entering the Silence: Becoming a Monk and Writer*. The Journals of Thomas Merton, Vol. 2. San Francisco: Harper, 1996.
———. *Run to the Mountain: The Story of a Vocation*. The Journals of Thomas Merton, Vol. 1. San Francisco: Harper, 1995.
———. *The Seven Storey Mountain*. New York: Harcourt, 1948.
———. *The Sign of Jonas*. New York: Doubleday, 1953, 1956.
Mott, Michael. *The Seven Mountains of Thomas Merton*. Boston: Houghton, 1984.
Padavano, Anthony T. *The Human Journey: Thomas Merton, Symbol of a Century*. Garden City, NY: Doubleday, 1982.
Shannon, William. *Silent Lamp: The Thomas Merton Story*. New York: Crossroads, 1992.

2

Dorothy Day's
The Long Loneliness

DOROTHY DAY tells us that the motif for her autobiography came in part from a letter her daughter sent telling about the loneliness of being a mother of small children (243). Day embodied the motif in the title and in the epigraph from Mary Ward, founder of a seventeenth-century order of nuns in England: "I think, dear child, the trouble and the long loneliness you hear me speak of is not far from me, which whensoever it is, happy success will follow" (iii). But the meaning of the phrase "the long loneliness" for Day did not limit itself to merely social isolation. As she told the psychologist Robert Coles many years after completing her autobiography, " 'I meant a spiritual hunger . . . a loneliness that was in me, no matter how happy I was and how fulfilled in my personal life' " (Coles 62). Here she aligns herself with Augustine, whose *cor inquietum* includes a spiritual hunger or restless need for God, and with C. S. Lewis, whose "joy" proves to be a dissatisfaction happier than any earthly satisfaction. But the solution for Day is not mystical union with God ("alone with the Alone"); rather, "The only answer in this life, to the loneliness we are all bound to feel, is community" (243). Thus, her story suggests that her primary experience and directional image are a dynamic emotion—a "loneliness" seeking "communion."

The reader is introduced to *The Long Loneliness* through a brief introduction entitled "Confession." Perhaps echoing Eliot's *Little Gidding* ("you are here to kneel / Where prayer has been valid"), she uses the half-personal, half-impersonal "you" to indicate the Catholic experience bridging the loneliness of sin with the communion of Eucharist through the sacrament of confession:

When you go to confession on a Saturday night, you go into a
warm, dimly lit vastness, with the smell of wax and incense in the
air, the smell of burning candles. . . .
  Going to confession is hard—hard when you have sins to con-
fess, hard when you haven't, and you rack your brain for even the
beginnings of sins against charity, chastity, sins of detraction, sloth
or gluttony. You do not want to make too much of your constant
imperfections and venial sins, but you want to drag them to the
light of day as the first step in getting rid of them. (9–10)

Ever the journalist, Day evokes all the senses as integral to the
experience of the sacred moment of overcoming the loneliness of
"ugly, gray, drab, monotonous sins" (10). Just as she will end her
story in the "Postscript" by showing how the solution to loneliness emerges from informal conversation ("We were just sitting
here talking . . ." [285]), so now her escape from moral loneliness
takes place in a formal conversation with an "impersonal" mediator in the ritual of conversation. But, as she moves from the description of the sacrament to her autobiography, she uses the
power of ritual as an essential step in overcoming the isolation of
the self—both in religion and in her life story. Just as she finds it
difficult to "worship, adore, praise and thank" God in the company of others "without a ritual, without a body" (10), so, too,
she finds it difficult to write a book about her "self" without an
autobiographical ritual. And the narrative rituals she uses—the
directional image, the circular narrative, the tension of parental
influences, the sequence of conversions, and especially the use of
writing as a sacramental resolution to inner conflicts—all are similar to those employed by other twentieth-century seekers.
  As a woman born into an American Victorian household, Day
finds the exposure of self in a public story to be difficult: "Writing
a book is hard, because you are 'giving yourself away.' But if you
love, you want to give yourself. You write as you are impelled to
write, about man and his problems, his relation to God and his
fellows. You write about yourself because in the long run all
man's problems are the same, his human needs of sustenance and
love" (10). Here she immediately apologizes for self-revelation by
universalizing her experience and by following this up with biblical reaffirmations of human worth: " 'Thou hast made him a little
less than the angels' " (10). She further apologizes for writing

"only of myself" and not of associates or friends, but justifies her
personal story by invoking Augustine's prayer, " 'Lord, that I may
know myself, in order to know Thee' " (11). But, as Patricia
Spacks has suggested, Day writes her life story from the vantage
point of a woman who has discovered and asserted her deeper self
far more strongly than most female autobiographers in the first
half of the twentieth century (130). In fact, Day's attribution of
her life story to God—twenty-five years of floundering and
twenty-five of building the Catholic Worker movement with
Peter Maurin—leads her to the ultimate experience moving her
from loneliness to communion: being " 'haunted by God' " (11).
From her childhood pious moments through her socialist years,
even the name of God made her heart leap up. But the leap was
not into ecstasy but into years of long loneliness in a quest for a
way to spell out that name in her life.

    The answer to the quest comes in various forms of "commu-
nion"—first her family, then friendships, then social movements,
then marriage, and, finally, an unexpected combination of all
these forms in the Catholic Worker communities. But the me-
dium of the final movement will be—like her autobiography itself—the ritual of conversation. For in the "Postscript," she
reveals that all the elements of Catholic Worker life—Peter
Maurin's leadership, Day's own transformation of Maurin's ideas,
"the service of the homeless, the rural farms and retreat, the newspaper—all emerged from 'just sitting there talking' " (286).

    This image of persons sitting around a table talking, often over
a meal, moves ahead of the reader throughout Day's life story as
the directional image of her search. The opening chapter of Part
One begins with a picture of Dorothy and her brothers and sister
sitting around the supper table listening to their mother talking
about her childhood. Two chapters later, her mother appears
again "reign[ing] over the supper table as a queen" with her children as her court, after a long day of housework in the early days
of family hardships in Chicago (27). The main image of Day's
chapter on her adolescence consists of the family gathered around
a table in the family library "with plates of apples to eat as we
read" (30). When she lives with a near-destitute family during
her university years, Day regrets that she cannot share a meal with
them (44). When she becomes a teenage reporter in New York,

she prides herself on her ability to "make a quick meal off a push-cart in the winter" and on spending time in small restaurants "where one could get good bean soup and plenty of bread and butter for ten cents" (57). In fact, one of the clearest images she gives of the breaks in her journalistic grind is of going "with some of the men from the copy desk to the restaurant on Park Row where we sat over pancakes and applesauce and talked for hours" (58). When her college friend Rayna visits her in New York, they entertain at supper parties and breakfast parties, even bringing home strangers while she and Rayna remain "sitting up all night, continuing to talk" (69). Perhaps the most memorable image from her chapter on her "freelance" years is of herself, Eugene O'Neill, Michael Gold, and others sitting in the back room of a saloon in Greenwich Village, all listening to O'Neill's poetry recitations or in "afternoons and evenings of talk and banter" (84–85). In her year as a nurse, one of her difficulties is having to work without eating or with just a snack (91). In Part Two, Day describes some of the idyllic moments of her early relationship with Forster Batterham in imagery of "sitting and talking": "[W]hen Forster and I shared an apartment in winter with my sister, Allen Tate and his wife Caroline Gordon lived across the street, and Hart Crane used to drop into all of our homes for coffee and conversation" (113). In dramatic contrast to these images of conversational meals are the two stark pictures of her hunger strike in jail during a march for women's suffrage (74ff.) and her part in the Hunger March on Washington during the Depression (165). She then begins Part Three with her first portrait of Peter Maurin, whom she meets sitting and talking in her kitchen when she returns from the march (169). All these images of "sitting and talking" are united in the eloquent parallel sentences of the "Postscript": "We were just sitting there talking when Peter Maurin came in . . . when lines of people began to form . . . and people moved in on us" (285). The fulfillment of these images of a ritual of meal and words is, of course, the Eucharistic meal, which becomes for Day the center of each day of her later years with the Catholic Worker.

Even a casual reading of *The Long Loneliness* suggests the aptness of the title, for Day repeatedly weaves her life story together with the thread of her experiences of loneliness. Loneliness, in fact, drove her as a child both toward God and eventually away from God. In portraying her early childhood in Brooklyn, she describes herself adventuring off alone one day when she was very young: "[O]n one occasion I went away alone, spending what I felt to be long hours one sunny afternoon, blissful enchanted hours until the sudden realization came over me that I was alone, that the world was vast and that there were evil forces therein. . . . I ran all the way home" (19). She remembers "the joy of being alone" in her girlish play in the garden and yard, and describes the later "sense of holiness in holding the book" of the Bible, alone in the attic of her home in Berkeley (19–20). This Wordsworthian attractiveness about being alone with nature and God, combined with her fear of the unknown, leads her to be a heightened consciousness of death. She wakes up sweating and crying for her mother after dreaming of God as a great noise in her ears. She describes her ambivalent attitude toward God at this time: "I was alternately lonely and smug. . . . I remember these dreams only in connection with California and they were linked up with my idea of God as a tremendous Force, a frightening impersonal God, a Voice, a Hand stretched out to seize me, His child, and not in love. Christ was the Saviour, meek and humble of heart, Jesus, the Good Shepherd. But I did not think of Jesus as God" (20–21).

Day's first direct experience of death comes when she sees the bodies of a brother and sister drowned in a pool near Lake Michigan, after her family moves to Chicago following the 1906 San Francisco earthquake, but this experience does not move her as strongly as her fearful dreams. Her main consolation in the face of this fear is her love of nature and her family. Although her family does not attend church, she goes with friends to several Protestant churches, where, at ten years of age, she learns to love the psalms and hymns, a practice that, along with writing in her notebook, was her usual response to beauty: "I wanted to cry out with joy. . . . I always felt the common unity of our humanity; the longing of the human heart is for this communion" (29). During her later childhood, she acknowledges that she has much time to be alone and relishes her privacy, especially for reading and writing. The main family community events she recalls are the dress-up meals with her mother after a hard day of work, and the common reading in the house library:

To draw the curtains at night on a street where people bent against the wind, and where a steady whirl of snowflakes blurred the outlines of trees and shrubs, and made the trees black against the heavy gray sky, and to turn to a room where a fire glowed in the basket grate and a smell of bread filled the house—this was comfort, security, peace, community. (30)

When her younger brother is born in 1911, the fourteen-year old Dorothy falls in love with him and devotes much of her high school years to caring for him by herself. Some of her most vivid writing appears in her description of the early mornings alone with the baby, the songbird, and her classical homework in Virgil. Thus, her childhood feelings of loneliness lead to a directional motif of communion that remains her lifelong symbol in her search for ultimate answers to ontological loneliness.

When Day leaves her restricted home life for the University of Illinois at the age of sixteen, she is exhilarated at the prospect of being on her own, but is soon filled with a sense of what she calls "desolation and loneliness" (40) caused by her separation from her family, a type of loneliness relieved only by study and work. She describes her first experience of the existential loneliness in the break with her baby brother when she first leaves for college: "To know that this love was past, that John would grow up away from me, that I could not hold him, that I too had to go on, filled me with a sense of unutterable grief. I had a terrible sense of loss, and yet with it a sense of the inevitability of such losses in our lives" (41). When she encounters the challenge, loneliness drives her not toward God, as previously, but into herself and into a rage for social justice. She finds herself alone, separated from the communities of family, church, and friends: "I was seventeen, and I felt completely alone in the world, divorced from my family, from all security, even from God. I felt a sense of reckless arrogance and, with this recklessness, a sense of danger in which I rejoiced" (45). Her only sense of communion comes from a vague call emerging out of the literature and philosophy she was reading—to feel "one with the masses" (47), a feeling that leads her to temporary community in a socialist club and in close friendships with other student writers.

The attraction of these temporary communal experiences proves less than her desire to be with her family and to immerse herself in the world. For she follows her family to New York City, where she finds a job as a reporter on a socialist newspaper. "During that time I felt the spell of the long loneliness descend on me. In all that great city of seven millions, I found no friends; I had no work: I was separated from my fellows. . . . I wanted to weep my loneliness away. . . . And yet, as I walked these streets back in 1917 I wanted to go and live among these surroundings; in some mysterious way I felt that I would never be freed from this burden of loneliness and sorrow unless I did" (51). It is during the years of her work as a reporter that Day solves her problem of social loneliness by pouring herself into the frantic community of work, politics, and partying that make up the lives of the radicals and bohemians with whom she associates on the Lower East Side. She discreetly sums up her life with Mike Gold, Eugene O'Neill, and others: "No one ever wanted to go to bed, and no one ever wished to be alone" (84). It is also during these years that she first experiences the isolation of jail in Washington, D.C., as a protester for women's rights. She describes her feelings in the cell, "I lost all feeling of my own identity. I reflected on the desolation of poverty, of destitution, of sickness and sin. . . . I was a petty creature, filled with self-deception, self-importance, unreal, false, and so, rightly scorned and punished. I was willing not only to say two and two were five, but to think it" (78–79). This Orwellian experience of total moral isolation and its degradation of her sense of identity and self-worth never leaves her memory, although its immediate effects of turning her to prayer do not endure. She continues her fringe involvements with various radical movements, but her journalistic detachment and exhausting overwork prevent her from finding any lasting community support. Her romantic liaisons, which she describes only as "my own personal joy and heartbreak" (95), though later revealed in her novel *The Eleventh Virgin*, provide no solutions to the enduring loneliness of her spiritual hunger. When her emotional confusion leads her to unhappy relationships—and even into an abortion, as her biographer tells us—she suffers a near breakdown, from which she recovers by taking work as a nurse during the last years of World War I (Miller 141).

Loneliness eventually leads Day out of her breakdown and into a naturally happy common-law marriage with Forster, an anarchist who teaches her the beauty of creation but will not allow her to continue her religious search. She loves him, despite his antisocial and lonely temperament, and even tells us that "his ardent love of creation brought me to the Creator of all things" (134). But his social isolation and fear of commitment do not allow her to grow. She waits and waits, but when he eventually deserts her and their daughter, she is left to search out a lonely path to faith in Christianity: "I felt all along that when I took the irrevocable step it would mean that Tamar and I would be alone, and I did not want to be alone" (145). Although she eventually experiences great joy in the sacramental life of the Church, her conversion to Catholicism brings her a sense of social isolation and a feeling of betrayal of "the class to which I belonged, the workers, the poor of the world, with whom Christ spent His life" (144). As a Catholic, she finds support from a few priests who serve as spiritual directors, but she finds no permanent faith community and knows no active Catholic for several years. In fact, her conversion gradually leads to a deeper loneliness at times, as she describes on her travels west after her baptism into the Church in 1927: "I was lonely, deadly lonely. And I was to find out then, as I found out so many times, over and over again, that women especially are social beings, who are not content with just husband and family, but must have a community, a group, an exchange with others. . . . Young and old, even in the busiest years of our lives, we women especially are victims of the long loneliness" (157–58).

It is at this low point of her personal, family, and religious loneliness that she undergoes a second stage of her religious conversion. Like Merton, she became a personal convert to Catholicism but lacked a close community and a means to bring together her communal commitment to social justice and her community commitment to the Church of "the masses." Her transformation begins as she prays at the National Shrine during the trip to Washington, D.C., in 1932 for a Hunger March in the Depression. "How little, how puny my work had been since becoming a Catholic, I thought. How self-centered, how ingrown, how lacking in sense of community! . . . I offered up a special prayer, a prayer which came with tears and anguish, that some way would open up for me to use what talents I possessed for my fellow workers, for the poor" (165–66).

Thus, the dynamic of loneliness-seeking-communion that drove Day from her childhood reclusiveness into the hurly-burly of university and newspaper life, and later into her unhappy relationships and her common-law marriage, now drives her as a Catholic toward an image of what she later calls the only answer to the long loneliness—"a community"—expressed in shared work and conversations around a supper table. Here she has to create, with Peter Maurin and a few others, the community of the Catholic Worker. Ironically, the focus of the group is not on themselves but on the needs of the laboring poor, the homeless, and the unemployed during the Depression. But, in the process of giving themselves away, they find themselves no longer alone or lonely. Even though she is to experience bouts with the long loneliness again, especially at the death of fellow workers such as Steve Hergenhan, or much more poignantly at the death of Peter Maurin, she is never defeated by them. In fact, although Day does not lose a close relative or friend to death in the years of her search for God, she does record a series of separations or losses that were the equivalent of "deaths." She describes several of them as leading immediately to feelings of loneliness—the separation from her baby brother when she leaves for the university, the separation from Rayna when she leaves college for New York, the separation from her "heartbreak" relationships (identified as with Lionel Moise and Berkeley Tobey), and especially the separation from Forster when she baptizes her daughter. All these are compounded by the "death" of her relationship with her father, partial in childhood, complete after her college years. Finally, during the days of the Second World War, when she feels herself deserted by many who could not go along with her Christian pacifism, Day does not despair. She is now strong enough to face the long loneliness.

Thus, the drive for self-realization leads Day out of her partial selves—as journalist, as radical, as nurse, as lover, as wife and mother—all of which are filled with restlessness and loneliness, into a new self that is no longer alone. She faces the varieties of loneliness in the human condition—personal, social, familial, and religious—and, through the experience of each, is driven on in her search for "communion." The personal loneliness of her childhood and adolescence allows her to wander into years of searching and moral confusion, but she is faithful to the drive to go beyond the lonely hour. Through friendship and work, she searches for the fulfillment of her personal self and finds only partial completeness. Then the social loneliness of the laboring poor in the tenements of New York develops in her a concern that can identify with those around her and draw her out of her fear and shyness. When she tries to find a way to overcome her loneliness through a common-law marriage, she grows dramatically for several years in her life with Forster, but he, in his own tragic isolation, tries to block her search for more than what she calls "natural happiness." His own loneliness and fear of society make him possessive of her, not permitting her to follow her faith. Finally, in her basic ontological loneliness—what she later calls her "spiritual hunger" for God—Day finds in Catholicism a gradual way to community and communion. At first, the Church provides only personal nourishment, but, after she meets Peter Maurin, Day finds a prophet of community and ministry who teaches her a way to a full life of communal service and witness in the Catholic Worker movement, which they establish together. Like Augustine, she follows her restless heart in its loneliness until it is emptied out of all consolation and then is filled with what she calls "a harsh and dreadful" love (285). She learns to relate the loneliness of the self to the community of Christian believers in the Ultimate as a God of love who has identified through Christ and his "mystical body" with the lives of the poor.

MEDIATORS OF COMMUNION IN THE VALLEY OF LONELINESS

Because, as Spacks says, "the story she tells in its large outlines belongs to a pattern as characteristic of men as of women" (131), it is difficult to show that Day's journey differs essentially from the journeys of modern male spiritual autobiographies. But if we dive down from the heights of the "large outline" (to be discussed in the next section) to the details of her relationships with "mediators" of conversion, we discover significant differences. These differences do not show, as some interpreters of female autobiographies suggest, that only the female "I is mediated by the agony of a significant other(s) and originates as an Other in itself" (Watson 181). This general description can apply to the role of mediators in the autobiographies of Merton, Gandhi, Cowan, and perhaps Malcolm X. But, what Greer sums up as the feminist theory of Friedman and others seems to apply distinctively to the role of "others" in Day's life story:

> Predominant in women they find is the consciousness of a collective identity; thence of a dual consciousness, a "self" represented in the hall of mirrors of a culture, as well as in their own sensibility; a sense of the importance of interpersonal relations in the formation of a sense of self. Not least among these is the "mother–daughter" relationship which has been so thoroughly obscured by the Freudian emphasis on "father-figure," the Oedipal construct, the phallic cult. (174)

Postponing the mother–daughter relationship to a subsequent section, let us examine Day's early religious guides and then the three most important personal mediators in her self-realization—Rayna Proehme, Forster Battenham, and Peter Maurin. Day's guides to religion during her childhood were all outside her family. Her acquaintance with Catholicism came through servants and friends. The first one she recalls is Mary Manley, a servant who lived with the Days in Brooklyn until Dorothy was six and who once took her to Mass. The second is Mary Harrington, a friend in Chicago who was the eldest of nine children in a hard-working family and who told Dorothy about the saints and thus gave her a desire for what she calls "spiritual adventure" (24). The third is Mrs. Barrett whom Dorothy accidentally encountered saying her prayers and whom she felt impelled to emulate. Her acquaintance with Protestantism comes through a vibrant Methodist family in Oakland who teach her the "sweetness of faith" in Sunday school and hymn-singing (20). This piety is confirmed by her occasional attendance at the Episcopal church during her later childhood years in Chicago, where she develops a love of Scripture, especially the Psalms, and of the local boy soprano. Although these childhood experiences never left Day, at the time they remained part of what she calls a religious "game."

During her lapse from faith in college, Day's main mediators are the novelists and radical authors she learned about from her brother Ronald—Jack London, Eugene Debs, Upton Sinclair, Peter Kropotkin, Vera Flynn. These become the mediators of her first major transformation—from romantic adolescent to socially conscious collegian with a new sense of "a call, a vocation, a direction" (38): "I felt even at fifteen, that God meant man to be happy, that He meant to provide him with what he needed to maintain life in order to be happy, and that we did not need to have quite so much destitution and misery as I saw all around and read of in the daily press" (38). This conversion also pulls her away from her middle-class Protestantism, which she sees as out of touch with the misery of the poor and as a refuge of the weak or the "opiate of the people." She begins to take on a religion of the "masses": "I was in love now with the masses. I do not remember that I was articulate or reasoned about this love, but it warmed and filled my heart. The poor and oppressed were going to rise up, they were collectively the new Messiah, and they would release the captives" (46). Her baptism into radicalism comes when she joins the local Socialist Party, but, like Merton, her official enthusiasm soon wanes and she stops attending meetings.

In place of radicalism Day develops a college friendship with Rayna, who becomes a mediator of her affective growth and later an inspiration toward political commitment. At the university, Rayna's intense and dedicated personality captivates Day and frees her from her own lack of self-confidence: "Whatever she did she did with her whole heart" (48). She teaches Day to be "single-minded, one of the pure of heart" (48). Not yet political in these days, Rayna brings Dorothy into a small community of sophisticated students and writers, thus fostering her vocation as a writer. Later, in the mid-1920s, Rayna marries a communist leader, William Prohme, works for revolution in China, and ends up immortalized in Moscow after her early death. Thus, she provides Day with both an intellectual and social Other who helps her become mentally and emotionally confident, and a political Other who evokes in Day the self-esteem to become the leader of a movement paralleling in its small way the early years of the party in the Soviet Union.

If Rayna Prohme mediates Day's affective growth and, unwittingly, her social transformation, Forster Batterham mediates her affective maturity and, also unwittingly, her religious conversion. After the seeds of her religious development had been haphazardly planted in childhood and then uprooted in college, Day wanders without religious practice for the decade of 1916–26. Even during that time, however, she visits churches, reads the Bible in desperate moments (such as in the Washington jail), and attends Mass with a friendly Catholic nurse. Even listening to Eugene O'Neill recite Francis Thompson's "Hound of Heaven" in the Hell Hole saloon gives her pause: "The idea of this pursuit by the Hound of Heaven fascinated me. The recurrence of it, the inevitableness of the outcome made me feel that sooner or later I would have to pause in the mad rush of living and remember my first beginning and my last end" (84). Her reading and rereading of Pascal, Dostoevski, Joyce, Huysman, and others indicates that she has undergone a sort of imaginative conversion over the years, but never enough to draw herself together sufficiently for a religious commitment. For that she will require a profound human relationship, which comes, ironically, from the very person from whom she will separate to follow her faith. Thus, Forster opens up to Dorothy Day the beauty and order of nature during the years of their marriage, but this beauty and order lead her back to the Bible, to prayer, and even to *The Imitation of Christ*. Day sums up his influence on her:

> His ardent love of creation brought me to the Creator of all things. But when I cried out to him, "How can there be no God, when there are all these beautiful things," he turned from me uneasily and complained that I was never satisfied. We loved each other so strongly that he wanted to remain in the love of the moment; he wanted me to rest in that love. He cried out against my attitude that there would be nothing left of that love without a faith. (134)

Along with Forster in this mediation of faith comes the subtle influence of their daughter, Tamar Teresa. For Dorothy, the presence of the child within her during pregnancy and with her after the birth evokes a sense of new life and confidence, whereas the same events burden Forster with responsibilities and confinement. Forster, as Dorothy says, "did not believe in bringing children into such a world as we lived in" (136), but for Day the birth of

Tamar brings with it a new power of creativity, expressed in her most famous article, an account of the childbirth that was published around the world in radical journals. Her exhilaration of this period is also expressed in the vivid prose picturing the mornings near the beach at their house on Staten Island: "I put her in her carriage and went out along the woods, watching, almost feeling the buds bursting through their warm coast. Song sparrows, woodpeckers, hawks, crows, robins, nuthatches and of course laughing gulls made the air gay with their clamor. Starlings chattered in the branches of the old pine in front of the porch" (137–38).

Whereas the child drives Forster to insecurity and fear of the world, Tamar impels Dorothy outward toward others. Day says of this period, "My very experience as a radical, my whole make-up, led me to want to associate myself with others, with the masses, in loving and praising God" (139). This impulse toward community eventually leads her (after a year of waiting for a change in Forster) to take religious instructions from a rigorous old nun and to have Tamar and herself baptized as Catholics.

This momentous step from isolation to Catholicism, which brought with it much relief and sense of sacramental participation, precipitates a new loneliness. As I have noted in the study of her directional image and motif, Day—like Merton, Malcolm X, Gandhi, and Cowan—required a two-stage religious conversion, not only to the community of the Catholic Church but also, later, to a fusion of this community with concern for "the masses." Just as she had experienced a crisis in her earlier search for social responsibility on the trip to Washington in 1917, so now in 1932 (three years after her baptism) she travels again to the Capitol and asks in prayer that a new "way would open up for me to use what talents I possessed for my fellow workers, for the poor" (166). The answer to this prayer, which leads her into the second phase of her religious conversion, meets her when she returns to New York—in the person of the third unlikely mediator in her life, Peter Maurin. This itinerant French peasant social philosopher provides Day with a vision of " 'cult, culture, and cultivation' " (171) that gives her the intellectual confidence she needs to embody her hopes for a socially responsible form of Catholic living in a movement that is to become the Catholic Worker. Maurin provides the impetus, but, as with Forster, Day transforms the dream into enfleshment in her own way: in a newspaper, in a series of social centers ("houses of hospitality"), an educational program, and a philosophy of work. What begins in Peter's mind as a rural anarchism becomes through Day's practical vision an urban labor pacifist movement with a "collective identity" that is to endure for the rest of the twentieth century—prophetic of the Peace Movement of the 1960s, of the Green Revolution of the 1970s, and of the various religious and family revivals of the 1980s. In contrast to male spiritual autobiographers whose stories do not fully integrate their personal conversion story with the content of their beliefs (such as Merton's juxtaposing story with sermon or Cowan's reticence about his creed or Malcolm X's long summaries of Black Muslim theology), Day's autobiography leads gradually from the intensely personal story of the first two sections, through the mediatory portrait of Peter Maurin, to a full exposition of the elements that make up the Catholic Worker movement. Unlike Gandhi, who jumps back and forth between chapters on experiments in private Truth (the ashram) and public Truth (politics), Day in her story shapes a three-part structure in the tradition of twentieth-century autobiography, but with a progressive relationship and continuity between the earlier private and later communal conversions. Let us now explore with Day this feminine version of the spiral pilgrimage.

THE CIRCULAR JOURNEY THROUGH LONELINESS

Although Day did not read Merton's *The Seven Story Mountain* until 1959, seven years after she had published her own autobiography (and even then found his view of the world "superficial and scornful"), she organized her narrative in a remarkably similar tripartite structure. Part One, entitled "Searching," divides into two sections—her childhood seeds of faith and her adolescent wandering, both similar to Merton's first part. Part Two, entitled "Natural Happiness," embodies, as we have seen, her struggle through her two-stage religious conversion, first to personal Catholicism and then to a socially responsible Catholic life. This part parallels Merton's struggle with the preambles to faith but is much less an intellectual conversion than an affective and moral battle. Part Three, entitled "Love Is the Measure," narrates her social-religious transformation through the mediation of Maurin, the raising of Tamar, and her own encounters with loss and death, all woven together with the story of the founding years of the Catholic Worker. This last is least similar to Merton's story, which spends much of his third part with his personal journey from rejection by the Franciscan order to his entrance into the Trappist monastery, but, like Day's, includes a less personal section describing the monastic life.

Day's circular journey exhibits many significant parallels and antitheses in its large-scale outline among the persons, events, and symbolic objects of her intermittently religious childhood (Ia), her secularized and socially conscious adolescence and early twenties (Ib), then her married years with Forster (II), and finally her conversion and Catholic Worker years (III). I have already traced the dominant motif of loneliness-to-communion (and its image of the supper-table conversation) through these four stages—from the hours of inner isolation in her confined house in Chicago, through the emptiness of her destitute rooms in college or the Lower East Side tenements, to the tense loneliness near the end of her marriage in the cabin on Staten Island, and even to the times of abandonment in the midst of the Catholic Worker community (after Tamar's marriage, after the deaths of Dan and Peter, and during antipacifist years of World War II).

As will be clear in the next section, many of Day's later relationships with others derive from the unresolved tension in her family. In her childhood, she is close to her mother but isolated from her father, and she ends Part One by becoming a journalist at age seventeen, a move that occasions a lifelong separation from her father. The main persons in her life during this early period were, of course, her entire family along with a few friends, but most of all her mother and her sister, Della. Similarly, in her wandering, she finds new mothers (Rayna, Peggy, and radical heroines like Emma Goldman) and new fathers (her editors, Mike Gold, even Lionel Moise), and, as earlier with her parents, she remains close to the former but separates from or is rejected by the latter. Although Day never mentions Moise by name but merely as the source of her "heartbreak" in New York and Chicago, her biographer has shown him to be an ironic reincarnation of the aloof, dominating male she feared and revered in her father (Miller 125–59). During these middle years, she also finds a new extended family of friends amid the socialists, journalists, and nurses with whom she works. Even in her years of "natural happiness" with Forster, Day finds greater stability and comfort in her relationships with women (Peggy, Freda, the nun) than in the frustrating love of her husband, who, so unlike her father in most ways, embodied the individualism and lack of religious empathy of John Day. Finally, in Part Three, Day finds a man who serves as an authentic father, one who teaches her but whom she can correct and transcend, and through whom she becomes her own person. In Peter Maurin, Day finds the authority and flair of her father, the closeness to nature and love of detail of Forster, together with the concern for others of her mother, Rayna, and others who nurtured her desire for community (along with the religious sensitivity of her childhood models and later favorite saints). Through Maurin, of course, her final family becomes the Catholic Worker, which she describes in great detail in the final chapters of her autobiography. It seems no accident that Part Three ends with the death of Maurin, just as the earlier three sections ended with separation from her father (Ia), Lionel Moise (Ib), and Forster Batterham (II). Thus, the larger narrative structure consists in Day's trying to find in four stages and in four places a community which will allow her a fully developed self, a commitment to the poor, and a new family—first in her childhood family in Chicago, then in her university and radical circles in the Lower East Side, again in her family life with Forster on Staten Island, and finally in the Catholic Worker family on Mott Street in lower Manhattan.

Within this general outline of the spiritual autobiography, Day reveals several recurrent patterns of intellectual and spiritual growth. In each of the four sections she tries to deal with what she describes in her childhood as the source of all moral issues— property and sex (18). The late-Victorian concern with money and reticence about sex (both forms of "private property" for males) lies at the heart of the tensions between her parents and between Day and her father. Radical leveling of behavior about sex and abolition of private property permeated the bohemian life of the journalists and writers Day associated with in Greenwich Village in the 1920s. In Part Two, the inability to resolve Forster's anarchic views of both sex and property (he did not believe in marriage and only occasionally held jobs) brought about his separation from Dorothy. Finally, in her conversion to Catholicism and the family of the Catholic Worker, Day created a new lay form of life that lived without vows the long tradition of sublimating the tension between property and sex through religious lives of "poverty, chastity, and obedience." Day traces her concern for the poor to specific incidents in each part of her life story: to the common sharing and concern for the homeless shown by her mother and others after the San Francisco earthquake; to the humiliating jail experience during her years as a radical journalist; to her common life with Forster amid the alcoholics and beachcombers on Staten Island; and finally to her daily contacts with the unemployed and homeless at the Catholic Worker in the 1930s and '40s.

Emotionally, Day weaves a thread throughout her story which begins with the infatuation of her first love (for a park bandleader and later for her baby brother), stretches across her close college friendship with Rayna and her barely mentioned erotic involvements as a journalist during her wandering years, reaches the peak of human happiness in her common-law marriage, and then takes an unexpected direction in the form of lifelong *caritas* for her community and the urban poor of New York, as well as for her daughter, in Part Three. This last stage, of course, is appropriately entitled "Love Is the Measure," a phrase taken from a Catholic Worker retreat given by Father Pacifique Roy (249). All the theology of the Gospel and social responsibility which Day weaves through these final chapters is an extension of that phrase. The movement from infatuation to eros to married love to all-embracing *caritas* is not an easy path, of course, for Day. In each section, she recounts discreetly but significantly the struggle between what she calls, in language from St. Paul, the flesh and the spirit. In a long letter written when she was at fifteen, which she calls "self-conscious" and full of "pomp and vanity and piety" (34), but which shows a remarkably reflective, if dualistic, adolescent mind, Day says: "It is wrong to think so much about human love. All those feelings and cravings that come to us are sexual desires. We are prone to have them at this age, I suppose, but I think they are impure. It is sensual and God is spiritual. We must harden ourselves to these feelings, for God is love and God is all, so the only love is of God and is spiritual without taint of earthliness" (34). Her adolescent struggle for affection in a family that is "withdrawn and alone" becomes, as she acknowledges, a lifelong conflict for her (35), a conflict recurring in each of the intense relationships we have seen in each period of her life story.

Her life, however, is driven by an even deeper dynamic. In each of the four periods, she records a vocational moment. In childhood, it is her awaking to life as a "spiritual adventure" reflected in the lives of the saints described by a young Catholic friend. This takes place in the middle of one of her childhood religious enthusiasms. In her later teen years, her reading of Upton Sinclair's The Jungle leads her to what she refers to as "a call, a vocation, a direction to my life" (38). But, sensing the hypocrisy in the Christians she knows, Day rejects her religious enthusiasms to follow this new vocation, which she links with her desire to become a writer. This life as a radical writer leads her to the devastating experience of loss of self-identity during the jailing at the suffragette march in Washington, but she is supported by a brief burst of religious fervor and Bible reading. In Part Two, she regains faith in the form of her conversion to Catholicism, but, once again in Washington, undergoes a definitive vocational call to unite her previous desires to be spiritual adventurer, advocate of the poor, writer, and Catholic. In Part Three, her prayer is answered.

Besides these characteristics of her evolving religious self, Day shows a peculiarly Catholic trait—also evident in Merton—of *sacramentality*. She describes this value in the life of the Catholic Worker artist Ade Bethune: "She has such a sense of the sacramentality of life, the goodness of things, a sense that is translated in all her works whether it was illustrating a missal, making stained-glass windows or sewing, cooking or gardening. To do things perfectly was always her aim" (191). This trait of reverence for the sacredness of physical detail and beauty as symbolic of the religious can be traced back not only to Day's description of the church and ritual of "Confession" in the introduction to The Long Loneliness, but also to each of the four stages of her spiritual pilgrimages. In Part Ia, Day's love of nature, work, writing, literature, psalms, and rituals becomes the ground for what she will later see in Catholic terms as sacramental. In particular, she loves to describe the details of water scenes on Lake Michigan or the winter evenings in her home. In Part Ib, she deliberately gives up the rituals but retains a love of nature and art, especially as expressed in her craft as a writer. Here she describes in great particularity the Lower East Side streets and tenements along the East River, as well as the grimy details of the lives, rooms, offices, taverns, and causes of her circle of journalists and radicals. In Part II, she moves from describing these secular concerns to painting the natural scenery on Staten Island with its beaches, cabins, exotic mix of cultures, and especially her hours spent exploring and fishing alone or with Forster. Finally, in Part III, she records Ade's teaching her "sacramentality" and then exhibits this virtue in her description of the sacred details of life in the houses of hospitality and on the retreats of the Catholic Worker. Mixed in with these four phases of sacramental writing are the numerous allusions to books, many of which served as mediators of her writing and her conversions. In Part Ia, she mentions the Bible, Wesley's sermons, St. Augustine's *Confessions*, Latin and Greek classics, and Victorian novels by Scott, Dickens, Hugo, Stevenson, Cooper, and Poe. In Ib, she is radicalized by London, Sinclair, Gorky, Tolstoy, Dostoevski, and socialist thinkers. In Part II, she returns to faith through reading: the Bible, *The Imitation of Christ,* St. Thérèse's *Autobiography*, Pascal, Joyce, and, again, Victorian novels. At the end of each of the four sections of her autobiography, Day records her own best writing at the time, as if to frame her life story in what is her primary way to resolve the tensions of the spiral pilgrimage. Near the end of Part Ia, she shows us a long letter summing up her childhood; in Ib, she tells us that she has written *The Eleventh Virgin* and sold it to Hollywood; in Part II, she ends with an account of her world-famous article on childbirth; and Part III concludes with a request from a fellow Catholic Worker to tell everyone about Peter Maurin's burial as the cause of nourishment for new spiritual life. Along with these important closing passages on her writing, Day concludes each section with a passage on nursing (her brother in Ia, the elderly in Ib, her daughter in II, and the world in III). Like Gandhi, she combines the vocation of her father (journalist) with that of her mother (homemaker and caretaker of others). Thus, it is appropriate at this point to examine these final two traits of Day's more closely—her struggle with inner parental tensions and her use of writing. Both will provide clues to the inner structure beneath the tripartite, four-stage outline of her journey from loneliness to communion.

TRANSCENDING THE LONELINESS OF A VICTORIAN FAMILY

At first sight, no one appears less the child of her parents than Dorothy Day. Neither of them practiced any religious faith, and her father, a prejudiced crank, went so far as to call Dorothy "the nut of the family" (Miller 311). Neither became socially active or politically involved. Neither grew beyond the late nineteenth-century post–Civil War world into which they were born. But Day's portrait of her mother in her autobiography reveals a strong mother-daughter relationship that may lie at the psychological source of Day's mature sense of herself. The opening chapter of Part I indicates that on her mother's side she came from three generations of strong women. Her great-grandmother bore eighteen children, raising the six who survived after her husband cracked his head in a fall on the whaler he was captaining. Her grandmother raised five children with little help from her invalid husband. Her mother raised Dorothy and her three brothers and sister with a husband who worked nights and rarely saw his whole family. Day pictures her mother as a woman determined to provide a home in the difficult circumstances of her sportswriter husband's career—moving from Brooklyn to Chicago to San Francisco to Oakland and back to Chicago and eventually to New York during Dorothy's youth. Having worked as a factory girl in her youth, her mother taught Dorothy the dignity of physical work to produce a livable home, gave her an example of helping the homeless during the earthquake of 1906, consoled her during times of bad dreams and the fear of death, knew how to dress up to overcome the shabbiness of poverty, and survived near-breakdowns and blinding headaches caused by the pressures of family responsibilities under her husband's regimen. From what Dorothy tells us of her mother, one discerns that the daughter received from the mother the seeds of devotion to the poor, to the sacredness of work and beauty, and to commitment to her goals, and a sense of her identity. Although Day goes through periods of self-doubt, most of her accusations of "selfishness" against herself in her autobiography can be attributed to the confessional genre common to most spiritual autobiographies by men and women since Augustine.

What excessive self-abasement she may have undergone can be traced in great part to the lack of affection from her father. In a family in which "[w]e kept ourselves to ourselves," as Day says (35), she felt especially estranged from her father. Her portrait of him, however generous and vaguely drawn ("he was a good and happy man in his own circle"), reveals by its lack of detail his remoteness and prejudiced character as an alcoholic Southerner trying to survive as a racetrack reporter in the North. He treated his daughters like children until they went to college, restricting their reading, keeping them away from school activities, never eating with them and the family, centering his household around his own privacy and self-image as a great journalist and neglected novelist (whose supreme moment was "making" the *Saturday Evening Post* with a short story). Dorothy's venture into journalism so violated his picture of propriety for his daughter that he did not let her live at home. She never mentions him in her autobiography after that early separation.

What Day, along with her brothers, gained from her father was a lifelong desire to be a writer. Nearly all other virtues she developed came from her mother, unless we were to reverse all of her father's prejudices and see him as a counter-example against which she fashioned herself. A case can also be made that her frustrations in love derived in part from her attempts with men as different as Lionel Moise and Forster Batterham to reconcile herself with men who had the one-sidedness of her father, particularly his aversion to religion and to women's individuality. Even Peter Maurin had to be refashioned by Dorothy Day to become a realistic model for her social conscience to follow, but by the time she met him she had a solid sense of her religious self and was beyond any emotional dependence on Maurin. She had by then integrated all the "others"—her dominating father and her caring mother—in her deeper Self.

"We Settled Some Problem . . . While We Wrote About It"

If Day's life can be seen as a circular journey to resolve the tensions between the father and the mother within her (and within American society), her way to resolve those tensions, like other tensions we have noted, was through writing. This begins at an early age: "When I was a child, my sister and I kept notebooks; recording happiness made it last longer, we felt, and recording sorrow dramatized it and took away its bitterness; and often we settled some problem which beset us, even while we wrote about it" (115). Noteworthy, of course, and typical of Day, who assures her readers several times that her conversions came not from rejection but from joy, is her insistence that she wrote first to express joy and second to resolve tensions. She repeats this in her first account of her writing, which she sees as essential to her pilgrimage toward community: "Whenever I felt the beauty of the world in song or story, in the material universe around me, or glimpsed it in human love, I wanted to cry out with joy. The Psalms were an outlet for this enthusiasm of joy or grief—and I suppose my writing was also an outlet. After all, one must communicate ideas" (29). Whether in her childhood diaries, her teenage letters, or her university stories and reporting, Day says she "became immersed in writing" (44). Interestingly, both in college and in her journalism, she writes about the experience of hunger, the physical hunger perhaps a symptom of the lifelong spiritual hunger she terms "the long loneliness." After every major turning point in her life, Day turns to writing as celebration or release—after her social conversion in college, during her years of confronting the "appalling poverty" of New York City, after her break up with Moise, after the birth of her baby, during the tensions after her conversion to Catholicism, during the trips to the capital, and all throughout her years building up the Catholic Worker. In fact, like Merton, she sees herself as fundamentally a *writer*, using her talent to create both her public self and her religious movement. One of the reasons the Catholic Worker became what she calls "a permanent revolution" (186) is that it had a permanent living voice in the paper, which Day edits and for which she writes much of the copy. Thus, as writer, she becomes the motivator of the movement. Even in the act of writing her autobiography, however, Day admits the difficulty of both her own motivation and the project of writing: "Was this desire to be with the poor and the mean and the abandoned not mixed with a distorted desire to be with the dissipated? I write these things now because sometimes I am seized with fright at my presumption. I am afraid, too, of not telling the truth, or of distorting the truth" (59).

In fact, one might say that the form of the last part of *The Long Loneliness*, with its plethora of names, places, and events about the movement, is Day's attempt to purify her autobiography of the "hypocrisy" she finds implicit in writing one's story on the central expression of a movement dedicated to *caritas*, concern for others as expression of love of God. She is caught in the triple bind of a woman and an autobiographer and a "Catholic worker"—the first afraid to assert her "self" in a male profession, the second committed to tell the truth of the Self, and the third called to work for the "cult, culture, and cultivation" of a society for others. Throughout the autobiography, she links the story of her self with the wider stories of her past—of the Bible, or great novels, of Peter Maurin's life story—thus avoiding self-aggrandizement. By disappearing during the last section from the circular journey and ending simply as a recorder of others' lives, Dorothy Day becomes part of the "we" who overcome loneliness not by self-glorification but by the strengthening of the deep Self in community. As she sums up the movement of her life and that of the Catholic Worker in the final page, using the directional image of the supper-table once again:

> We cannot love God unless we love each other, and to love we must know each other. We know Him in the breaking of bread, and we know each other in the breaking of bread, and we are not alone any more. Heaven is a banquet and life is a banquet, too, even with a crust, where there is companionship.
>
> We have all known the long loneliness and we have learned that the only solution is love and that loves comes with community.
>
> It all happened while we sat there talking, and it is still going on (285–86).

REFERENCES

Coles, Robert. *Dorothy Day: A Radical Devotion*. Reading, MA: Addison-Wesley, 1987.

Day, Dorothy. *The Long Loneliness*. New York: Harper, 1952.

Greer, Germaine. "Autobiography." Olney 170ff.

Jelinak, Estelle, ed. *Women Autobiographies: Essays in Criticism*. Bloomington: Indiana UP, 1980.

Miller, William. *Dorothy Day: A Biography*. San Francisco: Harper, 1982.

Olney, James, ed. *Studies in Autobiography*. New York: Oxford UP, 1988.

Spacks, Patricia M. "Selves in Hiding." Jelinak 112ff.

Watson, Julia. "Shadowed Presence: Modern Women Writers' Autobiographies and the Other." Olney 180ff.

3

The Psychology of Conversion in G. K. Chesterton and C. S. Lewis

"A YOUNG MAN who wishes to remain a sound atheist cannot be too careful of his reading." C. S. Lewis makes this remark in *Surprised by Joy* (191), just at the point where he describes his reading of Chesterton. At the time, Lewis was a nineteen-year-old second lieutenant in the British infantry recovering in 1917 from trench fever in a hospital at Le Trepart. Although Lewis disagreed with Chesterton's essays at the time, he admits that the humor, paradox, and goodness of the author made "an immediate conquest." In fact, the book led him to regard Chesterton as "the most sensible man alive 'apart from his Christianity' " (223). Nine years later, while teaching philosophy and English back at Oxford, Lewis read Chesterton's *The Everlasting Man*. This book led him to affirm "that Christianity itself was very sensible 'apart from its Christianity' " (223). Thus, at two crucial periods in his life—the first during a moral conversion in World War I, the second during his final conversion to belief in God—Lewis read G. K. Chesterton. Any study of the psychology of conversion in their religious autobiographies might well search out the similarities and differences in their respective stories of the journey from unbelief to Christian faith.

By "psychology of conversion," of course, I do not mean to reduce the authentic religious transformations of Lewis or Chesterton to mere psychic or emotional phenomena. Lewis himself was the first to recognize and discard any merely Freudian interpretation of his experiences. As he puts it, "If [Freud] can say that it [Joy] is sublimated sex, why is it not open to me to say that sex is sublimated It?" (W. Griffin 64–65). Likewise, he was aware of Jungian and archetypal interpretations but did not see these as incompatible with historical and realistic interpretations of Christian experiences. Just as he found Christianity to be a myth but a true myth, so his own experiences were perhaps archetypal but nonetheless valid. A more helpful approach to understanding Lewis (as it was in reading Merton) is to use some of the broader and friendlier categories of developmental psychology to explore the stages of the faith journeys of these two British autobiographers. Whatever the method, the use of psychological categories does not necessarily preclude a theological interpretation; in fact, as Emilie Griffin has shown in her excellent study of conversion experiences, *Turning*, any theology in which grace builds on and transforms nature calls for a natural psychological pattern to be present in the development of the religious self.

Here is the burden of the present chapter. I will begin by discussing the similar routes (through other genres) taken by Lewis and Chesterton to the writing of their autobiographies. Next, I will examine four common literary elements within their autobiographies proper: namely, (a) the circular journey form of their narratives; (b) the directional images and emotions of each author; (c) the influence of family and deaths; (d) the mediation of friends and books. In the final section, I will provide a preliminary examination of Lewis's autobiography as a movement through the five levels of conversion identified in religious development: the levels of imaginative, affective, moral, intellectual, and religious conversion.

Chesterton once said: "If [autobiography] is really to tell the truth, it must . . . at all costs profess not to. . . . [A] touch of fiction is almost always essential to the real conveying of fact . . ." (*Dickens* 139–40). The similarity in the use of "a touch of fiction" in various genres for autobiographical purposes by Chesterton and Lewis (as also by Merton, Day, and Wakefield) deserves a separate study, for the similarity is too remarkable to be merely coincidental. Both Chesterton and Lewis first wrote the story of their intellectual and religious conversions around age thirty-three in allegorical form—*The Man Who Was Thursday* (1908) and *Pilgrim's Regress* (1935), respectively. The use of such a form suggests, perhaps, similar psychological insecurity about revealing their deepest personal transformations in direct first-person autobiography, but it also reveals the intensity of their convictions about their conversions. Their next attempts were through a second literary form, the argumentative essay; for Chesterton in *Orthodoxy* (1908), for Lewis in a series of short books beginning with *The Problem of Pain* (1940). Both came to the use of formal autobiography only at a later age, Chesterton in his early sixties, Lewis in his mid-fifties. Even in these later books, however, both shied away from revealing personal details not directly relevant to their religious conversions. Chesterton, in fact, relegated his religious conversion to relatively few pages of *Autobiography* (1936), a book that is primarily a series of memoirs on the influence of others. Lewis concentrated on events and persons directly relevant to his movement away from and back to Christian faith. Thus, they both created autobiographies that are, as Gary Wills says, "a series of symbols rather than a prosaic account of fact" (6). But the general movement from allegory to apologetical essay to conversion autobiography reflects the relatively private character of these very public Christian converts.

Other studies of Lewis have shown in detail how *Pilgrim's Regress* embodies in its allegory what Lewis summed up in his 1943 preface: "On the intellectual side my own progress had been from 'popular realism' to Philosophical idealism; from Idealism to Panteism; from Pantheism to Theism; and from Theism to Christianity" (5). What is significant for the present study is that Lewis highlights the allegorical journey as primarily intellectual. Chesterton also uses the allegorical form of *The Man Who Was Thursday* and the essays of *Orthodoxy* (both published in 1908) to express his intellectual conversion to Christian faith. In the former, Chesterton describes in a detective story the search for ultimate meaning and reality by a poet who is much like the young Chesterton. The autobiographical impulse is so strong in both *Orthodoxy* and *The Man Who Was Thursday*, however, that they provide a much clearer picture of the stages of Chesterton's conversion than his later *Autobiography* does. Thus, in an allegory and in a book of essays which he describes as "unavoidably affirmative and unavoidably autobiographical," Chesterton heralded the way for Lewis to follow thirty years later.

The Circular Romance and Its Directional Image

Orthodoxy (1908) and *Surprised by Joy* (1955) exhibit notable common patterns, in spite of the fact that no two books of Chesterton and Lewis may seem less alike than the books that they each claimed and disclaimed to be an autobiography. The former is a series of essays written when Chesterton was thirty-two and not yet a Christian; the latter, a conversion story written when Lewis was fifty-eight and a longtime convert to Anglicanism. Yet both books take the reader on a circular romance narrative in which the author arrives where he started, only to recognize the place for the first time. This form, familiar to students of autobiography from the time of Augustine's *Confessions*, lent itself to these two authors, who had common childhood experiences of a quasi-religious nature, who then spent many years of wandering in search of an adequate version or fulfillment of their first experience, and who finally arrived at a faith that did fulfill their earlier longings in a surprising but familiar manner. Chesterton describes the circular journey image as the motif of his story in his introduction to *Orthodoxy*:

> I have often had a fancy of writing a romance about an English yachtsman who slightly miscalculated his course and discovered England under the impression that it was a new island in the South Seas. . . . But I have a peculiar reason for mentioning the man in the yacht, who discovered England. For I am that man in a yacht. . . . The man from the yacht thought he was the first to find England; I thought I was the first to find Europe. I did try to found a heresy of my own; and when I had put the last touches to it, I discovered that it was orthodoxy. (14, 16, 19)

Chesterton discovers, as he tells it through the subsequent eight essays, a series of truths about his experience, only later to realize that these truths had previously been available under the title "Christianity."

Lewis's circular journey was much less an intellectual homecoming than an imaginative rediscovery of the ultimate meaning of his early emotional experiences. He begins his story with a central childhood experience of what he calls "Joy," then loses the experience for many years, only to rediscover it in a way that leads him to the surprising joy of Christianity. Like Augustine, with his repeated experiences of a "restless heart," both Lewis and Chesterton move through an odyssey of islands on their journey to discovery of their true and first home.

Green and Hooper have shown that Lewis first tried the circular sea voyage form of Chesterton's in an unsuccessful attempt in 1932 to write a long narrative poem on his own conversion. The only remaining thirty-four lines of the aborted autobiographical epic contain the verses: ". . . to follow the retreating shore / Of this land which I call at last my home, where most / I feared to come" (Green and Hooper 127). Lewis picks up the sea voyage imagery only occasionally in *Surprised by Joy*—for example, at his mother's death near the end of "The First Years": "It was the sea and islands now; the great continent had sunk like Atlantis" (21).

At the start of their circular journeys, Chesterton and Lewis each describes a basic "mental picture" (as Chesterton calls it) from his childhood, what psychologists might call a directional or "intentional" image, a sort of archetype that leads one on one's lifelong search for ultimate meaning. For Chesterton, it was a "toy theater" built by his father; for Lewis, it was a "toy garden" made by his brother. Chesterton describes the toy theater in chapter two of his 1936 memoirs:

> The very first thing I can ever remember seeing with my own eyes was a young man walking across a bridge. . . . I saw it through a window more wonderful than the window in the tower: through the proscenium of a toy theatre constructed by my father. . . . And the scene has to me a sort of aboriginal authenticity impossible to describe; something at the back of all my thoughts; like the very back-scene of the theatre of things. (*Autobiography* 24–25)

For Chesterton, this theater provided a heuristic picture ("something at the back of all my thoughts") of several qualities he searched for during his life and eventually found in Christianity: a sense of limits and connections amid the mysteries of human life; a sense of romance, creativity, and imagination; and a sense of personal meaning symbolized by the man with the golden key in the theater's story. Not only did Chesterton use childhood images to open and close his *Autobiography* (24, 355), but he even transformed them into philosophical qualities that he discovered on his journey through the intellectual and religious landscape of *Orthodoxy.*

Lewis tells us of the similar archetypal importance of the "toy garden" in the first chapter of his autobiography:

> Once in those very early days my brother brought into the nursery the lid of a biscuit tin which he had covered with moss and gar-nished with twigs and flowers so as to make a toy garden or a toy forest. That was the first beauty I ever knew. What the real garden had failed to do, the toy garden did. It made me aware of nature. . . . As long as I live my imagination of Paradise will retain some-thing of my brother's toy garden. (*Joy* 7)

At the time, Lewis recalls, this was an aesthetic experience, but throughout his journey such aesthetic moments gradually merge with and then become distinguished from religious moments. The "toy garden" sums up for him both his love of romance and his love of nature. In both he found a combination of satisfaction and dissatisfied desire which was the central emotional experience of his childhood. From this experience, all the energy for his life journey flowed; the experience provided the name and center of his autobiography, simply called "Joy": ". . . an unsatisfied desire which is itself more desirable than any other satisfaction. I call it Joy. . . . I doubt whether anyone who has tasted it would ever . . . exchange it for all the pleasures in the world" (18).

Lewis had already described this experience, which he then entitled "Romanticism," in the 1943 preface to his quasi-auto-biographical allegory, *Pilgrim's Regress*: "The experience is one of intense longing . . . yet the mere wanting is felt to be somehow a delight. This hunger is better than any other fullness; this poverty than all other wealth" (7). He goes on to describe the importance of this "joy" in human experience, as well as in his own allegory: "It appeared to me therefore that if a man diligently followed this desire, pursuing the false objects until their falsity appeared and then resolutely abandoning them, he must come out at last into the clear knowledge that the human soul was made to enjoy some object that is never fully given—nay, cannot even be imagined as given—in our present mode of subjective and spatio-temporal experience" (10). This primal experience will serve Lewis as the recurring motif during the turning points of his autobiography, driving him beyond satisfaction with any partial good, inadequate meaning, or "false object."

The equivalent of Joy in Chesterton seems to be his notion of romance. Joy is also a driving emotion for Chesterton, but in a slightly different sense, one that he describes most fully not at the beginning but at the conclusion of *Orthodoxy*:

> It is said that Paganism is a religion of joy and Christianity of sorrow; it would be just as easy to prove that Paganism is pure sorrow and Christianity pure joy. . . . Christianity satisfies suddenly and perfectly man's ancestral instinct for being the right way up; satisfies it supremely in this: that by its creed joy becomes something gigantic and sadness something special and small. (294, 297)

In this focus on early childhood images and experiences as crucial to their later conversions, Chesterton and Lewis make similar statements about the role of memory. Chesterton speaks of his memory of the toy theater as "more our own memory of the thing rather than the thing remembered" (*Autobiography* 29). He gives several other examples of these lifetime-remembered images—one, the picture of his sister falling; the other, of a white horse. Lewis makes such "memory of a memory" the core of his autobiography, beginning with the toy garden and repeated in experiences of the currant bush on a summer day, of reading Squirrel Nutkin, and so on (*Joy* 16).

THE THREE-CIRCLED JOURNEY: JOY FOUND, LOST, AND REGAINED

This combination of satisfaction and dissatisfaction in the remembered experiences of both Lewis and Chesterton (not unrelated to the *cor inquietum* of Augustine) drives both the narratives and each man's movements through the levels of conversion in his autobiography. Both begin with "joy" in a "toy" romance; both end with "joy" in a real romance, Christianity. When Lewis was openly admitting in 1956 to his former student Alan Griffith that *Surprised by Joy* had this "Chestertonian quality," Lewis went on to acknowledge the more obvious *structural* plot of the book: "The gradual reading of one's own life, seeing a pattern emerge, is a great illumination at our age. And partly, I hope, getting freed from the past as past by apprehending it as structure" (*Letters* 266). Let us now join Lewis in "seeing a pattern emerge" in his autobiography, a pattern that helped him toward freedom from the formless past so apparent in his diaries or letters. What appears in his diaries of 1922–27 as intermittent insights on "joy" or the occasional use of a developing philosophical language about God becomes part of a recurrent tripartite structure found in all the autobiographies we are considering (cf. *All My Road* 48, 50, 112, 118, 142, 177, 328).

Although the middle of Chesterton's religious journey is too clouded with literary memoirs to provide a structural pattern, Lewis's search for Joy covers territory that can be mapped in a rough three-story spiral: I. Childhood Joy; II. Adolescent Loss of Joy; III. Adult Joy Regained. In each of the three stages, Lewis describes parallel events, persons, and symbolic objects. His psychological journey after the death of his mother and the loss of confidence in his father leads him on a quest for a permanent mother and a trustworthy father. He finds temporary substitutes in Kirkpatrick and, as Griffin and A. N. Wilson show in their very different biographies, in Mrs. Moore. However, after a period of what Lewis calls "my deep-seated hatred of authority, my monstrous individualism, my lawlessness" (172), he goes beyond both these mentors to religious humility and acceptance of divine mercy as a reluctant prodigal son (229). His way to the Christian Father is a way of dissatisfied satisfaction, a Joy found and lost in childhood (7, 16, 61), again in adolescence (72, 77, 168), and finally gained in an integration of the imagination, the rational, and the practical in adulthood (ch. 11, pp. 179, 196). In each stage, this Joy expresses itself in religious practice—first in the Anglo-Catholic fervor of his first schoolboy piety (33–34), then in the anti-religious sentiments and even blasphemous reception of the sacrament in adolescence (59–66, 161), and eventually recovered through participation in daily chapel and in weekly parish mass after his conversion to theism (233). This religious pattern finds its moral parallel in his childhood and adolescent cycle of conscientiousness followed by moral lapses, eventually leading to an adult moral conversion. Intermixed with both is his growth as an imaginative writer. Like other individual seekers of this century, Lewis becomes his own mediator through the power of his imaginative pen—first in the Animal-land of his childhood, then in the Boxen narrative of his early adolescence, and, finally, in the poetry of his early adulthood (as his biographers note, poetry is the primary obsession of his early adult writing).

"LOSING HIS SONS": DARKNESS AND THE FAMILY ROMANCE

Although neither Lewis's father nor his mother was a direct mediator of his religious conversion, each strongly influenced him in ways that produced a split in his personality. As he admits in a passage about his parents and their families, "the contrast of Lewis and Hamilton dominated my whole early life" (42). His mother, the daughter of a clergyman, came from an old English family in Belfast, known for their courtesy, calm personalities, sense of duty, and confidence in life. Lewis remembers her as showing him "a cheerful and tranquil affection" (4). Lewis's father, as portrayed in *Surprised by Joy*, was a well-meaning, bumbling, heavy-handed man, successful as a police solicitor (the first professional in a family of Welsh farmers), but with a volatile and insecure disposition—"sentimental, passionate, and rhetorical" (3). For young Lewis, the difference between his parents' personalities bred in him an intellectual control and fear of emotion that brought about a split within his psyche: "From my earliest years, I was aware of the vivid contrast between my mother's cheerful and tranquil affection and the ups and downs of my father's emotional life, and this bred in me long before I was old enough to give it a name a certain distrust or dislike of emotion as something uncomfortable and embarrassing and even dangerous" (4).

This split within Lewis became, of course, much wider upon the death of his mother in 1908 after a four-month bout with cancer, when Lewis was only nine and about to leave for boarding school. Although he seems to have gained some degree of what Erik Erikson describes as basic trust, autonomy, and initiative, these early childhood virtues were severely shaken not only by his mother's death but even more, perhaps, by his father's ineptness and emotional inability to console and support Lewis and his brother in their grief. Except for recalling intermittent periods of peace with his father, Lewis spends most of the many passages in his autobiography that deal with his father describing in a bitter comic fashion his eccentricities and oppressiveness. It seems as if Lewis's idealization of his mother led, after her death, to a lifelong resentment and anger toward his father, almost as if Lewis blamed him for the loss and for failing to be the ideal parent the highly imaginative son expected. In contrast to Thomas Merton (whose mother died when he was six), who idealized his surviving father at the expense of his mother, Lewis goes on at great length to portray his father as a bookish Belfast raconteur who could entertain adults with his stories and legal skills but who could not understand or communicate with his sons. Unable to handle his own grief, Lewis's father sent his son to his first (and most severely resented) boarding school in England only two weeks after his mother's funeral. During the vacations for the next ten years, Lewis finds his home world to be a series of refuges (with his brother or his friend Arthur Greeves) from the oppressive presence of his well-meaning but obtuse father. Yet, in the very years of finishing these portraits of his home life in his autobiography, Lewis could admit in a letter, " 'I treated my own father abominably' " (Wilson 114).

The religious effects on Lewis of the death of his mother and incompetence of his father were more serious than his autobiography suggests. During his first school year after the funeral, Lewis "became an effective believer" (33). While admitting he was afflicted by fear, he began to pray, to read the Bible, and to live by his conscience. However much this short-lived childhood conversion owed to his mother's memory and his father's sincere but sentimental practice of faith in the Church of Ireland, Lewis perseveres in his religious period for only two years. By the time he is thirteen, as he says, he "broadened [his] mind" and lost his childhood grasp on Christianity. This loss is occasioned by the assaults of puberty and his anxiety in attempting to force emotions in prayer, and by his first acquaintance with the Occult (61–68). As he summarizes this period, "And so, little by little, with fluctuations which I cannot now trace, I became an apostate, dropping my faith with no sense of loss but with the greatest relief" (66). In shaking off his faith, he was also shaking off the one consistent characteristic of his father—his piety. Later, in despair of finding any way to talk with his pious father, Lewis went through the motions of receiving communion and confirmation in the Church of Ireland, an event he calls "one of the worst acts of my life" (161).

Beneath this loss of faith lay what Lewis calls in several places in his life story the split within his personality, a split derived from the emotional contrast between his parents and from the loss of his mother and the ineffectiveness of his father in taking her place. The basic duality of his life, as he terms it, consisted in a split between his imaginative life of Joy and his practical life of school, family, and friendships (78). In a chapter entitled "Release," which deals primarily with his escape from boarding school, Lewis describes his life as "a story of two lives"—and then gives as his main example of this duality the practical life of oppressive conflict with his father (118–28) as contrasted with the imaginative life of Joy found in reading Norse mythology with his friend Arthur (129–31). This duality expressed itself in his intellectual life as a split between rationalism (fostered by his tutor Kirkpatrick and later at Oxford by his philosophical studies) and imaginative literature (fostered by his creative writing and by Norse mythology) (136–37). As he later sums up this contrast within his psyche:

> Such, then, was the state of my imaginative life; over against it stood the life of my intellect. The two hemispheres of my mind were in the sharpest contrast. On the one side a many-islanded sea of poetry and myth; on the other a glib and shallow 'rationalism'. . . . Such then was my position: to care for almost nothing but the gods and heroes, the garden of the Hesperides, Launcelot and the Grail, and to believe in nothing but atoms and evolution and military service. (170, 174)

The struggle for conversion is also a struggle to unite the two sides of his personality. When he comes to find Joy leading him toward Christian faith, the imaginative and practical worlds become one. This struggle for integration of the psyche and for faith was interrupted—as his autobiography is interrupted—by Lewis's second great confrontation with death, this time in the trenches of World War I. Like Chesterton, he had both a severe childhood loss and then no further brushes with death until the Great War. For Chesterton, the loss of his eight-year-old sister, Beatrice, when he was only three produced a grief he could not identify except as it became "the one dreadful sorrow of his [father's] abnormally happy and even merry existence" (*Autobiography* 29). More significant for Chesterton, the World War wounded him deeply by taking his brother Cecil, whose death passed on a legacy to Gilbert of heavy religious–political responsibility ("I went on editing [my brother's paper]; because he did not return"). Lewis also first confronted death in person in the same war. For him, however, the confrontation led him to only a narrow sense of social responsibility. As he says of the Great War: "I must not paint the wartime army all gold. I met there both the World and the great Goddess Nonsense. . . . Familiarity both with the very old and the very recent dead confirmed that view of corpses which had been formed the moment I saw my dead mother. I came to know and pity and reverence the ordinary man" (*Joy* 194–96). Paradoxically, the rest of the war appeared less than real to Lewis, who spent months in the trenches and even captured many German soldiers, but managed to detach himself from the war after his injury and return to England.

This distancing himself from death suggests that Lewis was still living with an inner dichotomy. His first encounter with combat occasions an "imaginative moment" more important than the direct realities of wounds and death. As he says of his first response to combat: "This is War. This is what Homer wrote about" (196). Even his own near-death is distanced by his rationalistic mind: "Two things stand out. One is the moment, just after I had been hit, when I found (or thought I found) that I was not breathing and concluded that this was death. I felt no fear and certainly not courage. . . . The proposition 'Here is a man dying' stood before my mind as dry, as factual, as unemotional as something in a textbook. It was not even interesting" (197). Significantly, Lewis identified his deeper self in this death experience as like Kant's Noumenon, and the outer events as mere Phenomena. This dualism was to reach an unexpected resolution only in his religious conversion. Ironically, in the midst of his description of the later stages of this conversion—when his imaginative and intellectual transformation came together in June 1929 (ch. 14)—Lewis casually mentions his father's death. But he immediately remarks that this death "did not come into this story" of his conversion to theism and prayer, probably because his father died in September

1929, several months *after* Lewis first knelt in prayer and faith. Although one biographer (Wilson 283) makes much of this event, its occurrence after Lewis's acknowledgment of God suggests that the death may have delayed rather than mediated his later conversion to explicit belief in Christianity in 1931.

MEDIATORS OF THE IMAGINATION

What helps Chesterton and Lewis along the way? Both received little formal help on their religious quests from either parents or parsons. Psychologically and culturally, both were men born into the modern age, an age that, as John S. Dunne describes it, suffers from a loss of spiritual and temporal mediation. As searchers without mediators from church or culture, Chesterton and Lewis were driven into their own inner experience to find their authentic selves and a sense of the transcendent. But, on their journeys through the islands of dissatisfactions, both Chesterton and Lewis found quasi-mediators in friendships and in books.

Because he writes a more traditional religious autobiography, Lewis provides for us a sketch of these mediators at each stage. Probably the most important mediator of his childhood was his brother, Warren, who receives only casual mention in the autobiography. The first and most important single mediator in his youth was Arthur Greeves, a classmate at Campbell's School near Belfast, who shared Lewis's love of myths of the Norsemen. In Lewis's words, "both knew the stab of joy and . . . for both, the arrow was shot from the North" (*Joy* 130). After the war, in early adulthood, Lewis found a "second friend" at Oxford in Owen Barfield. The difference between the two friends reveals the two sides of Lewis:

> There is a sense in which Arthur and Barfield are the types of every man's First Friend and Second Friend. The First is the alter ego, the man who first reveals to you that you are not alone in the world by turning out (beyond hope) to share all your most secret delights. There is nothing to be overcome in making him your friend; he and you join like raindrops on a window. But the Second Friend is a man who disagrees with you about everything. He is not so much the alter ego as the antiself (*Joy* 199).

Arthur helped Lewis in the imaginative level of conversion; Barfield, in the intellectual. A third friend, Neville Coghill, whom
Lewis met in 1922 while studying English in his fourth year at
Oxford, mediated his religious conversion. For Coghill was not
only "the most intelligent and best informed man in that class"
but also "a Christian and a thoroughgoing supernaturalist" (212).
Outside of his father and brother, who had strong but ambiguous
influences on Lewis, these three friends embody the three types
of friendships that, Lewis tells us, drew him from childhood imaginative Joy to the adult Joy of Christian faith.

Equal if not more powerful influences came to Lewis (as to
Chesterton) from his reading. As Lewis confesses near the time of
his final conversion:

> George MacDonald had done more to me than any other writer.
> . . . Chesterton had more sense than all the other moderns put
> together. . . . Johnson was one of the few authors whom I felt I
> could trust utterly. . . . Spenser and Milton by a strange coincidence
> had Christianity too. Even among ancient authors the same para-
> dox was to be found. The most religious (Plato, Aeschylus, Virgil)
> were clearly those on whom I could really feed. (213)

From the time of his first experience of childhood Joy, Lewis, as
he tells us, was "the product . . . of endless books" (10). In fact,
one of the three childhood examples he gives of his experience
of Joy occurred while reading "Balder the beautiful / Is dead, is
dead" in Longfellow's Saga of King Olaf (17). Later, at Campbell's
School, Lewis says that the most important event was reading
Arnold's Soharb and Rustum, perhaps the truest beginning of his
imaginative conversion through literature. But Lewis explicitly
denies this was an experience of Joy (72), for the title that called
him back to "the memory of Joy itself" was Siegfried and the Twi-
light of the Gods. As he describes this turning point of his life: "at
once I knew (with fatal knowledge) that 'to have it again' was
the supreme and only important object of desire" (73). Lewis
subsequently read all of Norse mythology and became a devotee
of Wagner.

Although Lewis read the Greek, Roman, and English classics
in his school years and developed intellectually under the tutelage
of his two great mentors, Smewgy and Kirkpatrick, he tells us that

the most important literary mediator in his spiritual journey was George MacDonald, the Victorian fantasy writer who was also a favorite of Chesterton's (Mackey 70). Lewis describes the October train trip when he first read *Phantastes*:

> It was as if I were carried sleeping across the frontier, or as if I had died in the old country and could never remember how I came alive in the new. For in one sense the new country was exactly like the old. I met there all that had already charmed me in Malory, Spenser, Morris, and Yeats. But in another sense all was changed. I did not yet know (and I was long in learning) the name of the new quality, the bright shadow, that rested on the travels of Anodos. It was Holiness. (*Joy* 179)

He goes on to describe this experience in language that echoes Chesterton's on the discovery of the familiar: "It seems to have been always with me . . . never had the winds of Joy blowing through any story been less separable from the story itself" (180). Finally, Chesterton himself was an important literary mediator for Lewis during the latter's respite from the war. Lewis sums up the cumulative effect of all his reading in a famous passage: "All the books were beginning to turn against me" (213).

Once all these writers had helped Lewis to an act of faith in God, Chesterton appeared again, this time to "make sense" of history in Christian terms in his *The Everlasting Man*. Lewis pulls together in one sentence all the mediators on his journey— experience, friends, and books—as he draws near the end of his autobiography: "And nearly everyone was now (one way or another) in the pack: Plato, Dante, MacDonald, Herbert, Barfield, Tolkien, Dysen, Joy itself. Everyone and everything had joined the other side" (225).

In contrast to Lewis, Chesterton followed literary mediators who were not at all Christian. As Chesterton tells it: "I never read a line of Christian apologetics. I read as little as I can of them now. It was Huxley and Herbert and Spencer and Bradlaugh who brought me back to orthodox theology. They sowed in my mind my first wild doubts of doubt" (*Orthodoxy* 154). Because his conversion story focuses most fully on his intellectual "argument" for Christianity, Chesterton finds its enemies to be his mediators. As he describes his thoughts after reading a series of lectures on atheism, "almost thou persuadest me to be a Christian" (154). Throughout his earlier books, he had debated against the giant freethinkers of his generation—from Kipling to Shaw to H. G. Wells—and in *Orthodoxy* he showed how these debates led to his personal philosophy, which turned out, to his surprise, to be the same as Christianity.

In fact, Chesterton gives almost no clues to any positive mediators among his readings before his conversion. With regard to the mediation of friends, however, he is slightly more helpful. Even in his *Autobiography* he credits four persons with mediating his conversion—his wife, his brother Cecil, his friend Hilaire Belloc, and his confessor, Father John O'Connor (the latter was also the model for Father Brown). His wife mediated his early conversion to Christianity and his affective conversion; Cecil and Belloc mediated his intellectual growth and social conscience; Father O'Connor mediated the final steps of his religious conversion to Catholicism.

STAGES OF CONVERSION

I have noted in passing that Chesterton gives glimpses of three aspects or levels of conversion in his autobiographies—intellectual, moral, and religious. In addition to these, Lewis's autobiography embodies the power of the imagination in the conversion process. His early experience of Joy at seeing the toy garden becomes a lifelong image of Paradise. It repeatedly emerges in his memory "as if from a depth not of years but of centuries" (*Joy* 16) and is associated with experiences of nature, books, friends. Even in the years of wandering, which make up most of the central chapters of his autobiography, Lewis finds that he tries in various aberrant ways to rediscover and control Joy, only to be disappointed and led, like Augustine, to further searchings. As he describes these middle years, "I was sent back to the false gods there to acquire some capacity for worship against the day when the true God should recall me to Himself" (77). Only later did he come to learn how to discern merely imaginative from religious symbols. As he says of his readings of the Norse sagas, "Only very gradually did I realize that all this was something quite different from the original Joy. . . . Finally I woke from building the temple to find that God had flown" (165). Like Wordsworth whose "glory" has passed away, Lewis had to learn the levels of conscience and faith: "I do not think the resemblance between the Christian and the merely imaginative experience is accidental. I think that all things, in their way, reflect heavenly truth, the imagination not least" (167).

From this distinction, Lewis learns two lessons—first, that he could not achieve Joy directly, and, second, that he could not produce or control it at all. Only later, when he read George MacDonald's religious fantasies, did he undergo a full-fledged conversion of the imagination. In Lewis's words, "That night my imagination was, in a certain sense, baptized; the rest of me, not unnaturally, took longer" (181). "The rest of me" included his moral, intellectual, and religious conversions. How important the imagination was for connecting these other conversions is revealed in Lewis's comment in his 1927 diary (two years before he accepted God) on the "truth that really is in the imagination." He calls this truth "rightness of feeling—the 'affective' side of cognition without the cognition" (*All My Road* 449). Thus, the imagination leads the way on the emotional level for a later transformation of the intellect of the religious searcher. But, like Chesterton, he gives little clue in *Surprised by Joy* to any affective conversion in relation to other persons. (In fact, Lewis explicitly sets aside his feelings for women as having little to do with his religious search. What biographer A. N. Wilson calls an "omission and evasion" may be one reason why reviewers of Lewis's autobiography in 1956 called the book "absorbing" but "singularly unsatisfying" or "strangely uneven.")

In contrast to this affective gap, Lewis gives a fairly detailed account of some of the circumstances of his moral conversion during World War I. This transformation was mediated by a man named Johnson, with whom he used to argue and who proved to be "a man of conscience." The result of these conversions for Lewis was a conversion to "strict veracity, chastity, or devotion to duty. . . . I accepted his principles at once" (192–93).

Lewis's intellectual conversion covered many years and many doctrines. Like Chesterton, he debated with and tried out a variety of theories—necessitarianism, absolute idealism, romanticism, etc.—but never found true and complete Joy in any of them. What was lacking, he later tells us, was any full notion of tran- scendence. In reading Samuel Alexander's *Space, Time, and Deity*, Lewis came to see the crucial difference between direct experien- tial awareness (which Lewis called "Enjoyment") and reflective consciousness (which he called "Contemplation"). He found this distinction "an indispensable tool of thought," especially for un- derstanding why and how he had lost his original Joy:

> I saw that all my waitings and watchings for Joy, all my vain hopes to find some mental content on which I could, so to speak, lay my finger and say, "This is it," had been a futile attempt to contemplate the enjoyed. . . . I knew now that the images and sensations were merely the mental track left by the passage of Joy—not the wave but the wave's imprint on the sand. (*Joy* 219)

From this insight into an aspect of the distinction between objec- tivity and subjectivity, Lewis came to appreciate the presence of God, not as merely subjective human experience itself or as scien- tific object of consciousness "out there," but as the implicit, un- known, undefined source and goal of human desire. Joy, then, proved not to be a delusion, but, as he says, "its visitations were rather the moments of clearest consciousness we had, when we became aware of our fragmentary and phantasmal nature and ached for that impossible reunion which would annihilate us or that self-contradictory waking which would reveal, not that we had, but that we were, a dream" (222). But he did not remain in this state of merely intellectual conversion.

Lewis's final and specifically religious conversion followed soon upon reading another book, Chesterton's *The Everlasting Man*. This final move was not merely an intellectual insight or judg- ment. Rather, faith came as a choice.

> The odd thing was that before God closed in on me, I was in fact offered what now appears a moment of wholly free choice. I was going up Headington Hill on the top of a bus. . . . I felt myself being, there and then, given a free choice. I could open the door or keep it shut; I could unbuckle the armor or keep it on. (*Joy* 224)

Like Augustine in the garden or Chesterton at his desk, Lewis was left to choose whether to believe in God. His religious con- version was not merely a final step in an imaginative or intellectual process; rather, it was a choice of belief in a personal God, a choice that felt like a letting go—"I chose to open, to unbuckle, to loosen the rein." The result of this choice, of course, had its emotional and imaginative aspects, neither of which was pleasant, as Lewis recalls, using an image from his 1926 diary: "Then came the repercussion on the imaginative level. I felt as if I were a man of snow at last beginning to melt. . . . I rather disliked the feeling" (225; cf. *All My Road* 412.) Unlike Chesterton, however, who reportedly said he became a Catholic "to have my sins forgiven," Lewis deemphasizes the importance of salvation in his religious conversion (Wills 162).

In rereading Lewis in the light of other modern religious autobiographies, one might make three reflections on his final stage of religious conversion. First, in the final stage of Lewis's conversion—as in Chesterton's—the more difficult step was to "admit that God was God"; the second step from Theism to Christianity (although two years long in his life) takes up no more than a few pages of *Surprised by Joy* and ends with the description of the drive to Whipsnade one sunny morning: "When we set out I did not believe that Jesus Christ is the Son of God, and when we reached the zoo I did. Yet I had not exactly spent the journey in thought. Nor in great emotion. 'Emotional' is perhaps the last word we can apply to some of the most important events" (237).

Second, unlike Chesterton, who had a remarkable social consciousness from his youth and developed a political philosophy of "distributism," Lewis never seems to have undergone a political-social transformation in his moral or religious life. He speaks of himself as "vaguely socialist" in the 1920s (173), later writes strongly against Fascism and Communism, but, as Wilson and others have noted, he never became politically sophisticated (Burton 160ff.). Third, the lack of ecstatic or even pleasant emotions in the final movement to faith suggests what Emilie Griffin has noted in her study of Lewis and other converts—"the conversion does not automatically convert the emotions as well" (140). Unlike what is suggested by some contemporary psychologists of religion, holiness is not necessarily wholeness. This was especially true of both Lewis and Chesterton, who continued to struggle, as most humans do, with disagreeable and even bizarre emotional patterns. As Lewis wrote to one of his correspondents, " . . .

genuine religious emotion is only a servant. No soul is saved by having it or damned by lacking it" (*Letters* 269). Although A. N. Wilson tries to make a great deal of the possible sexual involvement of Lewis with Mrs. Moore in the 1920s, it seems more likely that the relationship was that of a deep psychological dependency, an emotional fixation on a surrogate mother (cf. Beversluis). The episode is one more instance of Lewis's submerged emotional struggles. This lifelong struggle for emotional integration, however, did not prevent either Lewis or Chesterton from showing in their autobiographies the truth of Chesterton's words at the conclusion of his life story: "Man is more himself . . . when joy is the fundamental thing in him" (*Autobiography* 296).

References

Beversluis, John. "Surprised by Freud: A Critical Appraisal of A. N. Wilson's Biography of C. S. Lewis." *Christianity and Literature* 41 (1992): 179–95.

Burton, John David. "G. K. Chesterton and C. S. Lewis: The Men and Their Times." *The Riddle of Joy*. Ed. Michael H. McDonald and Andrew Tadie. Grand Rapids, MI: Eerdmans, 1989, 169–72.

Chesterton, G. K. *The Autobiography of G. K. Chesterton.* New York: Sheed and Ward, 1936.

———. *Charles Dickens.* London: Methuen, 1906.

———. *Orthodoxy.* New York: Dodd, Mead, 1908.

Conn, Walter. *Christian Conversion.* New York: Paulist, 1986.

Dale, Alzina Stone. "C. S. Lewis and G. K. Chesterton: Conservative Defendants as Critics." *The Taste of Pineapple: Essays on C. S. Lewis.* Ed. Bruce L. Edwards. Bowling Green, OH: Bowling Green State UP, 1988.

Green, Roger, and Walter Hooper. *C. S. Lewis: A Biography.* New York: Harcourt, 1976.

Griffin, Emilie. *Turning: Reflections on the Experience of Conversion.* New York: Doubleday, 1980.

Griffin, William. *Clive Staples Lewis: A Dramatic Life.* New York: Harper, 1986.

Lewis, C[live] S[taples]. *All My Road Before Me: The Diary of C.*

S. *Lewis, 1922–1927*. Ed. Walter Hooper. San Diego: Harcourt, 1991.

—————. *Letters of C. S. Lewis*. Ed., with a memoir, by W. H. Lewis. New York: Harcourt, 1966.

—————. *Pilgrim's Regress*. Grand Rapids, MI: Eerdmans, 1943.

—————. *Surprised by Joy*. New York: Harcourt, 1955.

—————. *They Stand Together: The Letters of C. S. Lewis to Arthur Greeves*. Ed. Walter Hooper. New York: Macmillan, 1979.

Mackey, Aidan. "The Christian Influence of G. K. Chesterton on C. S. Lewis." *A Christian for All Christians: Essays in Honor of C. S. Lewis*. Ed. Andrew Walker and James Patrick. London: Hodder & Stoughton, 1990.

Wills, Gary. *Chesterton: Man and Mask*. New York: Sheed and Ward, 1961.

Wilson, A. N. *C. S. Lewis: A Biography*. New York: Norton, 1990.

4

The Dual Plot of Gandhi's
An Autobiography

THE SUBTITLE OF GANDHI'S *An Autobiography*—"the story of my experiments with Truth"—gives the reader a clue to why it is difficult to follow its plot. Written periodically during and after a prison term from 1921 to 1924, the narrative of Gandhi's "experiments" appears episodic and disorganized, in part because it was composed as a series of newspaper columns to edify his followers.[1] Only Judith M. Brown, in her excellent *Gandhi: Prisoner of Hope*, makes sense of the complex tensions in the development of Gandhi's life and thought in a manner consistent with his own story. Yet even Brown does not try to untangle the narrative knots of the *Autobiography*. The plot remains to be unraveled.

Beneath what one biographer calls the "erratic and disturbing" (Payne) appearance of the book, and another critic its "slapdash method" (Meyers), I have uncovered a coherent principle of narrative organization. This principle is not easy for Westerners to discover, because the autobiography uses a mixture of cultural patterns and narrative forms from the three contexts of Gandhi's life—India, England, and South Africa. His reading in Hindu and Western literature in South Africa and later during his prison years in India led to his use of patterns from Augustine's *Confessions*. But Gandhi reshaped these patterns to fit Indian newspaper columns, each of which called for a moral message for a religiously

---

[1] With the lack of an obvious narrative structure in Gandhi's *Autobiography*, critics have concentrated their interpretations on a few psychologically memorable episodes (Erikson), on the mood of the author during the writing (Malhotra), on several differences between Eastern and Western writing (Parekh), on some bizarre aspects of Gandhi's vows (Mandel), on the feminine and political effects of his asceticism (Rudolph), or on select moral or political statements taken out of context and integrated with his voluminous other writings (Iyer, Chatterjee). Most of Gandhi's biographers draw upon the autobiography for information but fail to analyze its format closely (Desai, Fisher, Nanda, Payne).

diverse readership. Other Western influences from his reading included James's *Varieties of Religious Experience*, Thoreau's *Civil Disobedience*, and the New Testament. From India, of course, he incorporated his own version of the stages of Hindu life-patterns and the asceticism of the *Bhagavad Gita* and other Hindu classics (Bhattacharya, ch. 14). Although no historical evidence seems forthcoming, it is also possible that Herman Hesse's *Siddhartha*, published in 1922, may have influenced Gandhi in the use of Eastern pilgrimage patterns.

The result of these multiple influences is a back-and-forth, almost dualistic, version of the circular journey which I find to be the central plot of the *Autobiography*. In place of the dramatic shifts of a Merton or the sequential conversions of a Malcolm X, Gandhi describes a series of "experiments with Truth" which, I will show, are torn by tensions coming from several dualisms in his life and culture. The dualisms inherent in his goal of "self-realization" and in the experiments with Truth arise from two sources: his family background and his syncretistic religious framework. The family tensions stem from the contrary influences of his father and his mother; the philosophical tensions, from the paradoxes within his Hindu and other religious beliefs. For example, from the *Gita*, he holds in tension the principles of action and inaction, of the ultimate and the individual self, of eternity and history. Thus, his narrative is told as a circular journey upward between two poles of various dualisms. As he says in his *Autobiography*, he seeks "complete deliverance from the dual throng" (345). But these dualisms both reinforce and undermine each other. As Bhikhu Parekh has shown, Gandhi is writing the story of a "self" for whom the eternal "Self" is the primary reality. He is telling the story of private experiments for the purpose of public social revolution. He is reporting on empirical tests that lead him to what seem to be quite traditional methods and goals (27–28). In this struggle for personal, religious, and narrative integration, Gandhi the autobiographer learns the ways of higher synthesis, with the result that his story has what one Indian critic calls "dynamic stasis" (Chellapan 98).

Composed at a crucial period after the failure of his nonviolent experiment with a nationwide strike, the autobiography exhibits not only the ambivalences of Gandhi himself at this point of discouragement but also the two inherent sources of tension within his character. As he reveals most clearly in Part One, Gandhi experienced a serious psychic tension between the values imparted to him by his father (a secular, incorruptible devotion to Truth in public service of his people) and those modeled for him by his mother (a religious dedication and firmness through vows aimed at the restraint of personal passion and at nonviolent care and reconciliation). The tension between these two sets of virtues—or between what he called "the political field" and "the spiritual field" (xii)—led Gandhi into a lifelong series of deliberate choices in the practice of Truth as he struggled to integrate the double self-image embodying these virtues. Beneath these parental tensions lay a more fundamental philosophical dualism stemming from Gandhi's syncretistic understanding of reality. As his favorite Indian classic, the *Bhagavad Gita*, puts it, " 'The lotus leaf lies unwetted on the waves' " (V, 10). In his philosophical journey to unite the teachings of Hinduism, Buddhism, and Christianity, Gandhi tried to overcome the dialectic in two series of principles not precisely parallel to those embodied in his father and his mother: body/spirit, passion/reason, world/heaven, achievement of ends/nonviolence of means, activism/union with God, solidarity/individuality, urban industry/rural agriculture, politics/religion, and absoluteness of Truth/contingency of human knowledge. Like Merton struggling to preserve the distinctions between grace and nature, Gandhi never fully integrates these two sets of principles in human life and ultimate reality.

In the struggle for integration, he learns the ways of compromise, reconciliation, and transcendence. His lifelong attempts to follow the Truth of his father drives him on the philosophical level to seek ways to reconcile the "dual throng." He describes his goal on the last page of his life story: "The path of purification is hard and steep. To attain to perfect purity one has to become absolutely passion-free in thought, speech and action; to rise above the opposing currents of love and hatred, attachment and repulsion" (504). The moral conflicts of these passages suggest a tendency to think of ultimate principles in dualistic terms. Yet he was also the son of his mother, trying to reconcile and integrate peoples and values within a practical synthesis. Whereas other commentators, such as Erik Erikson, focus on the psychological contradictions or Freudian "ambivalences" in Gandhi, I will focus on the tensions in the narrative structure of the *Autobiography* as clues to the paradox in the overall development of his character and philosophy.

Despite these narrative tensions, the general structure of the autobiography follows the pattern of a circular journey in three stages. In the text of his life story, these three parts divide themselves as follows: Part One, Parts Two/Three, Parts Four/Five. Part One narrates the planting and uprooting of the values of paternal Truth (*satya*) and maternal Firmness (*graha*) during Gandhi's youth, first in India and later in England. Nearly all the episodes which he chooses to describe in Part One narrate the childhood loss (I, 1–2, 5, 10) or adolescent corruption (I, 3–4, 6–7–8–9) of these virtues. Even his often humorous account of his struggle for a legal education in London focuses on the struggle to retain his mother's values through the memory of his vow (I, 11, 13–14, 16–17–18) and to emulate his father's secular and political success through public adaptation (I, 12, 15, 19). Central to the narrative of this section, as of each of the subsequent four sections, are his marital struggles; here his child marriage and its tensions over lust, domination, and family integrity are highlighted. The entire autobiography, in fact, moves back and forth from experiments with "public" Truth and Firmness (law, politics) to experiments with "private" Truth and Firmness (marriage, family, ashrams).

Parts Two and Three tell of Gandhi's reawakening to his paternal and maternal virtues. Part Two awakens him primarily to the need for paternal Truth in society and in his private life through a series of experiences of the injustice and insults in the colonial legal system in Bombay, Natal, and again in India. Part Three awakens him to the discovery and use of maternal nonviolent methods of Truth and firmness, first in public (III, 1–4), then in communal or family life (III, 5–9), and finally in national Indian politics (III, 12–28). Parts Four and Five move from the discovery through experience to the large-scale practice (both public and communal) of *satyagraha* ("firmness in the Truth"), first in South Africa and later in India.

Gandhi as narrator also weaves together the three major divisions of his autobiography (I, II–III, IV–V) through a series of recurrent threads which can be listed as follows:

1. Mentors: mother and father in Part I; Rajchandra in II; Gokhole in III–IV; his inner voice in V
2. Religion: I, 20; II, 15; IV, 18
3. Deaths: father in I; mother in II; son Manilal in III; wife in IV; himself in V
4. Writing: I, 5, 19; II, 7 ; III, 10; IV, 11, 13; V, Farewell
5. Family Tension: I, 3, 4, 9; II, 23; III, 5, 7–8; IV, 10, 28–29; V, 21
6. Public Failure: I, 5; II, 8–9; III, 10; IV, 11; V, 33.

The subtlety of these patterns is reinforced by Gandhi's use of occasional metaphors, derived from three sources: nature (rootedness, storms, oneness of all life); health (purification, sickness, canker, sleep); and politics (slavery, conquering, ordeal). The significance of both the narrative patterns and the metaphorical threads will emerge as I now trace the sequential story of his experiments with Truth.

YOUTH (1869–91)

Part One begins with a brief description of Gandhi's parents and the values each bequeathed to him. From his father, who was a self-educated, secular "prime minister" in the princely state of Probander in western India, Gandhi received the central value of Truthfulness. In an occupation often marked by venality, his father was known for impartiality, incorruptibility, and truthfulness. Although short-tempered and sensuous, he conveyed his integrity to his son most effectively through his demonstration of fatherly love, not through angry punishment or the use of physical discipline. In chapter 8, when the fifteen-year-old Gandhi confesses his stealing to his sick father by means of a letter (an event that recalls the model sin of Augustine and the use of letter-writing for conveying a serious personal matter by Merton's mother), Gandhi describes the impact of the scene: "[My father] read it through, and pearl-drops trickled down his cheeks. . . . I also cried. I could see my father's agony. . . . Those pearl-drops of love cleansed my heart, and washed my sin away. . . . That was, for me, an object lesson in *ahimsa*" (27–28)

Here for the first time Gandhi shows the intimate link between Truthfulness (*satya*) and nonviolence (*ahimsa*). What is important for a study of the structure of his autobiography, however, is that Gandhi learns these values not through intellectual study or moral lessons but through the experience of the living image of his father. This image of his father as symbol of nonviolent love for Truth remains throughout the book as one side of the directional image for all Gandhi's "experiments." For this image of his sick father leads in the next chapter (I, 9) to the acutely embarrassing episode that same year of Gandhi's neglect of his dying father because of his own sexual desire for his child bride. In addition to the psychoanalytic reading of this episode given by Erikson, one can see in it the lifelong tension within Gandhi between his devotion to his father's image of integrity and his own lack of firmness in following that image. What for Erikson is primarily a sexual problem might more plausibly be seen on the psychological level, according to Judith Brown, as a lifelong "profound conflict" stemming from anger and aggression against his father, from his own idealism, and from all oppressive authorities (*Prisoner* 194–95).

If Truth for Gandhi is identified with his father, Firmness (or devotion to care) is identified with his mother. Unlike his father, who became a devout reader of the *Gita* only in his old age, Gandhi's mother is described in chapter 1 by her son as "deeply religious" (4). She showed her "saintliness" through her prayers, temple visits, and especially the practice of vows. This struggle for firmness through the taking of vows was her main legacy to her son, who experiences throughout his life a sense of his own shyness, laxity, and susceptibility to passion, all symptoms of a lack of firmness which he confronted by the taking of vows. The image of her in Part One is of a model of religiously firm dedication expressed in her vows to fulfill her duty to the divine and to care for other people in her "round of duties" (5).

All the episodes in Part One portray Gandhi's struggle to live out either his father's Truthfulness or his mother's Firmness. In the three incidents he recalls from grammar school (I, 2), Gandhi shows how he became known for his inability to tell a lie. The two lessons he recalls from this childhood period came from popular student plays—the first in a book about Shravana's "devotion to his parents"; the second, a live drama about Harishchandra's "truthfulness" (7–8). Gandhi describes his response to the latter play: "To follow truth and to go through all the ordeals Harishchandra went through was the one ideal it inspired in me." In high school, he remembers as his most embarrassing episode an instance when he was falsely convicted of lying. This false accusation pains him more than the "tragedy" of a bad friendship which led him into eating meat, smoking cigarettes, stealing, jealousy, a visit to a brothel, and even a suicide pact! What eventually stops him from eating meat is not any religious argument but the challenge to his integrity in the sight of his parents—"deceiving and lying to one's father and mother is worse than not eating meat" (20). Similarly, although criticizing his parents for giving him in a child marriage at the age of thirteen, and admitting his jealousy and mistreatment of his wife, Gandhi recounts his faithfulness to her in terms reminiscent of his father's Truthfulness: "The passion for truth was innate in me, and to be false to her was therefore out of the question" (11).

Thus, the main episodes in the first half of Part One (chs. 1–10) express Gandhi's youthful experiments in testing and living up to the image of Truthfulness implanted by his father. Even in his brief account of his early religious practice (which consisted in temple visits with his mother, a few prayers, and experiencing the tolerance between Hindus and Moslems), Gandhi states in a summary passage that, despite his lack of "any living faith" and an inclination "toward atheism," he learned a devotion to Truth: "One thing took deep root in me—the conviction that morality is the basis of all things, and that truth is the substance of all morality. Truth became my sole objective. It began to grow in magnitude every day, and my definition of it also has been ever widening" (34). In the next sentence, Gandhi adds a second precept which he carries from his childhood, that of compassion, as learned from his mother, whose firmness in her religion did not interfere with her maternal care for him and her extended family: "A Gujarati didactic stanza likewise gripped my mind and heart. Its precept—return good for evil—became my guiding principle.

It became such a passion with me that I began numerous experiments in it" (35).

Gandhi's metaphors in the opening ten chapters reinforce and complicate his interpretation of his parental influence on his directional image and consequent values. He speaks of his family and childhood experiences in three clusters of images: (*a*) as forces of nature (seeds, roots, sunshine, light/darkness, fire); (*b*) as bodily forces of health or sickness (purification, medicine, canker, blindness/sight), and (*c*) as political or physical forces (freedom/slavery, ordeal, conquest). However commonplace or submerged these metaphors may be (in the English translation or the original Gujarati), they reveal a strong sense of continuity between his youth and his maturity. Both the tenors of these metaphors—the influence on his character by forces outside or above him—and their origin—in nature, bodiliness, politics—remain at the heart of Gandhi's development and philosophy for the rest of his life. His later desire for a method that will accord both with nature and with healthy "self-realization"—spiritual, bodily, political— reveals itself in these early figures of speech. His very metaphors thus foreshadow the later tensions between his desire for "identification" through *ahimsa* with "the meanest creature" (504) and his struggle with the violence both in his own physical desires and in his political oppressors. Although attuned to the oneness of all natural life, Gandhi becomes aware of the realm of "sickness" and the need for "passion-free" politics to meet the tensions of the "dual throng."

Immediately after the passage in chapter 10 summing up his early love of Truthfulness and compassion, Gandhi gives a long account of his college years (chs. 11–25) in which he describes how he wandered far from many of his father's ideals but is gradually held in check by the triple vow he makes to his mother before leaving for years of legal study in London: "not to touch wine, women, or meat" (39). As he says later on, during a moment of discouragement after his arrival in England, "my mother's love always haunted me" (44). Her image of firmness haunted him so effectively, in fact, that despite his social ineptness and public temptations to become a worldly London barrister, he keeps his three vows. His temptation here is to experiment with the creation of a false identity, as suggested by the imagery he uses of "playing" the gentleman and later "awakening" from a dream. He also admits that he allowed a woman to misread his identity as that of an unmarried man. Although he deliberately tries for a time to learn social graces through lessons in dancing, French, and elocution, he soon "awakes" from this dream and begins a campaign of self-reform. Escaping from the three months of what he calls his social infatuation, he cuts his expenses in half, studies for a London matriculation as well as the bar exam, experiments with vegetarian diets, and overcomes the temptation to conceal his marriage.

Though each of these experiments (described in language of moral economics or health) flowed not from a religious or philosophical conviction but from his loyalty to his mother and from practical concerns, "the change harmonized my inward and outward life," making them "more truthful" (55). Only later does he admit that his dietary experiments, begun for reason of health and economy, grew from this "seed" to become the expression of his religious faith. His religion during this London period consisted in a little "knowledge" and no "experience," and he had only a vague sense of God's working in his life. For instance, on one occasion when he has been tempted to lust while playing the role of an English gentleman, he admits that, "I did not then know the essence of religion or of God, and how He works in us. Only vaguely I understood that God had saved me on that occasion. On all occasions of trial, He has saved me" (71).

During this period of developing firmness through his dietary experiments and his vows, Gandhi manages to acquire what he calls a "nodding acquaintance with Hinduism and other religions of the world" (70). Just as he spends chapter 10 giving an account of his childhood religion, so he devotes chapter 20 to giving one of his religious reading in London. For the first time, he reads the *Bhagavad Gita*, becomes acquainted with Buddhism through *The Light of Asia*, and reads the New Testament, with special attention to the Sermon on the Mount. In all three readings, he finds a common principle linking him with his mother's practice of vows: "That renunciation was the highest form of religion appealed to me greatly" (69). Gandhi ends the first part of his autobiography with several chapters showing how his successful passing of the London bar did not give him what he needed to practice law: "But notwithstanding my study there was no end to my helplessness and fear" (80). With no practical experience and no knowledge of Indian law, he was "torn with doubts and anxieties." The only encouragement he receives comes from a Conservative member of parliament who is a friend of Indian students. This politician's moral advice reinforces Gandhi's lessons from his parents: "honesty and industry were enough" (83). With these paternal and maternal virtues—and with little else except a sense of failure—Gandhi ends the account of his youth.

APPRENTICESHIP (1892–1901)

If Part One is Gandhi's account of the basis of his experiments with Truth as founded on the values imaged by his father (Truth in active life) and mother (Firmness in care for others), Part Two is an account of his awakening: first, publicly to the ways of the world, especially its political and moral challenge to his parental values and to the need for radical public reform; and, second, privately to his own worldliness, to his own need for radical personal reform, and especially to the lack of firmness and Truth in his behavior and household, his way of practicing law, and in his religious convictions. In the opening chapter, Gandhi provides an image of the two awakenings in the two "storms" he encounters on his journey back to India from England: "The outer storm was to me a symbol of the inner" (87). The movement to and fro of his pilgrimage through these storms is revealed structurally in Part Two in the shift back and forth from the private awakening to inner storms (chs. 1, 2, 10, 11, 15, 22–24) to the public awakening to outer storms (chs. 3–9, 12–14, 16–21, 25–29).

The first storm Gandhi encounters is the news of the death of his mother, whom he mourns even more than he mourned his father. Although reeling from the second of five deaths or near-deaths described in his autobiography, Gandhi shifts immediately to a description of a new friend, the poet Rajchandra, who becomes almost his guru, embodying in the midst of a public business career the precise virtues Gandhi idolized in his lost mother and father: religious Firmness and devotion to Truth:

The thing that did cast its spell over me I came to know afterward. This was his wide knowledge of the scriptures, his spotless character, and his burning passion for self-realization. . . . [The center of his life] was the passion to see God face to face. . . . The man who, immediately on finishing his talk about weighty business transactions, began to write about the hidden things of the spirit could evidently not be a businessman at all, but a real seeker after Truth. (88)

Under the guidance of Rajchandra, Gandhi creates the rest of the story of Part Two as "How I Began My Life" (II, 2). His first step is a reform of his private life, first of the education of his wife and child, and next of his household diet and wardrobe. Both reforms, typically for Gandhi, were tragi-comic failures of an experiment at the time, but neither was as pathetic as his first legal case, which he describes in painful details: "I stood up, but my heart sank into my boots. My head was reeling and I felt as though the whole court was doing likewise. I could think of no question to ask. . . . I sat down and told the agent that I could not conduct the case . . ." (94).

But the foibles of his early family and barrister life proved to be insignificant in comparison to the series of public shocks he describes in chapters 4 through 9. The first shock, which, he says "changed the course of my life," came from being pushed out of the office of a British officer whom he had met in London and who was in charge of a case against Gandhi's brother. To his dismay, Gandhi learns from other Indians that that sort of public rejection was a common experience in colonial India. He also learns how to "pocket the insult" and avoid mixing legal matters with personal relations between colonials and natives. This lesson opens his eyes to the petty politics of power among the small princely states within his native area of Kathiawad.

Because of the limited legal work available in India, Gandhi takes a position representing an Indian firm in an important legal case in South Africa. Gandhi describes his arrival in the Natal port of Durban by recounting two public storms that awaken him to the social injustices experienced by Indians in South Africa. First he tells of his shock at learning that non-Muslim Indians were required to remove their turbans in court. The shock leads him to his first public action of his life—an open letter to the people—

recounted in chapter 7. This is also his first use of the handwriting mentioned in I, 5 and the first resolution of conflicts through the use of writing. This letter is followed two months later by the incidents that changed the course of his life and the history of nonviolent resistance—the ejection of Gandhi from a train to Pretoria, followed by a beating from a stagecoach passenger and the near-removal from a second train (chs. 8–9). The "storm" raised by these events was not merely the legal issues but the deeper questions whether Gandhi was committed to firmness in his pursuit of the Truth of human rights: "I began to think of my duty. Should I fight for my rights or go back to India, or should I go on to Pretoria without minding the insults, and return to India after finishing the case?" (112). The rest of his life would be a search for ways to "root out the disease" of racial prejudice and "suffer hardship in the process." Here public *satyagraha* is conceived.

As in Part One, these first nine chapters of his "awakenings" are followed by two chapters concerning religion. The issue for Gandhi in these two chapters is his awakening to his own religious identity when he is pressured by fundamentalist Christians and, later, by Moslem friends. Faced with the challenge to accept Christ, Gandhi begins to study the Bible, the Koran, and the Hindu scriptures. The result, as he describes in chapter 15, is a new path: "Though I took a path my Christian friends had not intended for me, I have remained for ever indebted to them for the religious quest that they awakened in me" (138). Here Gandhi remains firm in his search for a higher religious Truth, which he finds in all religions.

Gandhi gives a clue in chapter 12 to the connection between his religious awakening and his awakening to public service. In his first public speech, given to a meeting of all Indians in Pretoria, his theme concerns "truthfulness in business": "I strongly contested the position [that truthfulness is not possible in business] in my speech and awakened the merchants to a sense of their duty, which was two-fold. Their responsibility to be truthful was all the greater in a foreign land, because the conduct of a few Indians was the measure of that of the millions of their fellow-countrymen" (126). This theme of truthfulness in public life guides the next section of Part Two, chapters 12–21, which deals with the variety of Indian causes for which Gandhi struggles in his first years in South Africa. In succession, he describes his struggles with coolie life (ch. 13), Indian franchise (chs. 16–17), the color bar (ch. 18), the Natal Indian Congress (ch. 19), indentured laborers (ch. 20), and unjust taxes (ch. 21). In the middle of his discussion of these political struggles, Gandhi devotes a chapter to showing how he successfully won his company's legal case by means of arbitration. What is most significant here is Gandhi's awakening to the force of truth in legal matters: "Facts mean truth, and once we adhere to truth, the law comes to our aid naturally" (133). Beyond strict justice, Gandhi learns that nonviolent use of the law must include considerations for the effects of one's victory upon the defeated party; in this case he worked out a method of payment allowing the opposition to avoid bankruptcy: "I had learned the true practice of law. I had learnt to find out the better side of human nature and to enter men's hearts. I realized that the true function of a lawyer was to unite parties riven asunder" (134). He repeats this lesson when he is admitted to practice before the Supreme Court: "the very insistence on truth has taught me to appreciate the beauty of compromise. . . . Truth is hard as adamant and tender as a blossom" (148).

Gandhi ends these chapters on his public storms with a fourth chapter on the religious influences of this period of apprenticeship. Here he explicitly demonstrates the importance of his religious motivation:

> If I found myself entirely absorbed in the service of the community, the reason behind it was my desire for self-realization. I had made the religion of service my own, as I felt that God could be realized only through service. . . . I had gone to South Africa for travel, for finding an escape from Kathiawad intrigues and for gaining my own livelihood. But as I have said, I found myself in search of God and striving for self-realization. (158)

Here Gandhi uses a term from Hinduism which has a very modern ring to it—"self-realization." Although this term echoes the Hindu doctrine of union with the Atman or divine principle (or Self) within all things, it also reminds the reader that Gandhi is writing in the modern period when the individual, even one from a locally traditional society, must, without clear religious or political mediation, discover and create his authentic self in the midst of a pluralistic society. Just as Merton, Malcolm X, and Day try on a variety of roles or negative identities before discovering their deepest self, so Gandhi sees his life as a series of experiments for himself to discover Truth in action and service. For him this process is, of course, essentially religious, since realization of the self is directed toward what he calls in his introduction to his *Autobiography* "self realization, to see God face to face, to attain *Moksha*" (xii). *Moksha* refers to the ultimate state of freedom from the cycle of birth and death in which the individual Hindu reaches union with the Divine in itself in a state of total liberation. What is significant for the study of Gandhi's growth in Part Two of his life story is that at this point he was just coming to a clearer awareness of this process of "self-realization" as religious. During this period he is repeatedly debating religion with Christian friends. Despite their continuous proselytizing, Gandhi retains their friendship and grows in his respect for and study of both Christianity and Hinduism. In particular, he deepens his regard for his mother's faith by reading the *Upanishads* for the first time. However, he complements this study by reading both Islamic and Buddhist literature and Tolstoy's *The Gospels in Brief, What to Do?* From the last he gains an intensified desire "to realize more and more the infinite possibilities of universal love" (160).

In contrast to these religious ideals, Gandhi inserts a chapter on his failure to give proper attention to his household (parallel to similar familial failures in the other four sections of his narrative). This failure results in his betrayal once again by the false friend of his youth, who had led Gandhi into adolescent moral and religious wandering (I, 6) and who now brings a prostitute into Gandhi's household in Natal. After describing the break-up of this friendship, Gandhi, in chapters 24–29 narrates his return to India in 1896, where he awakens his country to the condition of Indians in South Africa and is himself awakened to the need for Truth in colonial India. In his travels in India at this time, he is appalled by experiences of plague, of temple uncleanness, and of the power politics of the Indian leaders. In visits to Bombay, Madras, and Calcutta, he meets the great Indian leaders in politics and culture—Gokhale, Tagore, and others—as well as an English editor, Mr. Sanders, who welcomes the young Gandhi for his "devotion to truth" (182). In the midst of recounting these public awakenings, Gandhi devotes a chapter to showing how his two passions, one linked to his father, the other to his mother, continually guide him: "I can see now that my love of truth was at the root of this loyalty [to the British Constitution]. . . . Like loyalty an aptitude for nursing was also deeply rooted in my nature. I was fond of nursing people, whether friends or strangers" (172–73).

PREPARATION FOR *SATYAGRAHA* (1901–1906)

Like the previous section, Part Three begins with a double storm. Here the physical storm affects the ship bringing Gandhi and his family back to Natal. The "real storm," however, comes from the South African whites, who, enraged by Gandhi's public criticism of them during his trip to India, almost kill him as he tries to slip into Durban. He barely escapes, with the help of the wife of the chief of police, only to be forced to use a disguise later the same night to circumvent a hostile crowd. Gandhi's response to both storms is to produce a calm by refusing to prosecute his attackers. This act of nonviolence is the first of a series, the majority of which are recounted in his book entitled *Satyagraha in South Africa*, written just before the autobiography and containing a much more complete account of the public events mentioned here. A case can be made that *Satyagraha in South Africa* fits in the very center of the structure of the *Autobiography*, but its style and approach are of a very different genre. It seems that Gandhi realized that the first narrative of the *satyagraha* movement in its public phase required a genre focusing on the developing character of the process and not on the developing character of its author (IV, 25).

Structurally, Part Three of the *Autobiography* divides into two sections, each roughly similar to the two sections of both Part One and Part Two. Chapters 1–11 present his first (and unsuccessful) attempts at public nonviolent action (chs. 1–4) and then his even more unsuccessful attempts at private *ahimsa* (chs. 5–9), followed by a curious aside on the Boer War, the Zulu Rebellion, and sanitation reform (chs. 10–11). The second half of Part Three (chs. 12–23) shows Gandhi returning to India a second time, where he learns, among other things, to use nonviolence amid the complexities of Indian politics. Missing from Part Three are the chapter-length discussions of his religious development, replaced with only occasional but important references to spiritual insights.

The section on private *ahimsa* (chs. 5–9) continues the back-and-forth structure of the overall life story. After showing an important, if unsuccessful, breakthrough in his early use of public nonviolence in the opening chapters of Part Three, Gandhi switches to a discussion of his struggles with nonviolence in his family and personal life. Here his chapters give only a scattered glimpse of two profound personal struggles: first with his wife and children and then with his own passions. In chapter 5, while not regretting his attempts to teach his children at home, he admits the experiments were inadequate and extreme: "I have always felt that the undesirable traits I see today in my eldest son are an echo of my own undisciplined and unformulated early life. I regard that time as a period of half-baked knowledge and indulgence" (200). Even though Gandhi acknowledges that he went to extreme lengths, he nevertheless contends that his children's lesson in liberty was more valuable than any in mere literary training. Along with his home schooling of his four children come his experiments in nursing, first begun with his father during Gandhi's teenage years in Part One and continued in assisting his brother-in-law in Part Two. In these maternally inspired labors of caring for others, Gandhi learns the sufferings of Indians firsthand and prepares himself for nursing duties later during the Boer War.

The central chapters of Part Three, however, focus on Gandhi's slow circular movement toward the vow of chastity, *brahmacharya*. Here he is influenced, he tells us, by the views of his friend the poet Rajchandra, who had earlier taken the place of Gandhi's parents after the death of his mother (II, 1). Up to this point, Gandhi had practiced faithfulness to his wife as an essential part of his "love of truth." Now he shifts from his father's ethical motive to the more religious motives of his mother, moving from what he calls a "natural" devotion to a higher devotion not based on carnal desire (III, 7–8). For several years, Gandhi struggles to reach this deeper motive and source of strength for his vow. Only after long hours free for meditation during slack time in the middle of the Zulu Rebellion does he realize that his doubts about the vow of chastity indicate a lack of "faith in myself" and "faith in the grace of God" (207).

In his discussion of *brahmacharya* in chapter 8 Gandhi expressly links his vow with the hidden "foundation of *satyagraha*": "In about a month of my returning there [to Johannesburg during the Zulu Rebellion in 1906], the foundation of *Satyagraha* was laid. As though unknown to me, the *brahmacharya* vow had been preparing me for it. *Satyagraha* had not been a preconceived plan. It came on spontaneously, without my having willed it" (208). In all his struggles with diet and sexuality, which reflect in their rigidity his mother's religious firmness in observances, Gandhi makes it clear that only after many years in India does he realize that the achievement of *brahmacharya* is not primarily an ascetical practice to destroy passion, but a way to freedom of heart for union with God. Similarly, his use of *satyagraha* will appear to him not primarily as a political strategy to overcome an opponent, but as a way to transform oneself and others by eliciting the divine power in both oneself and one's opponent. In brief, the Gandhian tension between confidence in one's own grasp of the Truth and respect for the opponent's viewpoint demanded this rigorous self-purification through the most difficult of vows (Horsburgh 28–30; Mandel 91).

Along with chastity and fasting a simpler life emerges. Now for the first time Gandhi learns by experiment the "beauty of self help" (III, 9), which leads at times to what he calls "extreme forms" but also transforms his personal life to prepare him for nonviolent activity. In his efforts at personal nonviolent living, Gandhi shows how intimately he connects public with private virtues, his paternal and maternal values. As he says of his efforts to instill cleanliness in the South African Indian: ". . . the Indian community learnt to recognize more or less the necessity for keeping their houses and environments clean. I gained the esteem of the authorities. They saw that, though I had made it my business to ventilate grievances and press for rights, I was no less keen and insistent upon self-purification" (217). Once again, Gandhi's use of phrases like "more or less" and his concern for British approval suggests the complexity of his self-realization at the time he was writing his *Autobiography*.

Perhaps the most curious and least satisfying chapter of the second section is that dealing with the Boer War (III, 10). Here
Gandhi acknowledges that he felt a tension at the time of the
war—between his "personal sympathies" with the cause of the
Boers and his "loyalty to the British." Because of his disclaimer
of repeating his "inner struggle" over this matter, which he had
already dealt with, Gandhi opens III, 10 with a description of the
bravery of the nursing corps of 1100 Indians whom he organized
to assist the British. His main achievement from this point of view
as the founder of *satyagraha*, however, was the corps's power to
reconcile tensions—first, among the Indians of all castes, and, second, between the Indian and the British soldiers. The inner tensions of conscience and the public contradictions of Gandhi's
position were resolved, once again, through his use of *writing*, this
time in the account he calls here "my history of the *Satyagraha* in
South Africa" (214).

In the second half of Part Three, Gandhi presents himself once
again as a learner of political nonviolence through a second year-
long visit to India in 1901–1902. It is during this visit that he
becomes a full-fledged pupil of a new father/mother figure, Gokhale. After a chapter showing his struggle to free himself from
attachment to possessions by returning gifts (an effort he admits
he made clumsily and without regard for his wife), he returns to
India for his first active participation in the Congress Party. In
chapters 13–15, he comes to know the Congress and to obtain
support for his resolutions regarding South Africa. What he gradually realizes, however, is that mere oral support from a political
body that meets three days a year is of limited political or moral
force. In the subsequent chapter, he learns the deeper problems
of his own country by spending time with Gokhale. As he travels,
he is appalled at the ignorance, uncleanness, untouchability, viola-
tions of temples, and animal sacrifice he witnesses throughout
India. He also begins to have doubts for the first time of the legiti-
macy of the British Empire there. The patriotism that only two
years before had led him to organize an ambulance corps for the
British in the Boer War now almost completely disappears. He
concludes with a homely analogy from nature: "As the elephant
is powerless to think in terms of the ant, in spite of the best inten-
tions in the world, even so is the Englishman powerless to think

in the terms of, or legislate for, the Indian" (245). With this new attitude, mediated by Gokhale and others, Gandhi finds himself cut off from the last of his early certainties. Thus he breaks from his newly established law practice in Bombay and from his family in order to complete the struggle for Indian rights in South Africa. Before he leaves, however, his faith is tested by the nearly fatal typhoid fever of his second son, Manilal. Gandhi holds firm to his vegetarian principles in the treatment of his ten-year-old son, who recovers. Gandhi's prayer during the crisis of the fever reflects his sense of how deeply intertwined his very "honor" is with the outcome of this trial of his "faith" (III, 22). But his view of his public service as well as of his private care for his family takes on an expressly religious vision similar to that of his mother:

> I think it is wrong to expect certainties in this world, where all else but God that is Truth is an uncertainty. All that appears and happens about and around us is uncertain, transient. But there is a Supreme Being hidden therein as a Certainty, and one would be blessed if one could catch a glimpse of that Certainty and hitch one's wagon to it. The quest for that Truth is the *summum bonum* of life. (250–51).

SATYAGRAHA IN SOUTH AFRICA (1906–14)

A first reading of Part Four of Gandhi's *Autobiography* might lead one to suspect that he abandoned the structural plan he was following in the first three parts. Almost twice as long as Part Three, this account of his most active years in South Africa seems to try to cram together everything he did between his return in 1902 and his final departure in 1914. Part Four, unlike the previous three parts, also lacks an easily discernible division into religious and secular sections.

But chapter 5 of Part Four, if examined in the light of the overall directional image of a series of experiments with Truth as first learned from his father and mother, offers a clue to the thematic structure of this long section. For, in chapter 5, Gandhi finds the heart of his faith emerging in his mid-career study of the *Bhagavad Gita*. Here he describes this sudden deepening of his

Hindu soul as he reads and memorizes its scriptures in the original
for the first time:

> . . . the Gita became an infallible guide of conduct. It became my
> dictionary of daily reference . . . a dictionary of conduct for a ready
> solution of all my troubles and trials. . . . I understood the Gita
> teaching of non-possession to mean that those who desired salva-
> tion should act like the trustee who . . . regards not an iota of
> [possessions] as his own. (265)

The result of this reading is what Gandhi calls "a change of heart"
(265). He here formally and consciously begins to discover spiritual roots for his experiments in nonviolence. He discovers as well
the need to unite the spiritual with the political, the private with
the public. Particularly painful for him is the step to give up his
insurance policy and savings, for this step prompts an outcry from
his earnest but less spiritually minded brother. Gandhi tells us in a
phrase of great significance that this brother "had been as a father"
to him and had challenged him not "to be wiser than our father"
(266). Despite his brother's resistance and invocation of their
father, Gandhi manages to move ahead with a deeper understanding through the *Gita* and the doctrine of nonpossession toward a
spiritual grounding for his life project of *satyagraha*.

   This episode is the first of a series of incidents in the dual plot
concerned with private moral and religious conversion mixed together in Part Four with the long account of the public power
struggles with various opponents in South Africa after 1902: the
Asiatic Office (chs. 1–3); the South African Police (ch. 9); the
founding of *Indian Opinion* (ch. 13); the work among the plague-
stricken ghetto people (chs. 14–17); the Zulu War (ch. 24);
World War I (chs. 38–39); and his law practice (chs. 44–47).
What binds together the more private chapters in the very center
of the *Autobiography* is what Gandhi calls "a training in self-re-
straint" (286). For in chapter 10, while talking about his ease in
treating all people openly, he contrasts this virtue with his earlier
difficulties of "continuous striving" to cultivate *ahimsa* (nonviolence), *brahmacharya* (celibacy), and *aparigraha* (nonpossession)
(276). He then gives as an example of his difficulty with these
cardinal Gandhian virtues the chamber pot incident which shows
his lifelong conflict with his wife, a conflict stemming from the

"cruel kindness" of his male desire for pleasure and domination. Only later, when he has satisfactorily developed the three virtues, especially celibacy, can he say that Katurbai and he have become "tried friends" (278). Although Erik Erikson's psychoanalytic reading of Gandhi's life story uses IV, 10–11 to show some of the emotional abnormalities in the Mahatma, my structural analysis of the narrative suggests further reasons why this incident of conflict with his wife leads to a review of his entire purpose in writing the *Autobiography*. For, in the review of his motives undertaken in chapter 11, Gandhi shows a realization of the contradictions within himself and between his public dedication to Truth and his private lack of firmness or restraint. This contradiction leads him to wonder at the midpoint of his life story whether he should continue this literary "experiment with Truth." He eventually decides to continue, but only because of religious experiences that have transformed his earlier motives for writing the *Autobiography*:

> When I began writing it, I had no definite plan before me. . . . I write just as the Spirit moves me at the time of writing. . . . On the examination of the greatest steps that I have taken in my life, as also of those that may be regarded as the least, I think it will not be improper to say that all of them were directed by the Spirit. I have not seen Him, neither have I known Him. I have made the world's faith in God my own, and as my faith is ineffaceable, I regard that faith as amounting to experience. (279)

This faith, once again the legacy of his mother, must be modified by his own experiments with both public truth and private sensitivity and nonviolence. In the latter virtues, he shows repeatedly in Part Four that his most fundamental struggle is with control of the self that desires *power*. For if he is to enter public "power struggles" with the Asiatic Office or with the police in South Africa (or later with the British colonials in India in Part Five), he must learn to gain freedom of spirit from all attachment to power and its fruits. As he says most explicitly in IV, 11, the very act of *writing* his autobiography is one of his ways to resolve the tension and overcome the "dual throng" he finds in his struggle for the truth.

After wondering whether to stop writing his life story, he concludes, "Writing it is itself one of the experiments with truth"

(280). At the time, of course, his resolution through writing comes in the form of editing *Indian Opinion* (IV, 12). Thus, in his very teaching of *satyagraha* could be both its practice and a dangerous temptation to power.

Throughout the dual plot of Part Four, we can see the interrelatedness of his many battles against attachment to possessions (chs. 4–7), to taste (chs. 8, 27–31), to pleasure (chs. 10, 25), and to power (ch. 13). All these struggles sprinkled amid the chapters on his public battles in Part Four show Gandhi sacrificing his self for the major movement of his public life—the Satyagraha movement. In chapter 26, entitled "The Birth of Satyagraha," he explicitly sums up this theme of Part Four as central to his life:

> Events were so shaping themselves in Johannesburg as to make this self-purification on my part a preliminary as it were to Satyagraha. I can now see that all the principal events of my life, culminating in the vow of *brahmacharya*, were secretly preparing me for it. The principle called Satyagraha came into being before that name was invented. (318)

The other factor in this struggle for the integration of public and private virtues in Gandhi's life story emerges in the central section of Part Four leading up to the birth of Satyagraha (chs. 18–23): the founding of a *community* at Phoenix Farm in 1904. He places the settlement of Phoenix Farm immediately after his reading of John Ruskin's *Unto This Last*, which taught him a notion of the common good, a sense of egalitarianism, and the value of physical labor. As an alternative to the South African "locations" for Indians (which were similar to Native American "reservations" in the United States), the settlement of a community and farm seemed to Gandhi an ideal way to embody these three new values found in Ruskin's book. Although this community has its difficulties, it proves to be the first of several embodiments in communal form of the ideal of *satyagraha* through which Gandhi learns by experimentation to fuse together the primal values bequeathed to him by his father and mother.

In the middle of this account of the Phoenix Farm, Gandhi inserts his experiences during the Zulu rebellion in 1906. The importance of this episode in the overall structure of the autobiography is not that he again organizes a medical corps (as he did during the Boer War), but that, during this minor war, Gandhi, for the first time in South Africa, begins to question his paternally fostered virtue of unquestioning *loyalty* to the British Empire. Only when carrying on his mother's legacy of nursing the wounded Zulus does he awaken to the falsity of the British interpretation of the rebellion: "This was no war but a man-hunt . . . I often fell into deep thought" (315). What is crucial in this incident is that Gandhi's public insight into war is immediately followed by a private decision—his final step toward a vow of celibacy. His motives, dimly realized at the time, only later came to be seen as intimately linked with nonviolent resistance to force (outer or inner, war or passion) and as a gift of divine grace:

> I too took the plunge—the vow to observe *brahmacharya* for life.
> . . . Man is man because he is capable of, and only in so far as he
> exercises, self-restraint. . . . It begins with bodily restraint, but does
> not end there. . . . Today I may say that I feel myself fairly safe, but
> I have yet to achieve complete mastery over thought, which is so
> essential. . . . For perfection or freedom from error comes only
> from grace. . . . Without an unreserved surrender to [God's] grace,
> complete mastery over thought is impossible. (317)

Celibacy, then, for Gandhi is both a religious act and a step toward firmness in control of the mind and will to power, both legacies from his mother. Gandhi goes so far as to follow up his section on the vow of chastity leading to the "birth of Satyagraha" as the result of faith and grace by giving two chapters on his wife's growth in faith during three near-fatal illnesses. The tone of these chapters (IV, 28–30) is difficult to interpret, for Gandhi admits that he may have pressured his wife into following his remedies (a mixture of religious experiments and natural medicine) and that he was considered by many to be a quack.

The remainder of Part Four (chs. 26–47) can be read as a series of applications of the newly born principle of *satyagraha* (and its dependence on restraint of the power-self) to parts of Indian life in South Africa other than the political. Since the political aspects had already been described in his previous book (*Satyagraha in South Africa*), Gandhi tells us that the reader should be able to see the connections among the later chapters. First, in chapters 26–31, he describes in great detail his experiments in dietetics as an effort to gain freedom from passion and power; then, in chapters 32–36, his less successful attempts at educating the young people of Tolstoy Farm in character training. Here he tries to avoid some of the one-sidedness of his own father by combining the teaching of Truth with that of Firmness in religious faith.

What is most strikingly innovative in this experiment in "spiritual" education is Gandhi's attempt to integrate it into early literary, physical, and moral training. He calls the attempt to postpone spiritual education to the fourth stage of life, as sometimes taught by other Hindus, "superstition." This use of spiritual truth at an early age will be of importance when later on we examine Gandhi's *Autobiography* in its relation to the levels of conversion in other modern authors and in developmental psychology.

After a few transitional chapters on his return to London and India, Gandhi concludes Part Four with a discussion of two major spheres of life in which he seems unable to apply successfully the doctrine of *satyagraha* born in chapter 26. In chapters 38–39, he describes his lack of success in sorting out a theory of *ahimsa* that would meet the challenge of World War I:

> So long as he continues to be a social being, [man] cannot but participate in the *ahimsa* that the very existence of society involves. When two nations are fighting, the duty of a votary of *ahimsa* is to stop the war. He who is not equal to that duty, he who has no power of resisting war, he who is not qualified to resist war, may take part in war, and yet whole-heartedly try to free himself, his nation and the world from war. (349)

Even as Gandhi struggles to think up ways to resist the war himself—through a boycott of the British Empire, civil disobedience of war laws, or temporary participation in the war to gain position for resistance—he concludes paradoxically that he "lacked this capacity and fitness, so [he] thought there was nothing for it but to serve in the war" (350).

In the final chapters of Part Four (44–47), Gandhi includes in his "reminiscences of the bar" some of his success in attaining Truth in that profession. But he concludes with a warning that is to echo throughout all of Part Five, a warning about the difficulty of bringing *satyagraha* to confront the political problems of his colonial nation of India. In both a flawed legal system and a flawed colonial system, Gandhi believes "even truthfulness in the practice of the profession cannot cure it of the fundamental defect that vitiates it" (365).

SATYAGRAHA IN INDIA (1915–25)

Part Five of the *Autobiography* presents the most serious evidence against the thesis of this study. In Parts Three and Four, Gandhi seems to have reached a significant degree of integration of the paternal drive for Truth and the maternal religious care and firmness, exhibited in both private and public forms of *satyagraha*. In many ways, the story of his personal experiments with Truth is over; now he begins, as he says in the opening chapter of Part Five, "to place my new-fangled notions before my countrymen" (374). Although he thinks that he "should not find [the challenge] difficult," the following forty-two chapters prove it to be not only difficult but eventually inconclusive. As Gandhi experiments with national Satyagraha from 1915 to 1922, the task proves to be not only an extremely complex series of political experiments but also a supreme test of the religious and moral basis of *ahimsa* within Gandhi himself.

Structurally, the dual plot of Part Five begins with ten chapters reintroducing Gandhi to India, followed by thirty-three chapters of his seven major campaigns using a variety of forms of public Satyagraha. Once again as in the previous parts, he deals with the perennial aspects of modern autobiography—death, mentorship, writing, and religious conversion—but these are no longer the experience of others. The death he nurses is now his own near-death through fasting. The mentors who guided him in earlier years now disappear as he becomes a guru to his people. The writing is not that of occasional columns or a short history but this autobiography. Religion is no longer to be learned but lived and taught to others. Despite these changes, the familial legacies from his parents, the tensions within his own family, and the public failures remain central to his circular journey, and, as they did in the previous four parts, provide tensions within the dual plot of this final part.

In the opening ten chapters, Gandhi spends most of his time

fulfilling his promise to Gokhale that he would first gain experience and express no opinions about political questions. All this travel and research are aimed at answering the fundamental question posed by Reverend Charles Andrews as he travels with Gandhi after the death of Gokhale: "Do you think that a time will come for Satyagraha in India?" (383). Yet even before Gandhi moves on to Rangoon in the far east or Hardvar in the north, he begins small experiments with nonviolent action. In the first chapter, he begins to speak the Gujarati and Hindi languages instead of English. In chapter 2, he argues in favor of keeping communication open with the British governor of Bengal, precisely because such openness is in accord with his "rule as a Satyagrahi" (375). But Gandhi regards the first formal use of nonviolence in India to be the successful attempt through correspondence to remove the cordon at a customs house in Viramgam (ch. 3). What is of significance for Gandhi himself in this episode is that he learned of the injustice only because he was beginning to travel third class (in contrast to his insistence on having first-class rights in his early years in South Africa). This choice is one of his steps toward greater solidarity with the destitute (379).

During his year of travel and introduction to the Congress Party, Gandhi takes several steps that deepen his commitment to Satyagraha. For one thing, he withdraws his application to become a member of the secular education fraternity, the Society of the Servants of India, a decision made from mixed motives but partly because of the clash between his religion and the Society's principles. In his visit to the Kumbha fair and the Hardvar temple, he comes so deeply to realize the violence associated with many aspects of Indian culture that he strives for greater self-purification and for atonement for the religious abuses by making his diet even stricter. At Jhula, he confronts once again the abuses associated with untouchability; his response is to refuse the Hindu custom of wearing the sacred thread, his personal nonviolent protest against the caste system. All these cultural shocks drive Gandhi to found a Satyagraha Ashram in Ahmedabad in May 1915. Here he confronts the greatest scandal within Hindu culture by admitting an untouchable family to the ashram, a decision that cost the project a major benefactor.

Gandhi ends his ten introductory chapters (V, 1–10) with the admission that he is going "to skip over quite a number of things pertaining to this subject [the ashram]" in order to continue the thematic narrative of Part Five about the public experiments with the Truth "down to the days of non-cooperation" (399). He then proceeds to describe his experiences in seven campaigns:

1. the abolition of Indentured Emigration (ch. 11),
2. the six-month Bihar Campaign against the *tinkethia* farm system (chs. 12–19),
3. the difficult three-week Labor Strike in Ahmedabad (chs. 20–22), with its public fast and grave defeat,
4. the Kheda Campaign against an impossible tax during a famine (chs. 23–25),
5. the Campaign against the Rowlatt Bills of 1919, martial laws restricting human rights (chs. 29–35),
6. the Khilefat Issue about boycotting foreign goods to support the Muslim caliph in Turkey (chs. 37–38), and
7. the Campaign for Self-Rule through national noncooperation (chs. 42–43).

During these major campaigns in the experimental use of Satyagraha, Gandhi provides a more detailed account of the personal aspects of the method than of the political circumstances (the latter now available in Brown's biography). The Kheda Campaign, for instance, is noted primarily as an example of Gandhi's struggles to show civility toward a distasteful opponent. This episode is followed by the story of the Congress Party Conference in Delhi, where Gandhi begins his struggle for Hindu–Muslim unity, which he calls the severest test of his doctrine of *ahimsa*, a test still engaging him as he writes about the conference. This chapter leads into two strange incidents: in chapter 27, Gandhi gives a long justification of his recruiting volunteers to fight for the Allies in World War I, another example of the contradictions he admitted in his thinking on *ahimsa* in wartime; and in chapter 28, he describes a nervous breakdown, perhaps the result of the contradictions and sickness brought on by the recruiting. His recovery, procured with the help of what Gandhi calls "a crank like myself," leads him back to public life and the campaign against the Rowlatt Bills of 1919.

It is at this time that Gandhi has a dream of a new form of *Satyagraha*—an hartal, a general strike on a day of fasting and prayer. The method, which Gandhi uses for the first time on April 6, 1919, succeeds politically but leads to violence, first by his own followers, and later by the British under O'Dwyer at Amritsar. These episodes teach Gandhi that he had committed a grave error—in his words, "a Himalayan miscalculation"—of timing and lack of preparation of the people (ch. 28). His explanation shows the difficulty and depth of practice he must use to implant the nonviolent spirit on a national level:

> A Satyagrahi obeys the law of society intelligently and of his own free will, because he considers it to be his sacred duty to do so. It is only when a person has thus obeyed the laws of society scrupulously that he is in a position to judge as to which particular rules are good and just and which unjust and iniquitous. . . . My error lay in my failure to observe this necssary limitation. I had called on the people to launch upon civil disobedience before they had thus qualified themselves for it. (470)

This drastic lesson, derived from the failure of execution of Satyagraha, leads Gandhi into the use of journalism, as in South Africa, as a means of teaching nonviolence. Like other modern autobiographers, he resolves the dilemmas of his life through the use of writing.

The sixth campaign, that concerning the Khilafat issue, leads Gandhi to request Hindu–Moslem support for his boycott against foreign goods, and prompts him to another step in his practice of Satyagraha—the use of the spinning wheel as a practice or symbolic protest against foreign dependence and in favor of national self-help, as well as against industrial society and in favor of traditional crafts and businesses (Brown, *Prisoner* 65ff.). But self-help will expand its meaning to the political level, becoming *Hind Swarj*, self-rule. It is the final campaign of Book Five that gives the reader a glimpse of the movement from 1920 to 1925 toward self-rule. Here Gandhi sees that he has taken only the initial, but important, steps in a long political journey: Hindu–Moslem cooperation, transcendence of the caste system, and a pledge of self-help (*Khadi*). In December 1920, Congress passes resolutions concerning these three first steps, and, with recognition of this, Gandhi ends his autobiography.

In his "Farewell," Gandhi tells the reader that "all my principal experiments during the past seven years have all been made through the Congress" (503), but he does not end on a note of success. Writing in a mood of "depression and dismay," he acknowledges that he is writing from jail, he does not know how to control the violence of his own people in large-scale campaigns, and he realizes that the Hindu–Moslem unity is very fragile (Malhotra 496). Thus, Gandhi concludes his life story with several paragraphs once again linking his public paternal pursuit of Truth with his personal maternal religious quest:

> My uniform experience has convinced me that there is no other God than Truth. And if every page of these chapters does not proclaim to the reader that the only means of realization of Truth is Ahimsa, I shall deem all my labour in writing these chapters to have been in vain. (503–504)

Yet he does not waver in his struggle to unite the public and the spiritual fields. The crucial step is to learn, as he says, "to love the meanest of creation as oneself." This lesson will bring readers face to face with the divine "Spirit of Truth," not only in private religious experience but also in a political way: "My devotion to Truth has drawn me into the field of politics; and I can say without the slightest hesitation, and yet in all humility, that those who say that religion has nothing to do with politics do not know what religion means" (504).

But this personal and political identification with others calls for continuing self-purification. This struggle for *self*-purification, moreover, is always in tension with the call to "love the meanest of creation as oneself." This final paradox in the circular journey of Gandhi (which he found in both Hinduism and Christianity) lies at the heart of the tension in the very structures of his *Autobiography*. As he does in Parts One through Four, Gandhi follows a dual journey of transformation of *self* as simultaneously a transformation of *society*. The maternal firmness in care for self and others fuses with the paternal care for truth in society. The care for self in Hinduism, of course, unites with care for the Atman, the divine "Self" present in all things. But, even in concluding Part Five Gandhi admits that he has not fully achieved either transformation: "Ever since my return to India I have had experiences of the dormant passions lying hidden within me. . . . The experiences and experiments have sustained me and given me great joy. But I know that I have still before me a difficult path to traverse" (505). As he ends his autobiography, aware of the endless transformation of self and society, he, like Augustine, asks the reader to join him in prayer.

The tension of the ending of Gandhi's *Autobiography* suggests an underlying conflict far deeper than simply between the paternal and maternal values. At the core of the book and its unsatisfying midlife ending lies the basic tension of Gandhi's dualistic understanding of Hinduism and Christianity. He achieves, in the midst of the most active of political lives, a level of vision that tries to reconcile the dialectics of the *Gita* and the paradoxes of the Sermon on the Mount. But he tends to confuse paradox with what he calls the "dual throng" of genuine opposites. Thus, at times he struggles to overcome the moral dualism of love/hate with a higher love. At other times, he cannot find the language to overcome the tensional dualisms in body/spirit; public self/ deep Self; feeling/mind; engagement/freedom; union with God/ action in the world. Sometimes, like Merton, he tends to separate these double principles, at others to integrate them. The tension of the ending of his life story and the zigzag pattern of the structure of chapters (especially in Parts Three, Four, and Five) embody in literary form the very paradox that was Gandhi's experiment with truths on the way to Truth.

THE TANGLE OF CONVERSIONS IN GANDHI'S *AUTOBIOGRAPHY*

Just as it is difficult to make precise distinctions between Gandhi's use of the dualisms in his life story, so it is difficult to distinguish his moral, intellectual, and religious conversions. Perhaps one might say that Gandhi gives every change in his story a moral and religious explanation, with an occasional intellectual foundation mentioned through a reference to a book or author he had read during a particular period. Thus, as our study of the overall structure and sectional divisions of the book indicates, Gandhi himself underwent the following journey:

1. childhood reception of moral and religious values from both parents;

2. adolescent lapses from these values, with loss of faith and addiction to pleasure but with partial adherence by vow to religious practices;
3. major social-moral conversions (with some incipient religious change) in South Africa; and
4. major social, moral, and religious conversions to public and private Satyagraha practices in South Africa (IV) and India (V)

Gandhi, of course, does not use these Western categories for assessing his growth through his experiments with Truth. Instead, he uses the traditional four-stage Hindu scheme of the life-cycle: (1) Preparation for the World (Youth); (2) Maintaining the World (Householding); (3) Separation from the World; (4) Renunciation. What is distinctive about Gandhi's practice is that he comes to the insight that the virtues of the last stage (Renunciation) cannot be postponed until old age. He challenges the Hindu tradition on this matter, as he did on the caste system and the use of physical force:

> I am familiar with the superstition that self-realization is possible only in the fourth stage of life, i.e., *sannyasa* (renunciation). But it is a matter of common knowledge that those who defer preparation for this invaluable experience until the last stage of life attain not self-realization but old age amounting to a second and pitiable childhood, living as a burden on this earth. (338)

Thus, his attempts to train the spirit in his young followers and in himself brought about a tension between what he calls the "spirit" and the "flesh." Following his belief that "the essence of religion is morality" (xiii), he inculcates, first through effort, later through grace, the virtues of detachment from all appetite as part of a moral-religious transformation. As he says of his educational principles in Part Four, "to develop the spirit is to build character and to enable one to work towards a knowledge of God and self-realization" (338). The autobiography of Gandhi is his story of experiments—only partially successful—to reach what he calls "self-realization, to see God face-to-face, to attain *Moksha*" (xii). Since the means to this end (means that participate in the end) must be congruent with the end, Gandhi comes to the conclusion after struggling with a variety of dualisms that "the only means for the realization of Truth is *Ahimsa*" or nonviolent active Love

(503–504). This central value is based on the Truth of the oneness of all life and manifests itself in "the identification with everything that lives," an identification that calls for *ahimsa* achieved through a lifetime of "self-purification" (504). But self-purification (another name for Renunciation) requires stages—childhood seeds, householding control, mature separation. Thus, Gandhi takes on his vow of *brahmacharya* and his dietary experiments only in the latter half of his life. Although he finds partial success in these experiments, he never discovers a way to pass on the integrated virtue of the family "householding" stage, the form of "renunciation" appropriate to the husband, wife, and parent. Although he frequently attempted, through the Tolstoy and Phoenix Farms in South Africa, through the ashrams in India, and through his own extended family education system, to experiment with forms of *ahimsa* in the Householding stage, he admits that he failed in this regard. Perhaps he spent most of his creative energy in developing a way of *public* Householding by bringing through *satyagraha* a growth in human dignity and freedom in society in both Africa and India.

One source of his failures in this regard was his lack of mentors for the moral conversion necessary for what he calls "domestic *Satygraha*." As similar failures did with Lewis, Merton, Day, and others, Gandhi's failed experiments in Householding produced in him an aberrant emotional pattern. The tensions he found in the "dual throng" of body/spirit or passion/reason—while common to Hinduism and some forms of Platonic Christianity—were never fully resolved in theory or practice by Gandhi in his *Autobiography*. His struggle for total control of his mind through vows to eliminate influences from his appetites, however heroic in intention, produced a preoccupation with the minutiae of feelings, fear, and prescriptions that became a near-obsession.

And yet, Gandhi was never paralyzed by his preoccupations. He led an entire people in South Africa and an entire nation in India to eventual freedom. Perhaps the tension of his obsession with details of feeling and diet resolved itself as far as possible through the meditation of his writing. The act of meditating on his tensions led to the *recording* in detail of fears and failures in the context of his life story—both of which acts became his final form of "self help" leading to "self-realization." In addition to the act of writing, several mentors and books assisted Gandhi in transcending the dualism of his conversion process. His father, mother, Rajchandra, Gokhole, and others served as mentors; Tolstoy, Ruskin, the *Gita*, the New Testament, *The Light of Asia*, and other writings helped him appropriate personal and social values in the light of ultimate concerns. But the most important source of his conversion is his own experience—of conflicts, lapses, failures, insults, successes, all later seen to be "experiments in Truth" guided by an "inner voice." This later voice was his secret religious source, mediating his readings of and his discussions with all the major world religions.

What is perhaps most noticeably different in Gandhi's *Autobiography* from his popular image is the pervasiveness of *failures* in his life story, most of which are resolved through some form of writing (Erikson, *Life History* 137). Thus, in his childhood, he notes as a significant failure his inability to write well, to achieve good penmanship (I, 5). This peccadillo is mentioned amid a youth marked by failures in almost every virtue. Later, in his years as a barrister, he begins with a significant failure in his first case, a defeat that leads him to become a legal clerk who gains success by merely writing briefs and petitions (II, 3). This success occurs during a period when he is unsuccessful in his householding, as seen in tensions with his wife and in the failure of his relationship with his eldest son. When he first reaches Durban, he immediately fails in court to achieve equality in the matter of native dress (the turban dispute), but soon resolves the issue by writing a letter to the press, an act that gains him instant notoriety (II, 7). This recovery occurs in the same section in which his householding at Phoenix Farm is going badly, particularly when his old friend violates his hospitality (II, 23). Next, he experiences a significant failure to resolve the question of war during the Boer War, where he leads a nursing brigade despite his conscientious objections to the British side in the war. Once again, he tries to resolve his inner conflicts by writing a justification of his work in *Satyagraha in South Africa* (III, 10). This also occurs during a series of failures in education of his children (III, 5, 7–8). In the next section of his life story, he describes the failures of his domestic life, especially his difficulties in admitting equality in his wife. The description of this failure leads into the chapter on his justification for continuing the writing of the *Autobiography* itself (IV, 10–11). This justification of writing leads into the story of his resolution of public and private tensions through the founding of a newspaper, *Indian Opinion* (IV, 13). Finally, the failure of the use of public *satyagraha* on a national scale during the famous strike of 1921 leads Gandhi to admit he has made a "Himalayan miscalculation." At the same time, the jail sentence that follows soon after this event provides him with the opportunity to resolve the public and private tensions of this low period of his life and career—to resolve them once again through writing, this time, the dual plot of the *Autobiography* itself.

REFERENCES

Bhattacharya, Bhabani. *Gandhi the Writer: The Image as It Grew.* New Delhi: National Book Trust, 1969.
Brown, Judith M. *Gandhi: Prisoner of Hope.* New Haven, CT: Yale UP, 1989.
———. *Gandhi's Rise to Power: Indian Politics, 1915–1922.* Cambridge: Cambridge UP, 1972.
Chatterjee, M. *Gandhi's Religious Thought.* New York: Macmillan, 1983.
Chellappan, K. "The Discovery of India and the Self in Three Autobiographies." *The Colonial and the Neo-Colonial Encounters in Commonwealth Literature.* Ed. H. H. Anniah Gowda. Mysore: Prasarange UP, 1983.
Desai, Mahadev. *A Righteous Struggle.* Ahmedabad: Navajivan, 1951.
Erikson, Erik. "Gandhi's Autobiography: The Leader as Child." *The American Scholar* 35 (1965–66): 632–46.
———. *Gandhi's Truth.* New York: Norton, 1970.
———. *Life History and the Historical Moment.* New York: Norton, 1975.
Fisher, Louis. *The Life of Mahatma Gandhi.* New York: Harper, 1950.
Gandhi, Mohandas. *An Autobiography: The Story of My Experiments with Truth.* Boston: Beacon, 1929, 1957.

Horsburgh, H. J. N. *Non-Violence and Aggression: A Study of Gandhi's Moral Equivalent of War*. London: Oxford UP, 1968.

Iyer, Raghavan N. *The Moral and Political Thought of Mahatma Gandhi*. London: Oxford UP, 1973.

Malhotra, S. L. "A Study of Gandhi's Autobiography." *New Dimensions and Perspectives in Gandhism*. Ed. V. T. Patil. New Delhi: Inter-India Publishers, 1989. 495–512.

Mandel, Barrett J. "The Past in Autobiography." *Soundings* 64 (1981): 75–92.

Meyers, Jeffrey. "Indian Autobiography: Gandhi and Chaudhuri." *Biography East and West*. Ed. Carol Ramelb. Honolulu: U of Hawaii P, 1989. 113–21.

Nanda, Bal Ram. *Mahatma Gandhi*. Boston: Beacon, 1958.

———. *Gandhi and His Critics*. New York: Oxford UP, 1985.

Parekh, Bhikhu. "Some Puzzles About Gandhi's Autobiography." *Contemporary Crisis and Gandhi*. Ed. Ramamshray Roy. New Delhi: Discovery, 1986. 14–30.

Payne, Robert. *The Life and Death of Mahatma Gandhi*. New York: Dutton, 1969.

Rudolph, Susanne Hoeber. "Self-Control and Political Potency: Gandhi's Asceticism." *The American Scholar* 35 (1965–66): 79–97.

5

Malcolm X and the Black Muslim Search for the Ultimate

INTRODUCTION

THE LIFE OF MALCOLM X (1925–65) provides one of the most intriguing and prophetic stories of the search for ultimate meaning in the twentieth century. His life story and teachings, as expressed in his world-famous autobiography and his speeches and interviews, embody a range of experience as wide as any found in contemporary religious writers—Baptist Christianity, agnosticism and atheism, criminal hooliganism, Black Muslim ministry, and orthodox Islam. During his twelve years as a minster, he transformed the Nation of Islam, popularly called the "Black Muslims" in America, from a small sect into a large church. Even his break from the Nation of Islam and his move to orthodox Islam for one year before his assassination in 1965 proved to be prophetic of the movement of the majority of Black Muslims after 1975.

A study of Malcolm X's search for ultimate reality and meaning calls for (*a*) a brief chronology of his life in relation to the lives of the founders of the Nation of Islam, W. D. Fard and Elijah Muhammed; (*b*) a study of the circular journey form of his *Autobiography*; (*c*) a summary of his beliefs as a Black Muslim and later as an orthodox Muslim; and (*d*) several reflections on the social and metaphysical implications of his growth as a religious leader and thinker.

THE LIFE STORY

Malcolm Little, Wallace D. Fard, Elijah Poole

Malcolm X was born in 1925 in Omaha, Nebraska, one of six children born to the Reverend Earl Little, a Baptist minister and follower of black separatist Marcus Garvey, and his second wife, Louise Little, a mulatto from Grenada. After the violent death of his father in 1931 in Lansing, Michigan, and the breakdown of his mother in 1937, Malcolm lived for a few years in a white foster home and succeeded as a junior high school student until rejection by his favorite teacher drove him away from education. In 1941, he moved to Boston to stay with his half-sister Ella Collins, where he soon drifted into the hustler subcultures of Roxbury and, later, of Harlem in New York City. Imprisoned for theft in 1946, he was converted to the Nation of Islam in 1948. From the time of his release from prison in 1952 until his departure from the Nation of Islam in 1964, he was its leading preacher and the chief minister of its prophet, Elijah Muhammad.

Elijah Muhammad, born Elijah Poole in Sandersville, Georgia, in 1897, had moved his family to Detroit in 1923, where he did factory work until he was laid off in 1929. While on relief in 1931, Poole met Wallace D. Fard, a mysterious half-dark silk peddler who was preaching a mixture of black separatism, religious–racial mythology, and several practices claimed to be part of Islam. Fard, later believed by his followers to be the divine Allah in person, wrote two small books that became the primary documents of the Nation of Islam—*The Secret Ritual of the Nation of Islam* and *Teaching for the Lost Found Nation of Islam in a Mathematical Way*. Fard soon appointed Elijah Poole, whom he renamed Elijah Muhammad, to be Minister of Islam, and then disappeared in June 1934, never to be found again. Elijah Muhammad moved from Detroit to the Temple No. 2 in Chicago, where he rose to the status of "prophet" or "Messenger of Allah." Despite being jailed from 1942 to 1946 for sedition, Elijah Muhammed gradually expanded the Nation of Islam from a small cult in 1934 to a moderately large sect with some 40 temples in major U.S. cities and 400 members in 1952. Under the ministry of Malcolm X, the Nation of Islam grew to a peak of perhaps 40,000 members in 1960 and 100 mosques/temples in 1964.

In that year of 1964, Malcolm X split from Elijah Muhammad and, assisted by a pilgrimage to Mecca and the study of Islamic teachings, became an orthodox Muslim, taking the name El-Hajj Malik El-Shabazz. Between several trips to Africa, he eventually organized in Harlem a more open black nationalist movement entitled the Organization of Afro-American Unity. In February 1965, he was brutally murdered while delivering a speech to his followers in the Audubon Ballroom in Harlem. After his death, the Organization of Afro-American Unity declined, but in 1975, upon the death of Elijah Muhammed, most of Malcolm X's final orthodox Islamic teachings were taken up by Elijah's son Wallace Muhammad into the Nation of Islam. The ultimate legacy of Malcolm X is currently split between the new and larger American Muslim Mission under the leadership of Wallace Muhammad, which now teaches the orthodox doctrines of Islam, and the smaller but more intense Nation of Islam under Minister Louis Farrakhan of Boston.

THE AUTOBIOGRAPHY OF MALCOLM X

Although the teachings of Malcolm X appeared in national magazines in the early 1960s and many of his speeches have been reprinted in books by Epps, Lomax, Breitman, and Clarke, the most powerful exposition of his life and doctrines is his autobiography, written with the assistance of Alex Haley, a black journalist and author of *Roots*. The complex structure of the autobiography demands a closer study to see its importance in the history of modern autobiography and search for ultimate meaning.

With its ambiguous perspective and patterns, *The Autobiography of Malcolm X* has puzzled critics since its publication. Paul John Eakin has helped readers understand the shifting perspectives of the narrative by pointing out that Malcolm X began the autobiography as a militant Black Muslim but finished it as an orthodox Muslim. Despite the shifting perspective (complicated also by the third perspective of Alex Haley himself in the epilogue and as co-author throughout the book), at the time of his break from the Nation of Islam in 1964, Malcolm X did not revise his earlier version of his life but simply wove in comments from his later viewpoint. Other commentators have helped readers see various psychological and religious patterns in the narrative. James Fowler, for instance, has traced the religious growth of the author in light of Fowler's own theory of the five stages of faith development. John D. Groppe has more recently sketched out the psychological development in trust by Malcolm X in the light of Erik Erikson's six stages of personal growth. H. Porter Abbott has tried to find parallels between Malcolm X's story and the organic form of the autobiography of St. Augustine's *Confessions*, especially in the influence of the mother figures and in the Manichaean traits he finds in the Black Muslims. Albert Stone has nuanced the reading of the autobiography even further by showing how Haley has interwoven Malcolm X's life with the historical events of 1925–65 and by uncovering symbolic patterns of names, clothes, colors, rising and falling action, and the movement from west to east. More recently, Bruce Perry has uncovered details about Malcolm X's painful childhood that may have scarred him for life.

No commentator, however, has made much of the fact that the autobiography begins and ends with the same scenes—a trip to Africa, a murder threat, a burning house, a besieged family, a black community divided between separatists and integrationists, an exotic religion that calls for a refusal to eat pork, and, eventually, a dead father. What all these parallels suggest is that Malcolm X's autobiography is a variant on the ancient story form of the circular journey. In modern Christian autobiographies, such as those by G. K. Chesterton, C. S. Lewis, Dorothy Day, or Thomas Merton, this circular journey takes the shape of a movement though a series of painful early life experiences that raise problems that find resolution only though a number of "conversions" in later life.

In the journey of Malcolm X, the resolutions take place first on a lower and then on a higher level, thus forming a circular journey that moves downward and upward in the form of a spiral. Like Merton's or Day's three-part journeys, Malcolm X's life goes through three stages: the first is an upward circle of movement of childhood and early adolescence; the second is a downward circle of his adolescent life into crime and, eventually, prison; the third stage is a new upward movement into two successive communities of ultimate meaning. A study of these three stages of his life reveals the remarkable parallels in the first, second, and third stages with regard to the following traits found in many twentieth-century religious autobiographies

1. intellectual, moral, and religious conversion;
2. confrontations with loss and death;

3. struggle for personal identity;
4. concern for symbolism (here, black/white racial symbols);
5. struggle for self-understanding with the help of "mediators";
6. challenge by women to male leadership; and
7. resolution of tension through the use of words.

What drives Malcolm X throughout his life journey? What makes his life so intensely dynamic that he was never satisfied or defeated? Like the authors of other religious autobiographies, Malcolm X provides the reader with a "directional image" derived from his childhood feelings associated with his father and mother. In Malcolm's case, this image is two-sided, the dualism producing a tension that drives and divides him throughout his life. From his dark-skinned African-American father, he gains an image of black pride and the distrust of white power, both traits associated with a separatist movement, and a call for political action, with an emotional and religious base. From his lighter-skinned West Indian mother, he complements this image with that of a more trusting family circle, a visionary interest in learning, and a disciplined but intense moral commitment. With the loss of both parents by the time he was twelve, Malcolm X spends his life searching for a new embodiment of this two-sided image. Driven by this dynamic directional image, he struggles through a series of "conversions" told in a story of radically changing identities on his circular journey toward ultimate reality. Albert Stone has vividly summed up the metaphorical power of the black/white tension of the story:

> . . . none [of these metaphors] is more vividly a reflection of the inner self than the repeated pattern in Malcolm X's life of two persons face-to-face—one a dark-skinned Negro, the other a light-skinned or white partner or opponent. The variations of the dramatic pairing are numerous: Malcolm Little's father and mother arguing and fighting; his mother and Ella Collins embracing at the insane asylum; Malcolm himself dancing with Laura and then, on the same evening, with Sophia; his last handshake at the traffic light. . . . All these contrasting figures . . . represent forces and feelings struggling for balance within his own psyche. (255–56)

Childhood Nightmare

Malcolm X speaks of his childhood in Omaha, Nebraska, Milwaukee, Wisconsin, and East Lansing, Michigan as a "Nightmare." In this dreamlike world of violence, his earliest memories are of his black family besieged by the hostile white world but somehow providing him with affection, competence, and pride. He opens his autobiography with two dramatic scenes: first, an attack on his home in Omaha by the Ku Klux Klan when his mother was pregnant with him, and, second, the burning down of his house by whites in East Lansing four years later. Between these two scenes, he describes his father and mother. His father appears in memory as a dark Georgia Baptist minister who has become a disciple of Marcus Garvey, the black African nationalist; his mother emerges as a light West Indian whose white father had deserted her family. The tensions of his father's double vocation, as Christian revivalist and political separatist, and the friction between the two parents—one, educated, affectionate, visionary, and light; the other, simpler, violent, political, and dark—were embodied in the person of the child Malcolm.

Other tensions in his family also bind him, such as those from his struggle for survival among the large number of children. Malcolm fought with some of them but protected and cared for others, especially his younger brother Reginald. In the relative security of this family of tensions, Malcolm learned confidence as a thinker from his educated mother, enjoyed growing vegetables and meditating in his private garden, and figured out that "crying out in protest would accomplish things" (8). He also learned, while hunting with his cousins, how to be a strategist. All these childhood experiences are recalled because they sowed seeds that would develop in unexpected ways in his later life.

Why did these seeds not blossom immediately? The Edenic dream of his early childhood turns to nightmare in 1931 when his father is killed. Uncannily, his death is foreshadowed in a waking vision by Malcolm's mother, whose gift of prescience is one of her legacies to Malcolm. This death, when Malcolm was six (the first of four crucial losses in his life), leads to the emotional breakdown of his overworked and rejected mother five years later. The brothers and sisters are separated and sent to foster homes, with Malcolm left feeling that the ground of his life had been taken out from under him. He describes his feelings on seeing his mother during her worst days in a mental hospital: "The woman who had brought me into the world, and nursed me and advised me, and chastised me, and loved me, didn't know me. It was as if I was trying to walk up the side of a hill of feathers" (21). Thus, the parental support that normally provides the foundation for adolescent growth and transformation is removed from Malcolm's life at the crucial age of twelve. Just when he is beginning his search for identity (Erikson, *Childhood*), the movement to the level of abstract thinking (Piaget and Inhelder), and the construction of a moral sense of order (Kohlberg), Malcolm is thrown into the hostile world of a racist society with his two-sided directional image shattered and his life groundless.

Early Adolescent Mascot

The story of Malcolm's junior high school years is the story of a talented black youth who has lost his family security and been thrown on his own to try to measure up to the emotional, intellectual, and moral demands of the white world of semi-rural East Lansing during the Depression. In each of these three dimensions of his personal growth, Malcolm struggles to succeed, but is blocked at the last step by the forces of discrimination. His mother is replaced by a good-hearted white woman, Mrs. Swerlin, who accepts and supports him but unconsciously treats him as a "mascot," a less than full human being. At school, he succeeds academically by becoming one of the top three in his class, but the English teacher who gives him the most praise for his studies eventually denies him any further work except as a manual laborer. In response to Malcolm's announcement that he would like to become a lawyer, the teacher, Mr. Ostrowski, replies: "Malcolm, one of life's first needs is for us to be realistic. . . . you've got to be realistic about being a nigger. A lawyer, that's no realistic goal for a nigger. . . . Why don't you plan on carpentry?" (36). This conversation is the turning point in Malcolm's youth. The rejection of his dreams is followed by other more subtle rejections. Although he is popular enough among his classmates to be elected class president, he is not allowed to dance with white girls and is automatically considered by his peers to be sexually promiscuous. Throughout this crucial period, Malcolm's efforts to bring about any affective, intellectual, or moral change in himself are blocked by the limits set up by a hostile white world and undercut by the loss of a secure family grounding. The nightmare of his childhood becomes the waking bad dreams of his adolescence.

From Adolescent Homeboy in Boston to Detroit Red in Harlem

Just as he is withdrawing into his protective shell after the rejection by the white world, Malcolm meets the third and most important woman in his life, his older half-sister Ella Collins. Her strength of character, which dominated two marriages and Malcolm's own extended family, gives him his first most vivid image, after that of his father, of black pride. In moving in 1939 to Boston to live with her, Malcolm begins his search for identity as a teenager. Unfortunately but predictably, Ella can give him an example of black pride but not the means to embody the model in positive ways in his life. Barred from growth and success in the white world, Malcolm fixes on the distorted and self-destructive alternative in the black "hip" street culture of Roxbury and Harlem. As Fowler has shown, in rebelling against the conventions of the white world and the more successful but subservient black middle class, Malcolm models his new-found black pride on the swinging ghetto subculture of Roxbury. As "homeboy" from East Lansing, he follows his new friend Shorty by becoming super "cool"—with zoot suit, conked hair, lindy dancing, and a hip sex life, all the while remaining locked in a menial "slave" job within a black-hating-black ghetto cycle. As Abbott has shown, in Malcolm's first sexual escapades in Boston, he is acting out the fantasies of his white junior high friends who cajoled him at their dances. First he corrupts an innocent black girl, Laura, at the black dance hall, and then he jilts her for a loose white woman, Sophia, thereby reversing the patterns of his childhood ideals. In Abbott's words:

> Malcolm's attempts at white mimicry—the straightening of his hair, the preference for white women—throughout his descent through Roxbury and Harlem had been an unconscious worship of evil, blindness to the just evaluation his mother had made of his white grandfather. . . . It is a checkerboard pattern which he has already introduced through the feeling of his black father and light mother for his own light skin and which he will develop in a bizarre varia-

tion when he calls to memory the bordellos of Harlem where successful white executives pay to be beaten by black prostitutes. (133, 135)

Fowler has also shown that this stage of Malcolm's spiral journey downward can be seen as an unconscious turning of his anger against himself in his assuming what Erik Erikson calls a "negative identity." This identity occurs "whenever identity development loses the promise of a traditionally assured wholeness" (Erikson, "Development" 733; Fowler 14). This new negative identity is that of a Hustler. Malcolm reaches the extreme of this rebellious self-image in his role as "Detroit Red," the black con-man in Harlem. He becomes the master strategist who can manipulate the drug trade, prostitution rings, numbers rackets, and endless hustles that made up the underside of Harlem in the 1940s. He even goes so far as to initiate his younger brother Reginald into this corrupt subculture, the very brother whom he cared for as a sibling and who would later introduce Malcolm to his savior. In fact, all the emotional and intellectual talents fostered by his father and mother in his childhood now become inverted into a parody of his earlier self. This reversal of his image, of course, can be attributed largely to the hostile white world which limits his black growth and leaves room only for the self-destructive behavior of the hustler. All his childhood virtues of strategy, family trust, black pride, vision, and commitment to success now become the instruments for creating his own counter-world in the ghetto. Ironically, Malcolm learns the hard way that this counter-world is very fragile. He says of his days in Harlem, "What I learned was the hustling society's first rule: that you never trusted anyone outside your own close-mouthed circle, and that you selected with time and care before you made any intimates even among these" (87). This circle narrows so tightly for Malcolm that it leaves him back where he began: "I came to rely more and more upon my brother Reginald as the only one in my world I could completely trust" (115).

Early Adult: Transformation to the Nation of Islam

The most drastic change in his autobiography (or perhaps in any modern autobiography) occurs in Malcolm's prison conversion.

What is noteworthy for the structural study of this circular journey following a double-sided directional image is that nearly
every event, person, and book that influences his conversion in
prison parallels both the inversion of his adolescence and the seeds
sown in his childhood. Just as the end of his childhood security
came about from the death or loss of his parents, so his transformation to a new security in Black Muslim fundamentalism occurs
because of the loss of the streetwise models who are now separated from him, first by his fears of betrayal and, later, after his
arrest, by his imprisonment. In effect, he becomes one of the
living dead himself, cut off from all his former sources of life and
counter-life.

In the Massachusetts prison from 1946 to 1952, through a series
of unexpected mediators, Malcolm X recovers the seeds planted
by his father and mother. First, he begins a sort of moral second
transformation from drug addiction by recovering his mother's
aversion to eating pork. In doing this, he is responding irratio-
nally, for he begins this practice immediately after he has rejected
his brother Reginald's invitation to become a member of the Nation of Islam, which requires abstinence from eating pork. Following this sudden impulse, Malcolm X tells us that he was
unconsciously showing his "first pre-Islamic submission" (156).
He soon becomes a full-fledged convert. Just as he cared for Reginald in childhood and later corrupted him in Harlem, Malcolm
X now listens to him explain the mythology and code of the
Nation of Islam. What seems to have appealed to Malcolm X in
this sect are its echoes of his father's double faith—in the apocalyptic biblical God and in black separatism. The political separatism of Marcus Garvey is replaced by the demonological
separatism of Elijah Muhammad. Just as Malcolm X had contem-
plated in his own garden as a child, he now reluctantly bends his
knees and implores the forgiveness of Allah. His religious transformation leads him to withdraw into himself, as he had after his
rejection by Mr. Ostrowski in high school. But this time his with-
drawal enkindles rather than stifles his education. In prison for the
next few years, he gives himself the high school and higher education his junior high experience had interrupted. Emulating an
articulate fellow prisoner, Bimbi, Malcolm X reads widely and
chaotically books in history, philosophy, and religion. He also

takes part in prison debates, becomes a master of words, all the while using his education to give intellectual support to his new religious orientation within the Black Muslims. His junior high intellectual potential is now fulfilled in an unexpected way by what he calls his "homemade education." Even when his brother Reginald lapses from the Muslim code into immoral behavior and later insanity, Malcolm recovers through a "pre-vision" of his new grandfather, W. D. Fard, the anointer of Elijah Muhammad and replacement for Malcolm's white grandfather. This event parallels in reverse the vision Malcolm's mother had of his blood father before his death in 1931 (Abbott 132).

Adult Icarus

In the next twelve years (1952–64), Malcolm X lives out the mythology and ascetical moral code of Elijah Muhammad. In structural terms, Malcolm X regains his childhood dreams without the nightmares. Elijah Muhammad becomes his new father, preaches a new form of black separatism, this time with a non-Christian interpretation, complete with a black God, a prophet, a temple, a code, and a demonology. Sister Betty, his Black Muslim wife, soon provides him with the ground of affection and family he lost when his mother collapsed during his late childhood. His childhood sense of black inferiority in a dominant hostile white culture is replaced by a doctrine of black superiority to the excluded white "devil" culture. He regains brothers and sisters, some of them his own blood relatives who become members of the Nation of Islam. Chief among these is Ella, whose black pride now fixes itself upon the forms of the Black Muslim faith.

Malcolm X yields his entire identity to this new family and nation—going even so far as to become its main minister. He succeeds by using the "protest" skills and hunting "strategy" first noted in his account of his childhood. The separatist Nation of Islam becomes the famous Black Muslim movement in the United States, with Malcolm X as the spokesman for the prophet, Elijah Muhammad. But his twelve years of growth inside this movement reach a crisis in 1964 when Malcolm X confronts two limits similar to those he had met in his late childhood: the limit of restricted engagement with the wider world and the limit of the hypocritical model he discovers he is following. In his early teens, these limits were set by the white culture; now the limits in the 1960s come from the black subculture of the Nation of Islam itself. First, Elijah Muhammad refuses to allow Malcolm X to speak out on political issues or become engaged in the civil rights movement. When Malcolm X does speak out, he is abruptly censored and isolated, thus forced to withdraw into himself again as he had in early adolescence. Around the same time, in 1964, he discovers the moral vagaries of Elijah Muhammad and immediately becomes disillusioned in the "new father" and ground of his trust: "I felt as though something in *nature* had failed, like the sun, or the stars. . . . I first began to realize that I had believed in Mr. Muhammad more than he believed in himself. . . . I became able finally to muster the nerve, and the strength, to start facing the facts, to think for myself" (304, 306).

Once again Malcolm X experiences betrayal and the loss of a model so intensely that he is thrown back upon himself. Fortunately, at this time he has the support of his new family, some Muslim friends, and especially his half-sister Ella. She, again a woman present to him at the point of a radical conversion, had already moved out of the Black Muslims and discovered orthodox Islam. In fact, in April 1964, she steps aside from her pilgrimage to Mecca to allow Malcolm X to take her place.

It is significant to note at this point how dependent Malcolm X is on women throughout his life, and yet how independent he thinks himself to be from them. He has just finished telling Haley that "You can never fully trust a woman" (389) when the reporter asks him about his mother—thus raising the very question (and person) that makes a beginning of the personal revelations leading to the full autobiography. Throughout the story, at each stage, Malcolm X meets women of both strength and weakness—his mother and Mrs. Swerlin in childhood; Laura and Sophia in Boston; prostitutes and accomplices in Harlem; Elijah Muhammad's adulterous secretaries and his own faithful wife, Betty, in the Black Muslims in Chicago. Only Ella and Betty remain pillars of strength for him, yet he tells Haley that he trusts them only seventy-five per cent (389). Of the rest of women, Malcolm X generalizes from his experience in Harlem: "All women, by their nature, are fragile and weak: they are attracted to the male in

whom they see strength" (93). Although Ella compensates for the
loss of his mother, Malcolm as a teenager sees her through the
lenses of his male-dominant attitude and religious tradition; only
later, after his journey to Mecca, does he begin to transcend them.
In the final pages of his story, he recalls an earlier Black Muslim
episode in which he had rejected a white college girl's offer to
help in the racial struggle ("I told her that there was nothing she
could do"). The older Malcolm X shows a new attitude, "I regret
that I told her that" (376). He goes on to tell her and all white
supporters of racial equality: "Work in conjunction with us—
each of us working among our own kind" (377).

From this point on, the final chapter of Malcolm X's autobiography brings him to the top of his circular journey. Throughout
his life story, his imagination had followed a dynamic directional
image of tension between blackness and whiteness. This was embodied in the skin colors of his parents, in his own reddish-brown
skin, in the person of Ella, in his childhood school experiences,
in the racial conflicts and sexual tensions of the ghettos of Boston
and New York, and in the mythology of the Nation of Islam.
Only in chapters 17 and 18 of the *Autobiography* does he begin to
reach a vision that resolves this conflictual image. Only there does
he find what he calls "honest white-black brotherhood" (375).

Now on a literal pilgrimage to Mecca, Malcolm X discovers in
a new and higher form what had been hinted at but always limited
by unresolved conflicts in his childhood: (*a*) a fusion of ultimate
reality and black pride in a transcendent faith; (*b*) a universal
brotherhood and sisterhood that dispels the friction between his
black father and his semi-white mother; (*c*) an internationalism
that mutes the tension between black America and black Africa;
(*d*) a critique of America that allows for transformation of the
siege mentality of black and white antagonists (356, 365–71).
Blinded by his "anger" and the difficulties of "rearranging his
thought patterns" (340, 375), Malcolm X in 1964 struggles to
create a middle way between black separatism and integration,
but he finds the effort too much for his energy and creativity.
He dreams of shaping "an all-black organization whose ultimate
objective was to help create a society in which there could exist
honest white-black brotherhood" (375). In moving out of the
demonology of his Black Muslim years, he now calls for recogni-

tion of "rights and responsibilities" on the part of both races. But he feels the limitation caused by his lack of formal education. Thus, the final portion of his autobiography ends with a premonition of his own death. As he says, "Each day I live as if I am already dead. . . . And if I can die having brought any light, having exposed any meaningful truth that will help to destroy the racist cancer that is malignant in the body of America—then, all the credit is due to Allah" (381–82).

Here we see Malcolm X ending his story where he began, with the tensions between his father and mother brought to near-fulfillment but with frustration in his own life. Although he had transcended almost all the conflicts embodied in his father and mother, he could not find a way to communicate this transcendence to either the black or the white public. It was left to Wallace Muhammad, the son of the separatist prophet whom Malcolm X rejected near the end of his own life, to follow Malcolm's dream of a higher form of Islam. And it was left to Alex Haley in his long epilogue to insert a description of the final events of Malcolm's life. As we have seen, these events and their images parallel those in the opening nightmare of his childhood—a murder threat, a burning house, a besieged family, a black community divided between separatists and integrationists, an exotic religion, and eventually a dead father. Malcolm X died as his father had, an isolated prophet pointing to a new way and another country.

Again, like his father, Malcolm X does not die without leaving a legacy of "spreading words" (3). Even though he rejected his father's Baptist message, he sat as a child "goggle eyed" at the preacher's gestures and absorbed his love of rhetoric and power over an audience (5). At each stage of his life, as Albert Stone has suggested, Malcolm X learned and used words as a means of power. As a child, he learned from his verbally adept mother how to "cry out and make a fuss until I got what I wanted" (8). In school, his favorite class was English. When he dropped out and took to the streets of Roxbury, he quickly learned the language: "In no time at all, I was talking slang like a lifelong hipster" (56). In Harlem, he learned the art of conversation with everyone— customers, bartenders, cooks—in order to become, as he says, "indispensable" (80–81). In prison, he learned to study and became a master debater, getting his first taste of his father's power over a crowd with words: "I will tell you that, right there, in the prison, debating, speaking to a crowd, was as exhilarating to me as the discovery of knowledge through reading had been. Standing up there, the faces looking up at me, the things in my head coming out of my mouth, while my brain searched for the next best thing to follow what I was saying . . . I was gone on debating" (184).

This newfound power of words serves him well during his twelve years in the Nation of Islam, where he becomes the main voice of the prophet, Elijah Muhammad, first within the Black Muslim temples and later on the radio. Finally, he dies at the moment of preaching a new word, one of reconciliation among peoples along with the pride and promotion of black leadership. Even after his death, his immediately published autobiography gives his voice to an entire world. Thirty years later, his unpublished speeches and interviews are still appearing in print. Like Merton, Day, Gandhi, and others, Malcolm X expressed and later transcended the contradictions of his era and the frustrations of his life story by "talking" them out in words as well as in action.

Although a master of rhetoric, Malcolm X in the speeches included in his *Autobiography* gives away more about himself than he might have wanted to admit. For instance, in an excerpt from a speech to a university crowd (he was the most sought-after college lecturer in the 1960s after Barry Goldwater), Malcolm combines the clichés of a popular crowd-pleaser ("Time and time again . . . the sun has set forever. . . . The whole world knows") with a rich array of biblical allusions ("God's wrathful judgement is close upon this white man stumbling and groping blindly in wickedness and evil and spiritual darkness"), rhetorical questions ("Is it accidental that as Red Chinese visit Africa and Asian countries, Russia and America draw steadily closer to each other?"), balance and antitheses ("Look—remaining today are only two giant white nations, America and Russia, each of them with mistrustful, nervous satellites"), vivid caricaturing details (". . . that monocled, pith-helmeted resident colonialist, sipping tea with his delicate lady in the non-white colonies"), accumulating lists ("Memoirs, perfumes, autographs, titles, and even themselves")— all the devices of the popular orator (285). Beneath this rhetoric

and tying it together lies the fundamental imagery of racial contrast noted earlier—between "the black, the brown, the red, and
the yellow races . . ." and "the white man's small ability to understand the simple notes of the spirit." Malcolm concludes the same
passage by using his father's words about Christianity—but now
against the white audience: "The white man has perverted the
simple message of love that the Prophet Jesus lived and taught
when He walked upon this earth" (286).

THE MYTHIC STORY BEHIND *THE* *AUTOBIOGRAPHY OF MALCOLM X*

Despite the repetition of teaching in the words of Fard, Elijah
Muhammad, and the autobiography and speeches of Malcolm X,
it is not obvious how literally the believer is to interpret their
doctrines. Many teachings are cast in highly symbolic or apocalyptic language, apparently designed to appeal to the imagination
of the oppressed black audiences of urban America during the
Depression and postwar years. If taken at their word, the Nation
of Islam's teaching about God, prophecy, the afterlife, and human
history could be described as a *divine corporate racialism*. To test the
validity of this description, let us examine each of these four areas
of doctrine from the autobiography to see how they are also expressed in the moral code of the Black Muslims.

   The notion of God or ultimate reality in the Nation of Islam is
anthropomorphic. Unlike the transcendent divine Being of Islam
or Judaism, the God of the Black Muslims is the collective "Black
Man" embodied in all the black races of the earth. As Malcolm
X first heard from his brother in a Massachusetts prison, " 'God
is a man. His real name is Allah' " (158). Or as Elijah Muhammad
wrote many times, "God is a man, a flesh and blood being . . . a
being like ourselves" (Ansari 142). The ambiguity of these anthropomorphic terms stems in part from Elijah Muhammad's reluctance to admit the existence of either a transcendent Being or
a spirit, which he considered some imaginary formless "spook"
inferior to human persons. In addition, Allah is said by Elijah
Muhammad to be somehow identical with the entire black race.
As the leading exponent of Black Muslim theology puts it:

In the Black Muslim concept "Allah" seems to be identical with the collective entity of the Original People, the Black Nation, the Righteous. "We are the nation of the Creators or the Creator ourselves," says Elijah Muhammad. "Out of all nations the Black Nation alone is self-created. The fathers of the Blacks are believed to have created the heavens and the earth, and life and mankind, including the White or Caucasian race (or devils).
. . . All Blacks in the Black Muslim view, are Gods (Allah) and one of them is the Supreme Being. (Ansari 144–45; citing *Muhammad Speaks*, 1961; *Message*, 1968; *Saviour* 26)

This fundamental historicity of a finite "God" identified, almost Platonically, with the Black race both in its Original Man and its present descendants seems closer to a mythic story of origins than a literal theological statement. However, Elijah Muhammad preached and defended it as a central doctrine of the Nation of Islam and most of his followers accepted it at face value. The importance of this unique racial "God" is at the heart of Malcolm X's conversion and early faith. Blackness for the Nation of Islam is a divine perfection, the fullness of color and all other qualities.

The doctrine of prophecy in the Nation of Islam at first sight appears to be similar to that of orthodox Islam: "Muhammad is the messenger of Allah." The Muhammad in this statement, however, refers not to the seventh-century prophet of Islam but to Elijah (Poole) Muhammad of Chicago. The latter claimed that Wallace Fard was Allah-in-person and that he himself was merely his chief prophet ("I know Allah and I am with him"). Elijah Muhammad was given the titles and praise beyond any of the prophets of Judaism or Islam. According to Ansari, Elijah Muhammad himself gradually elevated his own status so that it almost equaled that of the divine:

Elijah Muhammad always maintained that he was different and separate from "Allah." On the other hand, he held that "Allah" is nothing more than a man, and that all Originals are Gods. Were this to be combined with the concept of "God-in-Person," it would be relatively easy to bridge the gap between "Allah" and His Messenger whenever the latter might choose to do so. . . . In some of his statements during the last years of his life Elijah Muhammad seemed to hint at a process of fusion and merging with or in Him. . . . Subsequently, he indicated in clearer terms that such a process was already in operation: "Allah is making me into Himself." (153; citing *Muhammad Speaks*, 1974.)

Given this status, Elijah Muhammad held power and authority over the scriptures, code, and beliefs of the Nation of Islam. The doctrine of the afterlife in the Nation of Islam was also radically transformed by Elijah Muhammad from its traditional metaphysical status beyond time and place (as in Islam or Christianity) into a political-historical status within the future of the earth, but with power and authority over others. The afterlife envisioned in literal language "a government of the righteous after the destruction of unrighteousness" (Elijah Muhammad, *Message* 303). According to Ansari, heaven and hell "signify conditions of earthly life rather than states of super-terrestrial, and post-terrestrial existence. . . . Heaven and Hell are the conditions which exist on this earth and which human beings experience during their lives" (158).

This doctrine of the afterlife is a corollary for the Nation of Islam to their most fundamental mythology or "hidden truth" gathered by Elijah Muhammad from Wallace Fard—the racial history of the black and white peoples. According to their theology of history, the Black Man is the Original Man, created by Allah and somehow divine. Although the Black Man is 78 trillion years old, he experienced a great explosion some 66 trillion years ago which separated the earth from the moon, and brought about the creation of an Eden for Blacks within the Nile Valley and around Mecca (Elijah Muhammad, *Message* 31). The white race, however, is only 6,000 years old, the creation of an insane Black scientist by the name of Mr. Yakub who challenged Allah and created through genetics a diabolical series of mutations resulting in the white race. Despite being excluded from his home near Mecca, Mr. Yakub lived for some 600 years in the Aegean, where he finally produced a white skinned, blue-eyed "devil." The destiny of this devil and his descendants was to rule the earth for 6,000 years, or until 1914, by using tricks, lies, and violence to conquer the colored races (Malcolm X 164ff; Lincoln, ch. 4; Ansari 161ff.).

As a result of this quasi-historical myth, Elijah Muhammad taught his most politically influential doctrine: the supremacy of the black race. Ansari sums up this doctrine:

Thus, the Blacks and Whites are fundamentally different. Their ancestries are different, and so are their natures. The former are inherently righteous and divine, whereas the latter are devils. . . . In some of his later writings, Elijah Muhammad seems to have relented somewhat towards the Whites since occasionally he does acknowledge that a number of Whites were Muslims, and were even sincere in their faith. Having acknowledged that, Elijah Muhammad is quick to point out that the White Muslims were Muslims by faith alone, not by nature. (165–66; citing *Saviour*, 119ff., 89ff.)

As a result of this teaching, racial integration and cooperation are not only impossible but theologically repugnant. To use the words of Elijah Muhammad that shocked Malcolm X in 1948: "The white man is the devil." With the appearance of Allah-Fard after 1914 and his prophet, Elijah Muhammad, the Nation of Islam was destined to carry out the racial separatism originally intended by divine history.

How far was this separation to go? What are the ethical and political consequences of the mythology of the Black Muslims? Despite rumors and violent language, the moral code of the Nation of Islam is almost fanatically rigid and generally non-violent.

First, the moral code is based on rituals similar to those of orthodox Islam. The Black Muslim prays five times a day, usually facing east toward Mecca, with each prayer preceded by ablutions. He or she also follows a strict diet, being allowed no pork, corn bread, or other "slave" food. The Nation of Islam also forbids smoking, drinking, drugs, and overeating; it requires attendance at the temple or mosque twice a week and expects regular time set aside for public recruitment of members. Sexual laws, dress, and customs are very strict, strongly favoring Black Muslim marriages and discouraging divorce, as well as forbidding dating, cosmetics, and dancing. This strict code has proven very successful in helping converts overcome previous lives of addiction, promiscuity, or criminality. Along with this private and family morality goes an ethic of hard work, economic savings and investment, and political aloofness. The last element—political aloofness—followed partially from the sectarian nature of the young Nation of Islam. To preserve its very existence as a distinctive religious group, Elijah Muhammad did not allow its members to mix in the political pluralism of American life. He even discouraged Black Muslims from voting and forbade military service. The primary reason for this aloofness derived, however, from the theology of black supremacy and apocalyptic separatism. Elijah Muhammad and Malcolm X, in fighting off the integration movements of the 1950s and 1960s, both taught that the rule of the white race was coming to an end, that the black people were owed a separate "state," and that ultimately the black race would regain its ancient "original" ruling power.

THE STORY BEYOND *THE AUTOBIOGRAPHY*

In the ministry of Fard and Elijah Muhammad, the use of Islamic vocabulary and select Muslim practices misled many members and observers in the West into thinking the Nation of Islam was truly connected with the religion of Islam. From the beginning, however, orthodox Muslims in the United States, especially black "Sunni" Muslims, challenged the right of the Nation to its Islamic title. Although Elijah Muhammad managed to make connection with several Islamic leaders in the Middle East and Africa, his teaching never gained status there as authentically Muslim.

As noted earlier, both Malcolm X upon his rupture from the Nation in 1964 and Wallace Muhammad upon the death of his father, Elijah Muhammad, startled their followers and the world by becoming orthodox Muslims. They both quietly abandoned the anthropomorphic view of a corporate black "Allah" and discovered faith in the transcendent spiritual Allah. They no longer considered Elijah Muhammad to be semi-divine or superior to the prophet Mohammed. They also renounced the realized horizontal eschatology of the "heaven" of black political domination in favor of the true Islamic belief in an afterlife consisting in the eternal justice of Allah. Most significant for their relations with the public was the embrace by both Malcolm X and Wallace Muhammad of the "universalism" of Islam. This doctrine called for them to reject the racial doctrines of black supremacy and white demonology in favor of a universal brotherhood and sisterhood (Ansari 173ff.).

Even as a Black Muslim, Malcolm X himself had begun to realize that the rigid black/white demonology of Elijah Muhammad might be open to a symbolic interpretation. As he said in one of his speeches in the early 1960s: "Unless we call one white man, by name, a 'devil' we are not speaking of any *individual* white man. We are speaking of the *collective* white man's *historical* record. We are speaking of the collective white man's cruelies, and evils, and greeds, that have seen him *act* like a devil toward the non-white man" (266).

After his conversion to orthodox Islam and his taking the name El-Shabazz, Malcolm X summed up the most important lesson he learned on his Hajj to Mecca in 1964: "The *brotherhood!* The people of all races, colors, from all over the world coming together as *one!* It has proved to me the power of the One God. . . . My pilgrimage broadened my scope. It blessed me with a new insight. In two weeks in the Holy Land, I saw what I never had seen in thirty-nine years here in America. I saw all *races*, all *colors* . . . in *true* brotherhood" (238, 262).

Among the first letters he wrote at that moment in 1964 was one to Wallace Muhammad, who had already begun to study orthodox Islam at the insistence of his father. Although Wallace remained within the Nation of Islam until his father's death in 1975, he startled the world by announcing in June of that year the end of racialism within the Nation of Islam. As the replacement of his father (now as a man and not as a prophet), Wallace began a gradual reinterpretation of the other basic teachings about God, prophecy, afterlife, and sacred history. Like Malcolm X, he came to realize the symbolic character of the myths derived from Fard and Elijah Muhammad. As Wallace said in a talk following a prayer service attended by Professor James Whitehurst in 1978: "There is no superiority in any color. The only superiority is that of obedience to God." (Whitehurst 228) Wallace also opened the Nation of Islam to white membership, a move that "had vast repercussions in the movement" (Mamiya 138).

Perhaps the most well-known public consequence of this theological and practical reinterpretation of color symbology has been the split between Wallace Muhammad's majority (later called the American Muslim Mission) and the militant minority under Louis Farrakhan (still called the Nation of Islam) The majority, with its doctrine focused on the Five Pillars of Islam (belief in Allah, prayer, fasting, alms, and the Qur'an), have entered into political activity in the United States. Calling themselves Bilalians instead of Blacks (after Bilal Ibn Rabah, an Ethiopian caller to prayer in the earliest Muslim community in Medina), they opened their movement to peoples of all races. Malcolm X was restored to a place of honor in the memory of the Bilalians, with their Harlem Temple No. 7 named the Malcolm Shabazz Masjid in his honor.

The result of this movement by the American Muslim Mission (Bilalians) toward centrist Islamic teaching and practice has been a wide fluctuation in membership. Among those who remained Black Muslims in the Nation of Islam, Louis Farrakhan, resembling his old friend and mentor, the early minister Malcolm X, has become more rigid and racist than any previous leader of the Nation. His actions and words, especially statements interpreted as anti-Semitic, have created tensions both within the Black Muslims and within the black political movements of the 1980s and 1990s which generally supported the presidential candidacy of Jesse Jackson, a Baptist minister and Democrat.

CONCLUSION

The remarkable revolution within the life of Malcolm X from 1948 to 1965 and within the Nation of Islam from 1931 to the 1980s suggests several conclusions for the sociology of religion. First, as Mamiya has shown, the economic and educational movement of Black Muslims from the lower to the middle class in the United States in the 1970s has influenced its shift from a mythic and separatist sect to a place within mainstream orthodox Islam. The previous symbolic and economic appeal of the Nation of Islam to the despairing and helpless underclass blacks of the 1930s through the 1960s was replaced by the more sophisticated beliefs and less rigid code of behavior of the American Muslim Mission. As Mamiya concludes his study of the evolution from Black Muslim to Bilalians:

> The barriers of racial doctrine and the restrictions of a strict disciplinary system have been removed by the American Muslim Mission. The way is now open for recruiting the Black middle-class more actively. The Mission has also moved toward major accom-

modation with the mainstream of American life. Political participation and voting are now encouraged. Muslims can be drafted. The red and white crescent and star flag of the Nation of Islam has been replaced by the American flag in all masjids. (148–49)

Second, the retention of Baptist Christianity by southern American blacks throughout the period of the rise of the Nation of Islam, as well as its important role in supporting social changes brought about by such leaders as Martin Luther King and Jesse Jackson, suggest that the Nation of Islam answered the needs primarily of urban blacks. In fact, in its early days in the 1930s, the Nation of Islam under Fard and the young Elijah Muhammad resembled other early twentieth-century black cults that gave identity and hope to displaced blacks lost in the depressed urban ghettos of the northern industrial cities of the United States (for example, Father Divine, Daddy Grace, etc.). With its strong discipline and black/white demonology, the Black Muslim movement answered the needs of the unstructured lives of an oppressed race excluded from significant urban leadership.

Third, and most important for a theological analysis of the Nation of Islam, is the movement of theology under Malcolm X and Wallace Muhammad away from a symbolic/mythic mode to a more intellectual/systematic mode of thinking. In particular, the black/white symbolism which had brought about racial separatism in the Nation of Islam (as it had also in Mormonism and some branches of fundamentalist Christianity) now became open to a less literal and racial interpretation in favor of a moral and spiritual interpretation. As Mamiya puts it, "After his father's death in February 1975, Imam Wallace Muhammad attempted to move the Nation in the direction of Islamic universalism by reinterpreting the basic racial doctrine in a symbolic manner. . . . Whiteness is a symbol of evil only when it is linked to the attitudes and values that characterize white supremacy and racism. Blackness, on the other hand, is a symbol for goodness and humaneness" (143). With this breakthrough in interpretation came the ethical insight into universal brotherhood and sisterhood, as well as the openness to a view of the divine or ultimate reality as transcending race, nation, or material world. Among the final words of Malcolm X were the following, which sum up the theological lesson of his life and movement: "Mankind's history has proved from one era to another that the true criterion of leadership is spiritual. Men are attracted by spirit. By power, men are *forced*. Love is engendered by spirit. . . . The only true world solution today is governments guided by true religion—of the spirit" (368–69).

REFERENCES

Abbott, H. Porter. "Organic Form in the Autobiography of a Convert: The Example of Malcolm X." *College Language Association Journal* 23 (1979): 125–46.

Ansari, Zafar Ishaq. "Aspects of Black Muslim Theology." *Studia Islamica* 53 (1981): 137–76.

Breitman, George. *Malcolm X Speaks: Selected Speeches and Statements*. London: Secker and Warburg, 1965.

Carson, Clayborne. *Malcolm X: The FBI File*. Ed. David Gallen. New York: Carroll & Graf, 1991.

Clarke, John Henrick. *Malcolm X: The Man and His Times*. New York: Macmillan, 1969.

Eakin, Paul John. "Malcolm X and the Limits of Autobiography." *Autobiography: Essays Theoretical and Practical*. Ed. James Olney. Princeton: Princeton UP, 1980. 181–93.

Epps, Archie, ed. *The Speeches of Malcolm X at Harvard*. New York: William Morrow, 1968.

Erikson, Erik. *Childhood and Society*. New York: Norton, 1963.

———. "The Development of Ritualization." *The Religious Situation: 1968*. Ed. Donal R. Culter. Boston: Beacon, 1968.

Fowler, James. "The Pilgrimage of Faith of Malcolm X." *Faith, Liberation, and Human Development*. Cambridge, MA: Harvard UP, 1974.

Groppe, John D. "From Chaos to Cosmos: The Role of Trust in *The Autobiography of Malcolm X*." *Soundings* 66 (1983): 437–49.

Kohlberg, Lawrence. *The Psychology of Moral Development*. San Francisco: Harper & Row, 1984.

Lincoln, C. Eric. *The Black Muslims in America*. Boston: Beacon, 1961.

Lomax, Louis E. *When the Word Is Given: A Report on Elijah Mu-*

hammad, Malcolm X, and the Black Muslim World. Cleveland: World, 1963.

Malcolm X. *The Autobiography of Malcolm X.* With the assistance of Alex Haley. New York: Random House, 1965.

Mamiya, Lawrence H. "From Black Muslim to Bilalian." *Journal for the Scientific Study of Religion,* 21 (1982): 138–52.

Muhammad, Elijah. *Message to the Blackman in America.* Chicago: Muhammad's Temple No. 1, 1968.

———. *Mr. Muhammad Speaks.* New York: Harlem, 1960.

———. "The Saviour." Malcolm X, ch. 12.

———. *The Supreme Wisdom.* Chicago: University of Islam, 1957.

Perry, Bruce. *Malcolm: The Life of a Man who Changed Black America.* Barrytown, NY: Station Hill P, 1991.

Piaget, Jean, and B. Inhelder. *The Psychology of the Child.* New York: Basic Books, 1969.

Stone, Albert E. *Autobiographical Occasions and Original Acts.* Philadelphia: U of Pennsylvania P, 1982.

Whitehurst, James Emerson. "The Mainstreaming of the Black Muslims: Healing the Hate." *Christian Century.* February 27, 1980. 225–29.

6

Black Elk Speaks:
A Century Later

READING *Black Elk Speaks* a century after its story ended at Wounded Knee raises issues quite different from those raised by other modern spiritual autobiographies. The primary problem for the reader is: what context to read it in? Some critics insist on placing the story solely within the historical culture of the 1890s, thus reading *Black Elk Speaks* as another document (alongside Red Cloud's speeches or letters from government agents) revealing the suppression of the Sioux culture by the American movement westward, expressed at its worst by the last episode of the book, the massacre at Wounded Knee in 1890 (J. Olson). Others focus on the context of the writing of *Black Elk Speaks* by Nebraskan poet John Neihardt in 1932, with the emphasis placed on distortions by the translator (Rice). Still other critics focus on the change of the oral narrative from a redemptive epic to a tragic autobiography (P. Olson). Others concentrate on the omission of the ritual and eschatological purposes of Black Elk (Hollar), or on the shift from oral, public, and mythic narrative to written, private, and historical document (Couser). Others emphasize the context of the extraordinary popular appeal of *Black Elk Speaks* in the 1970s, by showing its affinity with the "greening of America" movement and its similarities with other religions (Sayre, Diloria).[1]

---

[1] Julian Rice makes a very strong case against Neihardt for distorting the transcripts of 1931 into *Black Elk Speaks*. Using Neihardt's later writings as clues, especially *The Song of the Messiah*, and pointing out the additions to the transcripts, Rice attempts to show that Neihardt imposed a pattern of Christian universalism and a Platonic dualism on Black Elk's Lakota ritual religion. For Rice, the Lakota religion was tribal and particularist (not universal), earth- and health-centered (not otherworldly), creation-based without a notion of original sin (not salvation-based), and eschatological through one's descendants (not through personal immortality). Although Rice admits that Black Elk himself

While acknowledging the importance of these contextual studies, I will examine the book through the literary lenses I have
been using to read previous modern life stories. In particular, I
will focus on: (a) the *framing devices* used in *Black Elk Speaks* to see
how they bring out a special conflict between life stories within
traditional cultures and those within modern societies; (b) the
structural traits of modern spiritual autobiographies and their unexpected relevance to *Black Elk Speaks*; and (c) the conclusions to be
drawn about the untold story behind the text.

THE FRAMING DEVICES OF BLACK ELK'S CIRCULAR JOURNEY

Several commentators excoriate Neihardt for shifting the context
of Black Elk's oral narrative from "ritual" to "autobiography"
(Hollar, P. Olson). In fact, however, the opening chapter ("The
Offering of the Pipe") and the closing "Author's Postscript" include elaborate rituals. Although the pipe ritual is placed after
three fictional paragraphs of autobiography created by Neihardt,
it still occupies the place of prominence in the opening chapter.
Even some of the assertions of the fictional paragraphs merely
anticipate what Black Elk actually says later in the text. For instance, the statement that "all life . . . is holy" and all people "are
children of one mother and their father in one Spirit" is a para-
phrase of Black Elk's subsequent words. Yet, it must be admitted
that Neihardt's portrait of Black Elk as a recipient of "a mighty
vision given to a man too weak to use it" is the poet's own edito-

later in *The Sacred Pipe* (1947) showed many parallels between the Christianity
he had adopted and his Lakotan religion, Rice finds none of this in the 1931
transcripts (which were published only in 1984 as *The Sixth Grandfather*). Because Neihardt imposed Christian salvation patterns and universalistic assumptions, along with a Platonic dualistic worldview, on certain passages in *Black Elk
Speaks*, Rice considers it a distortion and, in fact, an inferior "literary text" (19)
to *The Sixth Grandfather*. While Rice admits that Black Elk in his life may have
found his Lakotan religion and his active Catholicism to be compatible, Rice
himself shows considerable animus against the consistency of such a position.
Perhaps one source of Rice's resistance to Neihardt's efforts is his own misread-
ing of Christianity as equivalent to Platonic dualism and merely an otherworldly
religion. Rice is reluctant to admit that Black Elk himself came to distrust the
Ghost Dance, a reluctance that suggests that Rice may not trust Black Elk's
Lakotan roots as much as he asserts in *Black Elk's Story*.

rial opinion. Furthermore, Neihardt's description of the holy tree that "withered" and a people's dream that "died" may be more pessimistic than Black Elk's original message, but Neihardt does allow him to say that his vision "is true and mighty yet" (2). Although Neihardt here and in chapter 25 overemphasizes the tragic "death" of the vision at Wounded Knee, it is clear from the phrase about the vision's being "true and mighty yet" that Black Elk's mission is still alive in 1931. This positive message is confirmed most strongly by writing the account of the ritual of the sacred pipe *in the present tense* (2–5). The account of the pipe recreates in description—in the moment of writing and also of reading—the form and origin of the pipe. The form (a red pipe, four ribbons, an eagle feather, a bison-hide mouthpiece) expresses and renews the six-directional unity (north, east, south, west, heaven, earth) of all nature as integral to the one Spirit of the entire sacred universe, both human and animal. This sacred unity is precisely the central message, as we will see, of Black Elk's vision at the age of nine. The origin story that follows the description of the sacred pipe is one form of creation and fertility narrative centering on the sacred bison-woman. In lighting the pipe, smoking it with John Neihardt and the reader, and praying to the eternal creator, "Grandfather Great Spirit," Black Elk invokes divine aid for all his people, for himself, and for union with the reader—so that "there may be only good between us" (5).

The power of this ritual opening in providing a transcendent framework for the subsequent narrative is matched by the ritual and prayer in the "Author's Postscript." In this latter, which completes the circular journey, Black Elk reenacts his vision by climbing to Harney Peak with Neihardt, where he dresses and paints himself, holds the sacred pipe, and prays to the same "Grandfather Great Spirit." He recalls to the Spirit, himself, and the reader that the objects of his vision are important, then ritually acknowledges his own failure ("I have fallen away and done nothing"), and finally prays for a renewal of the sacred tree in the sacred hoop:

"Again, and maybe the last time on this earth, I recall the great vision you sent me. It may be that some little root of the sacred tree still lives. Nourish it then, that it may leaf and bloom and fill with singing birds. Hear me, not for myself, but for my people; I am old. Hear me that they may once more go back into the sacred hoop and find the good red road, the shielding tree!" (233)

The prayer ends with a transfiguration. The sacred clouds gather, a cleansing rain falls, divine thunder is heard, and "[I]n a little while the sky was clear again" (234). However inadequate this passage may be to match the original oral event of 1931, it nevertheless shows a genuine attempt through poetry to re-create the ritual context of Black Elk's story. As ritual, the event invokes and makes present the timeless world of the Great Spirit to the historical world of Black Elk and his listeners.

As Todorov has shown with respect to the quest narrative in European literature, there is an unavoidable tension between "ritual logic" (transcending time, cause-and-effect, and private perspectives) and "narrative logic" (time-bound, causal, private). This tension occurs in many stories that attempt to portray religious events, for example, the Christian gospels, medieval allegories, eschatological epics, and so forth. A similar tension occurs in *Black Elk Speaks*, not merely because Neihardt omitted parts of the manuscript or tried to make the narrative fit Christian theological patterns, but also because of an inherent tension between the ritual framework and the subsequent temporal narrative. This tension recurs several times within the narrative itself, namely during the accounts of the Visions (chs. 3 and 15) and of the sacred dances expressing and renewing parts of the Visions (chs. 14 and 16). In these episodes, Black Elk receives several types of vision: a cosmological overview (of the six powers of the world, the six Grandfathers), together with a vocational gift-vision (cup, bow, herb, pipe, red stick, hoop, eagle), and a prophetic vision (four ascents), together with an eschatological vision (horse dance, hoop and world, flowering tree, procession through the Rainbow door of the tepee). In the first and last visions, he experiences symbolically the ultimate constituents of the universe of space (cosmological) and time (eschatological), which work by means of a "ritual logic" and are thus very difficult to interpret in a manner relating to history, as Black Elk discovers during the period of the Ghost Dances. In the other vision (the gift and prophetic vision), Black Elk sees specific objects and events that he will participate in but that work by a "narrative logic" more easily understood and followed once he takes on the identity of a young medicine man. Although the latter historical events are based on the ritual cosmological and eschatological symbolism, the relationship between the two is one not of identity but of a shift from one "logic" to another. The tension is expressed in "shadow" terms when Black Elk describes Crazy Horse's dream:

> My father . . . said that Crazy Horse dreamed and went into the world where there is nothing but the spirits of all things. . . . everything we see here is something like a shadow from that world. He was on his horse in that world, and the horse and himself on it and the trees and the grass and the stones and everything were made of spirit, and nothing was hard, and everything seemed to float. (71)

To compound the complexity of the framing stories, Neihardt had Black Elk tell his story within the ritual framework, but the story emerges as a mixture of two genres—epic and autobiography. As epic, told primarily in first person, Black Elk's main plot is the story of the growth of the young warrior during the Indian–White wars of 1860–90. Modeling his life after that of his cousin Crazy Horse, Black Elk experiences initiation into the tribe (ch. 2), into hunting (ch. 4), into relations with whites (ch. 5), into sexuality (ch. 6), into fighting and victory (chs. 7, 8, 9), into defeat (ch. 10), into the death of his model (ch. 11), and into exile (ch. 12). The hero's personal story fits, of course, within the rise and fall of his people's story, from the battle of Little Big Horn to the death of Crazy Horse. However, his preparation as a warrior proves to be a secondary story, for his family tradition (ch. 1) and his Great Vision (ch. 3) orient Black Elk to be not primarily a warrior but a medicine man, a vocation which he fears and avoids until he experiences a renewed calling at the age of seventeen (ch. 13). At this crisis point—in his life and in his tribe—Black Elk acts out his Vision in two dances (chs. 14–16), accomplishes his first cure (ch. 17), and gains the powers of both the bison and the elk (ch. 18). Unfortunately, the hero-as-shaman squanders his power by traveling to Europe in Buffalo Bill's Wild West Show (ch. 19), where he later recovers it through a new vision (ch. 20). Returning to his defeated people, he studies and joins the Ghost Dances of a new messiah (chs. 21–22), but realizes too late that this new vision makes him forget his original vision (ch. 23).

Thus, he concludes with his experience, along with his people's, of the butchery of Wounded Knee (ch. 24), where he is wounded and admits defeat (ch. 25). The epic-turned-spiritual-autobiography ends with a prayer for rebirth of his people ("Postscript"), which Paul Olson calls a "ritual attempt to reverse history."

Within the epic-autobiography tension lies the usual conflict of autobiography itself between life as a battle and life as a journey. The young Black Elk, as I have noted, struggles in an inner battle between his identity as a warrior and his identity as a shaman. At the same time, he finds himself caught in a series of outer battles—military and political—between his people and the Wasichus. Gradually he overcomes the battle for identity, and accepts his vocation as medicine man, only to revert at the end to a desperate attempt at becoming both visionary and warrior. Struggling to be both, he succeeds at neither, thus reaching the ambiguous ending of the story. This personal development and decline of the hero as autobiographer includes his passage through three differing theological frameworks. Chapters 1 to 6 introduce him to the tradition and sacred cosmology of his people within a primarily natural world, brought to its symbolic fulfillment in his vision. Chapters 7 to 18 introduce him to the transformative and redemptive powers of his vocation as medicine man, brought to its high point in the Horse Dance and the Dog Vision amid a violent outer world of victory and defeat. Chapters 19 to 25 plunge him into the eschatological world of ultimate conflict and movement toward a higher world, brought to its ambiguous climax in the Ghost Dance and the mistaken Vision.

A final framework for the story of Black Elk can be found in its fusion of both Native American and Christian theology and language. Without getting into the vexed historical question raised by Black Elk's conversion to Catholicism and his active role as a catechist after 1900 (a conversion in which he apparently found the beliefs of his Vision compatible with those of Catholic doctrine), I can try to account for two puzzling questions. First, why did Black Elk ask for his story to end with an account of his conversion to Christianity? Second, why does the use of biblical language, and even quotations from the Bible (some of which Neihardt omitted), interact with the use of Native American terms and symbols? From this interaction, the reader can feel some tension between the Christian echoes and the Native American framework, but a tension much less extreme when one considers the parallels between the apocalyptic imagery of the New Testament Book of Revelation and the Vision of Black Elk. Both include a sacred tree, white horses, an ascending road, all kinds of animals, a sacred nation, water and rainbows, armies and priests, a divine voice calling for a sacred dance, and so forth. These parallels and echoes do not lead the reader to identify the two visionary books, which differ radically in their plot and meaning. In fact, an analysis of merely the structure and form of the imagery is not sufficient to explain the significance of these parallels and echoes. Whether Neihardt imposed too strong a Christian redemptive motif on the last chapters of *Black Elk Speaks*, especially in emphasizing the doubts Black Elk felt about the Ghost Dance movement, or expressed an excessively pessimistic interpretation by emphasizing the "dead dream" of chapter 25—the overall pattern of *Black Elk Speaks* fits well within both a Christian and a Native American theology of ultimate transformation.

What is even more problematic about the narrative of Black Elk is that it reflects and embodies the larger conflict within which its events and its writing occurred—the violent clash between a traditional and a modern society. As traditional, the Sioux society of Black Elk's youth offered him a mediated way of life (through chiefs, parents, medicine men, rituals, legends, etc.) by which to find his identity as son of generations of medicine men. In experiencing violent conflict with a half-formed, expansionist, and pluralistic modern society (which lacks a tradition, a common culture, a single religion, and a class structure), Black Elk discovers that the traditional development into his role as shaman proves personally painful and socially ineffective. Despite his efforts, he cannot heal the social wounds and overcome the deaths of his people. In fact, as an analysis of the seven aspects of spiritual autobiography in *Black Elk Speaks* will make clear, the narrative *as story* gains its power by portraying Black Elk's struggle for identity, conversion, and religious authenticity in the very conflicts I have noted—between traditional and modern, Native American and capitalist American, ritual and narrative form, epic and autobiographical genre.

Is *BLACK ELK SPEAKS* A SPIRITUAL AUTOBIOGRAPHY?

If Black Elk's life story were merely a traditional Sioux story, its primary image would not be directional but static—that of the sacred circle within the cycles of nature. As a conflictual story, however, its directional image, like those of Malcolm X, Gandhi, and others caught in similar cultural clashes, expresses an impossible double bind. Black Elk follows the directional image of a "blocked" circular journey. As son of medicine men named Black Elk for several generations, he tells his listeners at the time of his first cure that "everything an Indian does is in a circle":

> . . . that is because the Power of the World always works in circles, and everything tries to be round. In the old days where we were a strong and happy people, all our power came to us from the sacred hoop of the nation, and so long as the hoop was unbroken, the people flourished. The flowering tree was the living center of the hoop, and the circle of the four quarters nourished it. . . . The sky is round, and I have heard that the earth is round like a ball, and so are all the stars. The wind, in its greatest power, whirls. Birds make their nests in circles, for theirs is the same religion as ours. The sun comes forth and goes down again in a circle. The moon does the same, and both are round. Even the seasons form a great circle in their changing, and always come back again to where they were. The life of a man is a circle from childhood to childhood. . . . Our tepees were round . . . and these were always set in a circle. . . . (164–65)

The symbolic depths and perfection of the circle conflicts, tragically, with the pragmatic individualistic culture of the white settlers ("Wasichus") expressed in the symbol of a square and a linear black road. In a passage following the one just cited, Black Elk laments: "But the Wasichus have put us in these square boxes. Our power is gone and we are dying, for the power is not in us any more" (166). As he concludes when describing the despair that led to his journey to Europe with Buffalo Bill: "All our people now were settling down in square gray houses, scattered here and there across the hungry land, and around them the Washichus had drawn a line to keep them in. The nation's hoop was broken, and there was no center any longer for the flowering tree. . . .

They were traveling the black road, everybody for himself and with little rules of his own, as in my vision" (181–83).

This conflict between the images of the circle and the square appears first in the dream of Drinks Water, the ancestral holy man who foresaw the coming of the whites who would put the Indian peoples on "little islands" in "square gray houses in a barren land" beside a web of linear forts and roads (8–9). The conflict continues in every chapter of the Black Elk's life story. Within the Great Vision, the central image of the sacred hoop surrounding the flowering tree holds the complex of other images together (ch. 3). Outside the vision, moreover, in the practical and ritual life of the Sioux, the circle underlies the patterns of their tepees, their villages, their hunting of bison, their dances, the sacred pipe, their sexuality, and so forth (3–4, 44–48, 78, 80, 136ff., 160, 175ff.). The sacred circle of life devolves, however, into the military circle of wagons and the circle of fired weapons (13–14, 78). As Black Elk repeats many times, his Vision guides him to preserve the sacred hoop and, if it is broken, to restore it, primarily through performance of his vision in ritual dances (174–75).

This circular directional image not merely provides Black Elk with an ideal for guiding his people in the patterns of their culture, but also offers him a map for the shape of the human life story: "The life of a man is a circle from childhood to childhood, and so it is in everything where power moves" (165). But the image of the circular journey comes into conflict with the events of history. Even the performance of circular ritual dances does not bring his life story to its rounded close in the narrative of his or his people's history. In the chronological patterns of the narrative between opening and closing rituals, as I have briefly noted, Neihardt has Black Elk tell his story as a religious autobiography in the shape of a circular journey upward and downward in four stages (similar to the stages of many other twentieth-century autobiographers). The four stages can be seen as (1) Initiation; (2) Search for Identity; (3) Acceptance of Identity; (4) Near Loss of Identity.

In the First Stage, Black Elk is initiated into his family, tribe, and vocation (chs. 1–3). As a member of a traditional society, he finds ready mediators in his mother, father, his cousin Crazy Horse, and the medicine man who tries to cure him during the sickness of the Great Vision. The first episode he recounts is the Battle of the Hundred Slain (1866), when his father is injured for life and where Black Elk first learns of the white expansionist and exterminating movements westward (6–7). It is significant that this long first chapter on his boyhood concentrates on a Sioux victory in which his father is injured and then forced to lie on a pony drag "like a baby" (12). For the image of the injured father reduced to infant helplessness haunts the entire narrative. After teaching Black Elk to hunt (53–54) and to fight (77), his father teaches him the futility of war (110), affirms his faith in Black Elk's spiritual power (128), and assists him in the Horse Dance (137). Thus, his father, who is both a medicine man and a warrior, passes along this double role to Black Elk, but later asserts the primacy of the vocation of spiritual healer. It is no accident that his father dies at a crucial low point of the story in chapter 21, just when Black Elk is trying to discern his role in the Ghost Dance movement.

> I did not believe yet, but I wanted to find out things, because all this was sitting more and more strongly in my heart since my father died. Something seemed to tell me to go and see. For a while I kept from going, but at last I could not any more. So I got on my horse and went to this ghost dance on Wounded Knee Creek below Manderson. (200–201)

Black Elk's mother also mediates his growth into identity, first by giving him two ancestors with names symbolic of his future— her mother, Plenty Eagle Feathers, and her father, Refuse-to-go, the latter to whom Black Elk tells all his young deeds (except his Vision). His mother later praises Black Elk for his first scalp as a warrior and then assists during his emergence in the Horse Dance as a shaman. But his parents' crucial role in the early stage of his life is keeping Black Elk alive and open to his calling as medicine man during his illness of the Great Vision. The role of the medicine man, Whirlwind Chaser, who assisted Black Elk during this illness is difficult to discern. In the narrative, the family ascribes his cure to Whirlwind Chaser, but the medicine man tells them afterward, "Your boy there is sitting in a sacred manner. I do not know what it is, but there is something special for him to do, for just as I came in I could see a power like a light all through his body" (41). After his recovery, Black Elk avoids the medicine man, because he fears to tell his dream to anyone. It has been argued that Whirlwind Chaser probably used symbols in his healing ritual that may have affected the form of Black Elk's vision.

After this stage of family, tribal, and historical initiation, Black Elk undergoes a longer Second Stage of adolescent search for his true identity. This stage begins with his fear of telling his vision, his first arbitrary killing (similar to Augustine's arbitrary stealing of fruit or Merton's rejection of his younger brother's love), and his initiation into the life of the hunter (chs. 4–6) and warrior (chs. 7–11). Throughout this extensive process of initiation (mediated primarily by the entire band and by Crazy Horse's leadership) Black Elk occasionally experiences reminders of his calling. For instance, he feels sorry for killing animals and offers sacrificial prayer (54); he refuses to throw stones at birds because they "seemed holy" (64); he prays alone at night (68); he discovers traces of his vision in his development as a youth (69); he finds similarities between Crazy Horse's vision and his own (71); and he is "lifted clear off the ground" while thinking of his vision before his first battle at Little Big Horn (89–90). When Black Elk confronts the problems of justice after his people begin to experience defeat in battle and some are eager to fight with the Washichus, he expresses his bafflement in the question, "How could men get fat by being bad, and starve by being good?" At this point, he begins to doubt his Vision and to wonder, "if maybe it was only a queer dream after all" (116). This doubt occurs just before the low point of his warrior initiation—the killing of Crazy Horse (ch. 11). This ends the wandering stage of his search for his identity, which coincides with the brief success and then decline of his people's fate in the struggle with the white settlers (chs. 8–12).

The Third Stage of Black Elk's growth—discovery and acceptance of his identity as a shaman—occupies the central chapters of the book, 12 to 18. This stage begins when the tribal fear of being penned up "on little islands" leads the band to walk the "black road" into exile. This disaster reminds the fifteen-year-old Black Elk of his vocation just after he had experienced the futility of his life as a warrior:

I was fifteen years old that winter, and I thought much of my vision
and wondered when my duty was to come; for the Grandfathers
had shown me my people walking on the black road and how the
nation's hoop would be broken and the flowering tree be withered,
before I should bring the hoop together with the power that was
given me, and make the holy tree to flower in the center and find
the red road again. (124)

That he is a boy and can say nothing suggests his inability to
resolve the tension between his double identity through words.
However, he begins to feel strange as he experiences his power
growing: he hears voices in the clouds (125), interprets coyote
howls (127), has premonitions of danger (131), and experiences
the power of prayer (133). But a year later, he goes through a
"terrible time" when he hears voices calling him without telling
him what to do. He tries on his own to link together the world
of his vision with the experienced world of earth and sky (134).
When he is seventeen, his parents, thinking he is lapsing into his
old illness, invite over the medicine man Black Road (whose
name ironically recalls his Vision of disaster), the first mediator to
whom he tells his Great Vision. Black Road responds with the
advice to follow his vision: "Nephew, I know now what the trouble is! You must do what the bay horse in your vision wanted you
to do. You must do your duty and perform this vision for your
people upon earth. You must have the horse dance first for the
people to see!" (135). Thus, in chapters 14 through 18, Black Elk
finds a way through the "speech" of ritual to express, appropriate,
and make public his Great Vision, thereby healing the broken
circle of the people by completing the circle of his own identity.
He repeats the positive content of his Vision from Stage One (ch.
3) in the ritual dance of Stage Three, after experiencing the negative content of the Vision (the four ascents) in Stage Two. As he
prays during the Horse Dance: "What you have said to me, I am
now performing" (143). In his act of losing his fearful self and
secondary identity as a warrior, Black Elk takes on the identity of
leader of the Horse Dance and later of Healer and Prophet (chs.
17–18). But this ritual alone is not the completion of his identity
or the final stage of his life story.

The Fourth Stage (chs. 19–25) presents the most controversial
part of *Black Elk Speaks*—his near loss of identity through a strug-

gle with an alternative Vision. Structurally, this stage includes
many formal parallels to the elements of the previous stages—a
central vision, a conflict between cultures, a tension between
warrior and shaman, a mediator, a ritual dance (all from Stages
One and Three); an exile, a treaty of betrayal, a straying from the
Great Vision, a death of a model (his father), a return of Black
Elk to the warrior role, and a battle leading to a slaughter (all
from Stage Two). Thus, as a circular journey, after Part One leads
downward to Part Two before returning upward to Part Three,
the movement of Black Elk Speaks in Part Four fluctuates between
an upward and a downward motion. After the three-year false
journey to Europe as a medicine man for the Buffalo Bill Wild
West Show, Black Elk has an authentic vision during a three-day
"spirit journey" in Paris (ch. 20), a vision of his homelands which
returns him to Pine Ridge to confront the most serious test of his
faith as a shaman. Here he meets an alternative vision—that of the
Paiute seer-savior Wovoha, who claims to have seen an eschatological scene in which the Indian people are returned to harmony
with the universe and with dead relatives, all freed of white domination. During the critical period when Black Elk tries to fit this
new vision with his own Great Vision, he loses his father, a fact
he mentions twice. At first, he refuses to join the public following
of Wovoha : "This was not like my great vision, and I just went
on working in the store. I was puzzled and did not know what to
think" (200). But the desire to see his father leads Black Elk to
join the ghost dances derived from Wovoka's vision, dances that
contain enough of the elements of his own Great Vision to con-
vince him to test their authenticity (especially the circle with a
dying tree and sacred hoop, the sacred pipe and eagle feathers,
and red paint). As he dances, Black Elk gradually see parts of what
"seem" to be his own Great Vision, but only, as he says, "maybe
the land of my vision" (204, 209). Although this "seeming" leads
him to take leadership in the dance and in the creation of ghost
shirts, and later to fight as a warrior at Wounded Knee, Black Elk
eventually admits that he went beyond his Vision:

> I have thought much about this since, and I have thought that this
> was where I made my great mistake. I had a very great vision, and

I should have depended only upon that to guide me to the good. But I followed the lesser visions that had come to me while dancing on Wounded Knee Creek. The vision of the Flaming Rainbow was to warn me, maybe; and I did not understand. (212)

After the final two chapters describe the butchering and consequent submission by his people at Wounded Knee, events in which Black Elk participates as both warrior and *waneka* (savior), he ends the narrative suddenly with two paragraphs added by John Neihardt as his interpretation of the final battle: "A people's dream died there . . . the nation's hoop is broken and scattered . . . the sacred tree is dead" (230). If the book ended at this point, critics like Hollar, Conner, and Paul Olson would be correct in seeing nothing but a truncation of epic into tragic autobiography. However, as I have noted earlier, the ritual in the "Postscript" indicates that the final word is intended to be redemptive. Even though Neihardt's translation clearly omits Christian references to Black Elk's life story and cuts out parts of his final prayer, the final ritual does show a sense of what one critic finds lacking: namely, "the teaching and real presence are alive in the ritual process of the community of faith" (Hollar 41). The gap is not within the overall 1931 text of *Black Elk Speaks*, where the ritual–narrative–ritual sequence is ultimately an upward spiral of transformation. The gap, rather, is in the context of the transmission of the traditional faith story to a modern skeptical audience. If the power of its directional image and its circular narrative form are sufficient to communicate the power of its ritual as well as its narrative "logic," then Black Elk still speaks efficaciously to his widening audience.

Thus, a closer study of the framework and structural parallels in *Black Elk Speaks* has shown that its original act and account, as Stone has demonstrated in other ways, are narratively powerful enough to overcome many of the limitations inherent in the speaker's use of a translator. The translation undergoes at least five steps—the temporal translation from 1890 to 1931, the verbal translation from the Oglala of Black Elk into the Indian-English of his son, the transcript's translation from the oral to the written by Neihardt's daughter Enid, the final poetic restructuring by

John Neihardt, and the final historical translation from a 1931 Depression context to a post-1960s audience. Despite all these translations, the personal and tribal spiritual life story of *Black Elk Speaks* still releases the enormous tension of the author and medicine man, Black Elk. In the very act of telling how he could not tell his story for many years, Black Elk re-creates the ritual and narrative words of his modern self raised in a traditional culture. Like a contemporary writer aware of the limits of words to recount the experience of the spirit, Black Elk can say, "Of course there was very much in the vision that even I can not tell when I try hard, because very much of it was not for words. But I have told what can be told" (174).

The consequence of "telling" is, as Dorothy Day says of her own autobiography, a "giving oneself away." This is a dangerous act, both personally and politically, as Black Elk acknowledges when he says, "I know I have given away my power when I have given away my vision. . . . But I think I have done right to save the vision in this way" (174). Even the failure of the original 1932 edition did not destroy the vision, for, although Black Elk did not live to see it, the ritual–narrative spiritual autobiography became what Neihardt calls in the 1971 preface, "the book that would not die." If it remains merely a "book" with a "message," as Neihardt describes it, *Black Elk Speaks* will not speak as it was meant to. For just as Black Elk had to learn to translate his Great Vision into the language of sacred tribal dance within a community of powerful faith, so now the reader must read beyond the narrative of the self caught between a traditional and a modern world. The reader must learn, as Black Elk learned, to read the vision with the "logic" of both narrative and ritual. In a word, all of us must learn—here even more than in reading other life stories—that "the life of man is a circle," a life to be read from the center. Perhaps the very act of reading will allow one to share in the ritual so profoundly that it becomes a contemporary ritual answer to Black Elk's final prayer:

> Hear me that they may once more go back into the sacred hoop and find the good red road, the shielding tree. . . . Hear me in my sorrow, for I may never call again. O make my people live! (233)

Perhaps in this way, "the sky will be clear again."

REFERENCES

Black Elk. *The Sacred Pipe: Black Elk's Account of the Seven Rites of the Oglala Sioux.* Ed. Joseph Epes Brown. New York: Penguin, 1971.

————. *The Sixth Grandfather: Black Elk's Teachings Given to John G. Neihardt.* Ed. Raymond J. DeMallie. Lincoln: U of Nebraska P, 1984.

Couser, G. Thomas. "*Black Elk Speaks* with Forked Tongue." *Studies in Autobiography.* Ed. James Olney. New York: Oxford UP, 1988. 73–88.

Diloria, Vine. Preface. *Black Elk Speaks: Being the Life Story of a Holy Man of the Oglala Sioux.* By Black Elk. Lincoln: U of Nebraska P, 1979.

Hollar, Clyde. "Lakota Religion and Tragedy: The Theology of *Black Elk Speaks.*" *Journal of the American Academy of Religion,* 52 (Mar. 1984): 19–45.

Neihardt, John G. *Black Elk Speaks: Being the Life Story of a Holy Man of the Oglala Sioux.* As told through John G. Neihardt. New York: Pocketbooks, 1972.

Olson, James C. *Red Cloud and the Sioux Problem.* Lincoln: U of Nebraska P, 1965.

Olson, Paul. "*Black Elk Speaks* as Epic and Ritual Attempt to Reverse History." *Vision and History: Essays on the Literature of the Great Plains.* Ed. Virginia Faulkner and Frederick C. Luebke. Lincoln: U of Nebraska P, 1982. 3–27.

Rice, Julian. *Black Elk's Story: Distinguishing Its Lakota Purpose.* Albuquerque: U of New Mexico P, 1991.

Sayre, Robert F. "Vision and Experience in *Black Elk Speaks.*" *College English,* 32 (Feb., 1971): 509–35.

Stone, Albert E. *Autobiographical Occasions and Original Acts.* Philadelphia: U of Pennsylvania P, 1982.

Todorov, Tzvetan. *The Poetics of Prose.* Trans. Richard Howard. Ithaca, NY: Cornell UP, 1977.

7

The Remaking of an American Jew: Paul Cowan's *An Orphan in History*

ALTHOUGH CALLED BY A *New York Times* reviewer "beautiful and moving," and applauded by a later critic as the greatest Jewish spiritual autobiography of the century, Paul Cowan's story remains somewhat of an orphan in the history of recent autobiography. It is overshadowed, of course, by great first-person Jewish novels by Chaim Potok or Isaac Singer, which portray similar American religious struggles across the generations. It also appeared in 1982 in the wake of more sophisticated and sensational autobiographies by secular Jewish writers like Irving Howe, Norman Podhoretz, and Arthur Miller. As I shall notice, Cowan's journalistic background and restrained personality make for a style that is, as one critic remarked, "curiously dull" in places or so "laundered" as to convey an image of an "earnest and somewhat pompous persona" (Wisse; Valentine).

But *An Orphan in History* cannot be dismissed that easily. For its peculiar narrative shape creates a circular journey that serves as a model for the journey of many Americans of Jewish heritage who have retraced the history of their ancestors over the past 150 years, a journey that ends for Cowan in what his subtitle calls "retrieving a Jewish legacy." In examining this spiral, I shall note the central importance of history—especially family history—as the theater of spiritual enlightenment. Although Cowan denies that Jewish experience depends on epiphanies or "spots of time," his story portrays a man coming to small insights by following a curious ancestral split image through family, parental, and personal history over five generations in a psychic and intellectual journey. Centered in the violent death of his parents in 1976, Cowan's life story is always aided by mediators and leads to a series of conversions, all of which are resolved through writing. This is a uniquely Jewish-American, but thoroughly modern, spiritual autobiography.

The Directional Image: Grandfather Jacob Cohen

Cowan's root metaphor throughout his autobiography grows out of a youthful experience of rootless dividedness. Although not attuned to the division in his early childhood in Dalton School in New York City or on Manhatten's East Side among people he calls "Jewish WASPs" (3), he begins his story with a series of phrases like "deeply conflicted," "poised tensions" (4), "amputated past" (5), leading up to the thematic sentence whose very suspensefulness and divided form expresses its main theme:

> I am reacting to the rootlessness I felt as a child—to the fact that for all the Cowan's family warmth, for all its intellectual vigor, for all its loyalty toward each other, our pasts had been amputated. We were orphans in history. (5)

This basic image of dividedness continues throughout the opening chapter and much of the book. For instance, when he is describing his feelings of being separated from his WASP schoolmates at Choate (a "human minefield of anti-Semitism"), where he is sent by his secularized Jewish father so that he can compete in the assimilated world of America. At Choate, he feels separated from both Jewish and non-Jewish classmates, for his looks and behavior simultaneously "dissociate me from other Jews" (14) and "separate me from my tribe" (15). He is forced to create a fantasy world of a small group of students separated from the majority of their classmates by an inner aloofness, for example when he attends compulsory Episcopal chapel services where he half-loves, half-resists the Christian rituals and prayers. After the experience of assimilated separateness at Choate, Cowan concludes, "I could never pretend that I was and wasn't Jewish" (15). Never again will he try to be an American on the surface and a secret Jew underneath, a Jewish "outsider" in American "disguise" (16).

Thus he begins a search for his deeper identity to overcome this feeling of separateness. The directional image that propels his search is of a man rejected but supported by his [Paul's] father—the grandfather and black sheep of the family, Jacob Cohen. As Cowan describes this chosen image: "It was at Choate that my fascination with my grandfather Jacob Cohen began. . . . I began to dwell on the fact that I was the grandson of someone named Cohen: an Orthodox Jew, an impoverished used-cement-bag dealer from Chicago. . . . while my teachers at Choate praised me for adapting so well to the school's environment, I began to feel impelled to search for a link between Jake Cohen's world and mine" (16). In the person of his grandfather—a practicing Orthodox Jew who had been unaccountably separated from Paul by his father, the latter having changed the family name from Cohen to Cowan—Paul finds an image that sets him off on the quest that turns this autobiography into the oldest of story forms, a mystery story about one's own identity. The mystery can be solved through the only link to Jacob Cohen—Paul's father, the CBS executive who created "Quiz Kids" on radio and "The $64,000 Question" on television, Louis G. Cowan. But his father rarely speaks of the grandfather. Only over many years does Paul overcome what he calls "the rift between our ancestors in Europe and the Cohens in Chicago, between Jake Cohen and Lou Cowan, [which] had been echoing in our psyches throughout our adult lives" (17). The peculiar shape of this search to heal this rift, as Cowan describes his "spiritual adventure," is the shape of another circular journey, but this one a pilgrimage through history.

THE SPIRAL THROUGH HISTORY

After the opening chapter in which he discovers during adolescence his mysterious Orthodox Jewish grandfather, who serves as a directional image for the rest of the autobiography, Cowan tells his story in an unusual variation of the three-part circular journey seen in other modern autobiographies: (1) chapters 2 to 5 narrate his search for the *causes* of his divided identity as found in the lives of his ancestors and parents from 1850 to 1976; (II) chapters 6 to 10 narrate his experience of the *effects* of the divided identity on his own life and family from 1960 to 1976; and (III) chapters 11 to 15 narrate the *healing* of the dividedness in himself and his family through the recovery of Jewish belief and practice from 1976 to 1981. Although this schema contrasts with the outline in other recent autobiographies in its long first section on the author's ancestors and parents (instead of on his childhood), its three-part form turns out to be another version of the circular journey. For, many of the persons, events, and themes of Part I appear in parallel form as *causes* of a rift whose *effects* appear in Part II, and which rift is *healed* in Part III.

In Part I, certainly the most fascinating because of its detective story format, the search for the causes of the dividedness in Paul takes him on a journey through the lives of his parents and their ancestors. The crucial discovery in chapter 2 is of the dividedness within the life of his grandfather, Jacob Cohen, and the subsequent rift between him and his wife, Hetty, as well as between him and his only son, Louis Cohen/Cowan, Paul's father. Paul learns through conversation with distant relatives that his grandfather, unlike his enormously successful great-grandfather, Moses Cohen, was a devout Orthodox Jew but a failed businessman who bankrupted the family, divorced his wife in 1930, and became a ne'er-do-well who lived off relatives for twenty years until his death in 1950. In 1931, Louis Cohen, just twenty-one, changed his name to Louis Cowan and began a successful rise to the top of the entertainment industry. Ashamed of his father, Jacob, Louis supports him financially but never allows him to visit Paul or his other sons and daughters. Paul interprets this split as his father's "trying desperately to rid himself of a demon" (42). Along the way of his journey of escape from the divided grandfather, Louis Cowan gives up nearly all his Jewish practices in 1939 and marries into a wealthy, secularized Jewish family, the Spiegels, where he finds a substitute father and brother in his wife's family (Mogie Spiegel, Sr. and Jr.). In 1942, when Paul is two years old, Louis and Polly Cowan leave their Jewish roots in Chicago and move to New York City.

The crucial discovery of chapter 3 appears when Paul delves into the secularized rise of his mother's ancestors. Her great-grandfather had been a practicing orthodox Jew in Germany but had joined the reformed Jews as an immigrant in Chicago. Her grandfather gradually gave up the practice of reform Judaism, and then her father left all forms of his tradition to join the Christian Scientists and move to the WASP suburb of Kenilworth near Chicago. As a result, Polly becomes a "stranger in both worlds"—neither a religious Jew nor a believing Christian. In response to this dividedness, she gains a strong sense of justice, from the Jewish tradition of fighting for their rights and from her revulsion against the Holocaust, as well as from her rejection of her parents' preoccupation with status and money. Paul sums up her religion as a form of "secular messianism."

In chapter 5, Cowan traces his parents' marriage, their work in radio, television, education, and political causes from 1950 until their death in an apartment fire in New York City in 1976. In these events, he finds a gradual shift from their American secular preoccupation with success and high-minded causes (television as education; the civil rights movement; private education) to their later concern for Jewishness, especially in his father's reminiscences and interest in his son's investigation into his roots. As he reviews their lives, Paul ends chapters 2–5 with an awareness that he received from his father his own concern for a rooted faith and from his mother a passion for justice. As he describes his mother:

> Her secular messianism—the kind of Judaism that shaped her beliefs—was a lonely faith. It demanded immense courage, for she had to overcome her own fears, her own innate sense of inadequacy, as well as take risks in the world. . . . As I thought about that creed, which had shaped me too, I became convinced that my own need to understand my past, to cease feeling like an orphan in history, to overcome my own recurrent feeling that I was an outsider wherever I went, was so deep that I had to find some version of the cohesive, communal Judaism that my father was beginning to rediscover. (97)

Structurally, Part II, chapters 6–10 parallels in Paul's life some of the patterns he found in his ancestors' and parents' lives. The dividedness he discovered in his grandfather and his parents between their "American" success and their "Jewish" loss of roots, between their concern for "justice" and lack of concern for "faith," between their being simultaneously insiders and outsiders in American culture he rediscovers in himself. Part Two begins with his struggle during the 1960s for his identity at Harvard, then in Israel, and finally in civil rights and Peace Corps work. Despite some growth during his Israel experience, he finds little religious faith and identity, while simultaneously losing faith and identity as an American, especially after the failure of the Great Society in the late 1960s. Just as his father had moved away from the practice of Orthodox Judaism by rejecting his own father and by marrying into a secularized Jewish family, so now Paul refuses to listen to his father's advice in all his major choices (regarding Israel, civil rights work, and journalism), and then marries a Protestant woman, Rachel Brown. Ironically, in Part II, the story of their married years shows both of them becoming more and more interested in the externals of Jewish life and identity. In particular, Paul, in chapter 8, uses a journalistic assignment to uncover some of his roots in New York City. When Part II ends, with the death of his parents in 1976, Paul promises himself to carry out his father's last wish that he explore the Jewishness of the Orthodox craftsmen in the Lower East Side of Manhattan.

Structurally, Part III begins with Paul's discovery of a new father—Rabbi Joseph Singer—who also replaces Jacob Cohen, the mediator of Part I, and Rabbi Joel Price, the mediator of Part II. From this new father, Paul learns the details of Jewish tradition—the prayers, ritual, history, and care for others—and begins to reassimilate them into his identity. Where he had recovered some Jewish family "history" in Part I and "consciousness" in Part II, now in chapter 12 he recovers Jewish practice. Just as his parents married in a secularized Jewish wedding in Part I, and he and Rachel in a secularized interfaith wedding in Part II, now in chapter 13 she converts to become a conservative Jew, thus bringing him back to a fully religious Jewish marriage. In chapter 14, which at first seems superfluous, Paul assimilates his mother's family history by visiting Ligonier, Indiana, and learning about their Jewish roots. Finally, in chapter 25, Cowan brings his circular journey to a coherent conclusion with the bat mitzvah of his daughter, whose choice of Jewish religious practice gives a fullness of identity to all the Cowans and structurally "heals" all the rifts that had been traced in Part I. Just as Parts I and II had ended with the death of Paul's parents, so Part III ends with the birth of his children's faith.

Geographically, the circular journey began in Part I with the family movement from Europe to Chicago and New York City, a movement that brought with it the loss of Jewish faith and practice; the movement of Parts II and III took Paul from New York City to Israel, then to Chicago, and back to New York, roughly retracing the pilgrimage of his ancestors, but now recovering Jewish faith and practice. Religiously, his great-great-grandfather had been a rabbi in Part I; his mediator in Part II was Rabbi Price; his mediator in Part III, Rabbi Singer. In Part I, Paul learns how the splits within his father's family led to his father's financial success in America but also to his loss of religion, and the splits within his mother's family led to her concern for justice but also to her loss of religion. In Part II, he follows his own version of his father's Americanization (Choate, Harvard, journalism career) and his mother's concern for justice (civil rights, Peace Corps, advocacy journalism). In following both, he gains an interest in the faith and practices they had abandoned. In Part II, Paul regains their lost faith but unites it with a more authentic pursuit of justice within a critical American identity. Underlying all the parallels of this circular journey is Paul's growth as a writer. For, as I shall explore later, he ends Part I with a pledge to write about Jews in New York, a pledge he renews at the end of Part II, and a pledge he fulfills in the very writing described and expressed in Part III.

PAUL COWAN: COHEN OR SPIEGAL?

Unlike the other writers in this study who lost their parents during childhood (Merton, Day, Gandhi, Malcolm X, Lewis), Cowan tells us that his father and mother remained alive in his psyche as in his life until he is thirty-six. Yet he also calls himself an "orphan in history." For, despite their closeness to his life (he called them daily from 1970 to 1976) and their strong influence on his inner tension, he discovers that his lack of identity stems from the lack of spiritual roots in his parents' lives. In his father, as Paul discovers during his detective search into the mystery of Jacob Cohen, he finds an "unbridgeable cultural gulf" caused by the split with his grandfather. In Louis Cowan, the warm father, devoted husband, and successful media entrepreneur, Paul discovers a secularized American man of integrity, but also a man nostalgic for his lost Jewish legacy. After uncovering the rift between Louis and Jacob Cohen, Paul reinterprets his father's idiosyncracies—his distaste for pork, his love of visiting old Jewish neighborhoods, his resistance to Paul's marriage to a Christian, and his discomfort during Christmastime. Cowan expresses this tension within his father in the very style of a series of questions about Louis Cowan's "deeply divided identity": "Was he a Smitz, a German Jew? . . . Or was he a Cohen, the descendant of the Lidvinova rav? . . . Was he Louis Cohen, a Jew who knew how to daven . . . or Louis G. Cowan, a cosmopolitan intellectual, a Jewish WASP?" (44). Within himself, Paul finds the same tension between the assimilated Jewish American and the nostalgic American Jew, but cannot at first understand why his father encourages his interest in his past as "a valuable spiritual adventure" (18). Only after his resignation from CBS leads him to spend time on Jewish causes does Louis reveal his own secret search for his identity. Both father and son become orphans in history.

The loneliness accompanying Paul's identity crisis as a divided orphan reflects the even more isolated soul of his mother. For Polly Spiegal Cowan, her son discovers, cut off entirely from her religious Jewish ancestors by parents who abandoned even nominal Jewishness for an affluent gentile suburb and a secular Jewish country club, feels herself totally isolated. Encouraged to be independent by her mother (whose domination by her husband Modie's brash ambition led to her breakdown and two years in an institution when her daughter was fourteen), Polly revolts against the country club creed of her family by becoming a socialist during her college years at Sarah Lawrence and a lifelong devotee of social causes. She spends most of the last decade of her life as a national civil rights leader. But she also, as Paul remembers, "became more openly Jewish in those years, too." She encourages Paul and Rachel in their first seder, gives generously to the United Jewish Appeal, and keeps the family aware of the long shadow of the Holocaust. While becoming close to other people in the struggle for justice, she never overcomes the loneliness of the secularized Jew separated from her past and her religion. In many ways, Paul sees more of his mother than his father in himself. Cowan again uses long sentences full of parallels to express in its form the multiple identities of his parents:

> I realize now that in many ways I was her child, more than my father's. I identified with her pain as much as I did with her principles. . . . She was the only girl in a male-dominated family—the only Jewish family in a gentile town; the daughter of a wealthy merchant, whose possessions may have been the principal reason her friends consented to play with her; the wallflower at the country club; the frightened Midwesterner in New York. . . . She had never really had a home in the first place. (95–96)

Thus, as Cowan concludes the long journey into his ancestors' world (chs. 2–5), Paul sees her as the loneliest orphan of them all. He admires her immensely as the inspirer of his own passion for justice, but comes to see after her death that "her secular messianism—the kind of Judaism that shaped her beliefs—was a lonely faith" (97). Paul concludes this passage with a series of images of the goal that he seeks on his voyage to discover the ultimate meaning of his directional model, Jacob Cohen. Here he finds in the positive metaphors in the lives of his parents some of the clues to his emerging theological values during his "voyage into the Jewish tradition"—cohesiveness, communality, tradition, and an historical identity (97). All these emerge as he learns to understand the rift between his father and his grandfather, and to heal the dividedness within his own psyche, a dividedness inherited from his even more divided parents. It is no accident, Cowan suggests by placing them at the end of his autobiography, that the prophetic lines his daughter reads at her bat mitzvah are a foreshadowing of the healing of this generational rift:

> *Lo, I will send the prophet Elijah to you before the coming of the fearful day of the Lord. He shall reconcile fathers with children and children with their fathers so that, when I come, I do not strike the whole land with utter destruction.* (246)

MEDIATORS AS NEW FATHERS

The person who calls Paul's attention to this passage from the prophet Malachi is Rabbi Wolfe Kelman, the erudite conservative leader who assisted the Cowan family in their final steps back from orphanhood to communal traditional practice. But he is only the third of three rabbis who appear in the last half of the autobiography as "new fathers" to guide Paul on his spiritual adventure. Just as he had resisted his father's advice about his career out of a feeling of being "overshadowed by him" and out of a need "to remain my own person" (101), so Paul has to find his own new fathers in his search for his Jewish identity.

Although Paul followed the example of a more Orthodox Jewish classmate, Joel Cassel, to resist briefly the anti-Semitism and assimilationist forces at Choate, he graduates from high school feeling like "a prototypical defenseless Jew" (13). This passivity about his amputated Jewish identity continues at Harvard, where his interest in studies wanes as he struggles for a deeper sense of his self. Paradoxically, it is that most fully assimilated of Jewish writers, Norman Mailer, who has what Cowan calls "an enormous influence" on him at Harvard. In particular, a short story, "The Time of Her Time," awakens Paul to the groundless self beneath his passive behavior. As he describes his response to the story: "I identified with Arthur in a very frightened way. . . . Passive Jews. Jews who don't fight back. Womanly men who can't make love as well as manly gentiles. Who are paralyzed with self-doubt and fear. Who go to gas chambers passively. Passive. That was the word that defined me. I had to change somehow" (104)

The mediation of Mailer leads Cowan to seek his identity by working for a year in Israel in 1961. Here the twenty-one-year-old Harvard drop-out experiences what he calls "an explosion" in his "consciousness" that gives him a new name—Saul Cohen—and a new pride as a Jew among Jews who "possessed a past they could use, a present they had created, a future they were building" (104–105). But the increase in pride also deepens the fissure in his identity, for he cannot imagine himself possessing the deep sense of a specific place and culture he sees among the Israeli people. Moreover, he gradually discovers that the younger Israelis experience a similar gap between their old world parents and themselves, or between the Orthodox and secular movements in the new nation. Although Paul overcomes his social passivity, he returns to the United States without having healed the rifts in his spiritual orphanhood.

Another mediator in his search for an integrated identity is Herman Wouk, whose novel *Marjorie Morningstar* awakens Cowan to his ambivalence about Jewish women. Afraid of marrying a woman like the apparently liberating but eventually dominating Shirley of the Wouk novel, Cowan admits that he stopped dating Jewish girls because of "fear that Jewish women would imprison" him (112). Instead, he begins searching, as he realizes later, for "a woman who would help me achieve my American dream and explore my Judaism" (113). He soon meets a Protestant woman with a Jewish name—Rachel Brown—whom he marries in 1965. To his surprise, she becomes a fellow "spiritual seeker," first during the search for "answers through politics" in the civil rights movement and the Peace Corps of the 1960s (117), and later through her interest in and eventual conversion to Jewish observances in the 1970s. It is she who articulates for Paul what he has been seeking all along: "I have always been proud to be a Yankee from New England. Now I'm proud to be a Jew" (224).

The most unexpected mediator of Cowan's eventual conversion to practicing Judaism is Father Daniel Berrigan. After the exhilarating 1960s work of tutoring and voter registration in Maryland and Mississippi had given way to the disillusionment of the racial conflicts and to Peace Corps frustrations of the 1970s, Paul and Rachel feel the impotence of their "secular creed" (118) leading to "a mood of angry despair" (133) within the movement and within themselves. Paul feels a new dividedness in his psyche as he comes to full circle on the downward spiral of his journey. As he bluntly pictures himself in 1968:

> I felt as if I had come full circle in a very few years. Just as I'd wanted to leave the Peace Corps that antagonized the Latins it was supposed to help, now I wanted to leave the part of the New Left that antagonized a substantial number of the Americans it was trying to reach. I wanted to keep opposing the war and fighting for social justice, of course, but from within a cohesive community, a spiritual home that offered the qualities of humanity and compassion—and the concrete ways to be useful—that had attracted me to the movement in the first place. (Cowan 138)

The person who propels him out of the circle and sends him back to his spiritual roots is Berrigan, the radical Jesuit priest whom he is unexpectedly asked to interview for the *Village Voice*. Berrigan startles Cowan by attributing his resistance to violence and his commitment to peace to "his own unabashed belief in God" (139), a confession that inspires Cowan to "question the atheism [he had] taken for granted ever since [he] left Choate" (140). As he continues to cover the Catholic radicals in the early 1970s, he is driven to examine his Judaism more closely. As he describes himself at this point, "I wanted to understand my roots, Jewish roots—to pursue the feelings that had awakened when I was in Israel, that slumbered during the years when the movement seemed like my spiritual home. But I still had to justify that feeling on political terms . . . by deciding to explore the Lower East Side of New York: to find the forces in my culture that had spawned generation after generation of socialist thinkers and organizers" (143).

In recovering this "buried past," Cowan uncovers and follows the three rabbis who replace his rabbinic great-great-grandfather. Each of these three teaches him about the tradition from which he had been orphaned. The first, Orthodox Rabbi Joel Price, introduces him to the Jewish poor of the Lower East Side, where he learns how secularism among successful Jews has alienated them not only from their religious identity but even from their fellow poor relations. Through a series of portraits (which appear in his *Village Voice* articles of this period), Cowan gives living flesh to the faith he is seeking—the poor but proud Moishe Kimmel, the rituals on Holidays at the schul, the plight of Rebecca Schwartz, all "part of a generation that was still lost in the desert" (154). Theologically, Cowan learns from Rabbi Price and his people the religious importance of *memory*. As he sums up his insights from this mediator: "There is no liberation without the memory of liberation, or the memory of oppression. . . . That precious feature of their religion—my religion—was entirely absent from the politics that had been my faith for nearly a decade" (152). Awakening to the similarity between these poor Jews on the Lower East Side and his father and grandfather's lost religious models, Cowan ends this journey into the past in the present of local Jewish poverty in his own city with the desire to "do a little to heal some of the rifts that had multiplied through a generation" (157). This desire was also, he recognizes, "one way of healing the rift between my father and my grandfather."

As a result of his awakening by Rabbi Price, Cowan and his wife begin teaching themselves and their children about Judaism. But their interest is still secular, an interest in Judaism as what Cowan calls a "rooted culture" with "the stability of religion, families, ceremonies" (158). Even after starting a Jewish weekly school for the neighborhood children, Cowan realizes that he is attempting "to teach tradition without teaching religion" (164). And the prospect of a religious conversion awakens in him and his friends the fear of a new split between their Jewishness and their assimilated American selves, between their private religious lives and their public careers. Even the beginning of a weekly ritual of lighting Shabbos candles on Friday nights begins to interfere with his journalistic career. Only after an assignment in Portugal where he meets Jewish *conversos* does Cowan decide that he must follow his father and cease being an "American style converso" (172).

Only in Part Three of the autobiography, which describes the years after his parents' death in 1976, does Cowan introduce the primary mediator in his religious conversion, Rabbi Joseph Singer, a tenth-generation descendant of a brother-in-law of Baal Shem Tov, the founder of the Hasidic movement. The secret of his mediation is not his teaching on the strict observance of the Talmud, which Cowan respects but does not follow, but his "spiritual power" and the "contagious joy" of his faith (177). Even though he is the "most important teacher" Cowan experiences outside his family, Singer teaches not so much theology as a lived faith, in particular the interdependent importance of ritual and care for the poor. For he seems to Cowan to be half-rabbi and half–social worker, uniting in his person the twin desire of Cowan himself for the faith of his grandfather and the passion for justice of his mother. In fact, although he can explain his faith in theological terms to Paul and Rachel, Singer explicitly avoids reducing the grounds for his practice to a "rationalized" theology. He remains a man of the word of God revealed in the Bible and explained by its Orthodox commentators. His primary justification of his faith and the Hasidic tradition is through telling his own

autobiography (183ff.), through performing the Passover ritual
with a mixture of adaptability and devotion (187ff.), and through
a hundred practical *mitzvahs* caring for the "troubles" of his poor
congregation (178ff.). Through these means, Singer gives back to
Cowan a way to integrate his "dual identity" as American Paul
and Jewish Saul. Singer, too, had experienced the severing of his
roots in Poland and now experiences the similar severing of roots
within his Jewish neighborhood and families. In his person, he is
a living balm to heal those rifts. But he is not out to proselytize
Paul to become an Hasidic Jew.

The final new "father" for Paul is a conservative rabbi, Wolfe
Kelman, who does not convert him but helps him discover and
create the new "home" Paul seeks, one where he can unite the
religious faith of Singer's world with the American pluralism of
his father's world. With the help of Kelman, Cowan gradually
takes on the Jewish prayer observances, the Shabbos, and even
the use of his grandfather's tefflin. Finally, after much struggle
and planning, Paul and Rachel revive a local synagogue which
combines in a primarily "conservative" form Jewish practices
with American equality, learning of theology with service of the
poor. Here they create what seems to be an impossible integration
of what Cowan calls "both a community center and a new sort
of pluralistic religious institution, a display case of faith, where
each kind of group . . . would pray in its own way" (217). Cowan
calls this effort one step in an old Hebrew tradition (*tikkun olam*)—
"repairing the world" (217). The climax of Rabbi Kelman's mediation comes, first, when he guides Rachel through her
conversion ceremony, which concludes with her reading of the
Torah, and, finally, when he leads the bat mitzvah of young Lisa
Cowan. Throughout Part III, the reader also comes to see that
Paul's recovery of his identity is also mediated by his wife and
daughter. His very family mediates his recovery from orphanhood
to community within his American family and his history.

TWISTS IN THE JEWISH SPIRAL: THE SEQUENCE OF CONVERSION

What appears most conspicuously absent from Cowan's spiritual
autobiography is the name of God. Cowan's mediators, unlike

those in the life stories of Augustine, Merton, or Lewis, do not lead him to a new notion of God or through theological debates. The "dialectic" of Cowan's pilgrimage fluctuates not between concepts but between persons, practices, and, most important, historical rifts. His earliest conversion, during his visit to Israel, is not religious or intellectual, but primarily psychological. He gains a valid pride in his Jewishness, not as a faith or philosophy but as an historical and emotional identity. Perhaps one could see this change as a moral transformation, a movement to a personal sense of power to act, both for himself and for others. He gives as his only example of this new sense of power an incident in which he stood up for a woman against her pimp who wanted her to strip in public in an Israel tavern. After this "conversion" from passive self-suffering Jew to proud activist American Jew concerned for others, Cowan undergoes what I see as three major conversions: first, a political–moral conversion to commitment to the rights of others (1960s); second, a political-religious conversion to the need for faith as a sustaining power for long-term social change (1970); third, a gradual religious conversion from merely Jewish "tradition" to Jewish "practices" and then to a final sense of shared family faith, which he comes to see is related to a wider ecumenical experience in the modern world (1980).

The political–moral conversion, Cowan sees as typical of the "spiritual seekers" of his generation, all persons who "believed . . . that we could find most of our answers through politics" (116). Mediators for this conversion were his mother, with her haunted memories of the Holocaust, and Cowan's "idol of the sixties," Bob Moses, the chief organizer of Student Non-Violent Coordinating Committee (SNCC) in Mississippi whose non-violent interracial leadership inspired the early years of the civil rights movement. Cowan's faith in merely political action begins to waver when Moses, Stokely Carmichael, and others shift the emphasis toward "black power" and confrontation, thus engaging the media but losing the cooperation of many students and local southern blacks. Cowan's political faith sinks to unbelief and "angry despair" after his two years of Peace Corps work with his wife in Peru end in a wave of anti-Americanism. As Cowan sums up his feelings of 1967: "I began to think of my country as the God that failed" (133).

This loss of an idol leads to Cowan's political religious conversion, occasioned by his contact with Dan Berrigan and the Catholic peace movement, a conversion, like that of Day or Gandhi, to a realization of the need for a spiritual ground for long-term radical social change. But because Cowan does not share the faith of the Catholic left, he is driven back to the Jewish "culture that had spawned generation after generation of socialist thinkers and organizers" (143)—a source that leads him to his "buried past" in religious Judaism. Eventually, as he recovers this faith, he sees how he can integrate it with his political-moral convictions:

> Rabbi Singer's campaign on behalf of the dead and their survivors . . . gave me [a] microscopic view of the interdependence between text and tradition which was, I believed, the religious foundation for the ethical quality of Judaism that had been so important to my family. That discovery of that Jewish source for my political ideas answered one of the questions that had sent me from Harrisburg to the Lower East Side, from the Catholic left to the Jews without money, some five years earlier. (192)

Cowan's eventual religious conversion, as I have noted, occupies most of Part III of the autobiography. What is most surprising in the stages of this final conversion is the lack of a sharp turning point. Unlike Augustine in the garden or Lewis on the bus ride, Cowan cannot point to a moment of epiphany when he moved from unbelief to belief. Instead, he recounts the slow process of his journalistic immersion in the Hasidic community, the gradual and tentative recovery of Jewish family customs, and the creation of a school and a place of worship—all begun for motives of tradition and only later lived for motives of faith. Using the language of the 1970s, Cowan describes himself as a "newcomer who decides to become part of [Judaism] slowly, one mitzvah at a time, in order to transform himself without losing himself" (206). His greatest tension lies between the demands of authoritative Orthodox Judaism, embodied in his mentor Rabbi Singer, and the demands of the best in American democracy, particularly the doctrine of equality, embodied in his parents. He desires to be both Jacob Cohen and Louis G. Cowan. The resolution occurs through his family's option for a conservative conversion for Rachel and a conservative bat mitzvah for daughter Lisa. In many ways, this "family conversion" proves ironic, as Cowan admits, for his wife severs herself from her past at the very time Paul is healing the severance of his own past. Likewise, he fears that his pressure on his daughter to accept her bat mitzvah may be a recurrence of his father's pressure on him to succeed in an assimilated Jewish life.

In the very style of the final pages of his life story, Cowan expresses the resolution of the tensions that his family conversion meant for him. As his daughter is reading her Haftorah ("I will make your government be peace / And righteousness your magistrate"), Cowan reflects: "Those words made me think of my mother. For what was her Judaism but an effort to embody Isaiah's prophecy . . . in her own actions. . . . Nothing could dilute my pride in those ethics. Only I wanted to convey them to my children, and my children's children, through the substance of Judaism, not the memory of oppression. I wanted those values to come from the joyous voice of the spirit, not the painful throbbing of the conscience" (244).

"I ALWAYS DEALT WITH TUMULTUOUS FEELINGS THROUGH WRITING"

It is no coincidence that Cowan's best writing occurs primarily at peak moments when he is describing the build-up and release of tension in his circular journey as a "wandering Jew." For as a journalist and a Jew—a man of words and of the Word—he resolves the conflicts and heals the rifts of his life by transforming them into a life story. After each of the conversions I have noted, Cowan—like Lewis, Merton, Day, and Gandhi—wrote essays and then narratives of his experience of transformation. His political–moral transformation appears first in articles about civil rights or the Peace Corps in the *Village Voice*, then later, once the conversion leads to despair, in the autobiographical *The Making of an Un-American* in 1972. His political-religious conversion appears in his articles on the Catholic peace movement. Eventually, his religious journey into his past begins with an article about Jewish poverty in New York; then, prompted by his father's last request, he embodies his search in articles on the lost Jewish craftsmen of

the Lower East Side, on Rabbi Singer, and on the Hasidic community of New York. As Cowan describes his method of writing,
"I'd always dealt with tumultuous feelings by writing" (175). Like
his mother, never a person of vivid emotional expression, he nevertheless releases his grief over his parents' painful death by writing about what his father most desired him to write—his lost
Jewish tradition. As a journalist, he begins his investigation with
a lack of commitment but in the writing finds himself believing.
In his writing, he comes to see himself becoming not merely an
idiosyncratic teller of a strange tale but also an exemplum for his
entire rootless generation of Americans of all traditions. He sees
his story as doing "a little to heal some of the rifts that had multiplied through a generation" (157). He longs to be the James Agee
and Chaim Potok of his era (3). Later, seeing his story as parallel
to the stories of alienated Italians, Scandinavians, or Latin Americans in the United States, he frames his autobiography with a
foreword that ends, "I hope the story of my search will help other
orphans in history find their way home" (x).

   In his avoidance of theological content and any revelation of
his inner spiritual life, Cowan, unlike Merton, feels safe in expos-
ing his deeper self only by recounting his response to the ritual
of his daughter's bat mitzvah, thus ending his autobiography in
Talmudic fashion by responding to the words of the prophets.
One passage from Isaiah removes all his worries about his daughter's future and makes him think of his mother. The next passage
strikes him as "a revelation"—a revelation of the fact that his
"days of mourning had ended" and he is now "free to possess the
spiritual land which had seemed so alien for so long" (244). As a
writer and believer, he finds that his final words on his life story
are overpowered by the words of Scripture. Like Merton and
others, he ends his account of his circular journey by recovering
his directional image of himself and recalling the stages of his
journey:

   I was on a lifelong journey to find faith; a journey through the land
   of the ancients; through Beersheba's shantytowns, built on the
   caves which Abraham inhabited; through the pawnshops of Chicago's ghettos; through the courtyard, shuls, and restaurants of the
   Lower East Side, the places that could have been Jake Cohen's
   haunts; through Rabbi Singer's New York, where Weiderman, the

tallis maker and Eisenbach, the scribe, could have been Rabbi Jacob
Cohen's neighbors in Lidinova. Now as I sat in our synagogue, I
realized I was no longer an orphan in time, but a wandering Jew
who had come home.

REFERENCES

Cowan, Paul. *An Orphan in History.* New York: Doubleday, 1982.
Valentine, Dean. Review of *An Orphan in History. Nation* 236
(Jan. 29, 1983): 117–19.
Wisse, Ruth R. Review of *An Orphan in History. Commentary* 75
(Feb., 1983): 70–74.

8

I, Rigoberta Menchú:
The Plotting of Liberation

READERS OF *I, Rigoberta Menchú* have been fascinated by the naïve intensity of the young Guatemalan woman's faith and perseverence in the face of atrocities that destroyed her Indian family. But her storytelling, first audiotaped and then rearranged by Elizabeth Burgos-Debray, seems awkward and confusing. As an autobiography, it is clogged with extensive details of her tribal Quiché life and with repetitive expressions of her feelings. Like Neihardt's structural framing of Black Elk's story, Burgos-Debray's version of Rigoberta Menchú's life calls out for redaction and interpretation. While not excusing the obvious repetitions and ideological slanting of the editing, I find that the plot of the text makes greater sense if read as a product of three forces not entirely within Menchú's control: modern autobiographical traditions, anthropological methods interpolated within its plot, and liberation theology. These three influences were undoubtedly more consciously within the control of the editor than of the narrator. Burgos-Debray used them to filter the transcribed monologues into a text about Rigoberta Menchú's birth of socioreligious consciousness. The resulting text contains numerous historical gaps, inaccuracies, and coalescences that further its political purposes (Stoll, *Rigoberta*). But the uniqueness of this testimonial in relationship to its three sources makes it what some critics have called a new form of oral-to-written literature (Beverley, "Margin").

I, RIGOBERTA MENCHÚ AS A MODERN
RELIGIOUS AUTOBIOGRAPHY

As this entire study of twentieth-century spiritual autobiography shows, modern storytellers of the self base their autobiography on a dynamic directional image. This rather untutored Guatemalan peasant is no exception. She writes as an unofficial witness to her growth from a naïve victim to a socially conscious religious activist. As the Spanish subtitle explicitly announces, this is an autobiography of Latin American native consciencization, told "from below." The first lines of the story indicate her status as a person giving testimony for a whole people:

> My name is Rigoberta Menchú. I am twenty three years old. This is my testimony. I didn't learn it from a book and I didn't learn it alone. I'd like to stress that it's not only *my* life, it's also the testimony of my people. . . . My story is the story of all poor Guatemalans. My personal experience is the reality of a whole people. (1)

Both Rigoberta Menchú and her native village in Quiché begin their journey into consciousness as passive, childlike victims of an oligarchical social system, with power held by *ladino* landowners, government officials, and the Guatemalan army. As Menchú tells her story in the framework of tribal and personal testimony, she and her people transform their self-image from that of passive traditionalists to that of active revolutionaries. This image, of course, is present from the start in the title, words, and narrative structure of the autobiography, present as an image created from her final standpoint as a committed Catholic and native liberationist (Beverley, "Margin" 96ff.).

Like other modern autobiographers, Menchú finds the seeds of her developing consciousness in the lives and words of her parents, who precede her in their own labor of consciencization, even to the point of martyrdom. From her father, an orphan who was "given away" by his mother to be a servant to a *ladino* employer, Menchú learned how to cope with life. As he tells her, " 'you must do what I do' " (31). As his favorite and most intelligent child, she imitated her father's early initiative, his steady work habits, his ability to fight, and his political strategies (ch. 26). But beneath these personal qualities, she built her character on his love of native traditions and his Catholic faith (81). On a long work expedition with him, Rigoberta recalls his lesson: "During the journey my father told us all about the marvellous things there were in our land (and thinking of our ancestors of course), and the closeness of the peasant to nature. . . . He dis-

cussed everything with me. When we went off to work, for instance, he'd have a conversation with me just as if he were talking
to a neighbour" (191, 193). Her father treated her as an adult
from her early years, giving her work to do with him and explaining the customs of their ancestors. Most of all, he helped her
overcome her timidity and fear of life, especially by defending her
and choosing her to speak at public meetings (194).

From her mother, she derived her love of nature and tradition
as well as the need not only to understand but also to challenge
the limits of women's roles in the villages and tribes of northern
Guatemala. Her mother talked to her encouragingly, even when
Rigoberta was a child in her womb, and said to her, " 'You must
never abuse nature and you must live your life as honestly as I
do' " (8) She later taught her to express her feelings and not to
avoid painful emotional scenes which her father and other men
could not face, especially the burial of the dead. In their mountain
village, her mother's duties included growing and fixing food,
accounting, health care, education, and introducing Rigoberta
and her brothers and sisters to their responsibilities. Each year,
when the family went down from the mountains to the coastal
plantations, or fincas, her mother taught her how to work hard in
picking coffee, cotton, and sugar cane. Most important, her
mother taught her the customs and values of her people—
marriage preparation, family living, tribal solidarity, sowing and
harvesting, predicting the weather, and the rules of gift-giving.
However, her mother's growth in social awareness was perhaps
her greatest legacy to Rigoberta. She taught her daughter how to
deal with machismo within a marriage and with other limits of
traditional women's roles in the village. She passed on the secrets
of communication within the emotional patterns of a native marriage, and the ways to deal with male anger. Also, Rigoberta
learned from her mother's practice how to become politically active: "My mother couldn't express her views about political
things; but she was very politicized through her work and
thought that we should learn to be women, but women who
were useful to the community" (218). This political involvement
of her mother came from her sense of the equality between men
and women, hidden beneath some quite unequal responsibilities.
Rigoberta considered her mother to be the stronger of her parents

in facing suffering in their lives (219). Her mother's greater courage in facing death inspired Rigoberta in her own encounters
with loss and death.

Whereas Dorothy Day first experienced death by viewing the
bodies of children drowned in an urban backwash in Chicago,
Rigoberta Menchú first confronted death when she lost her
younger brother to malnutrition and a close friend to spray poisoning in the coffee fields—victims alike of the hazardous life on
the plantations. Because her brother's burial interfered with the
family's work for two days, they lost both their jobs and their
back pay, events that made the child Rigoberta "mad with grief"
(89). As she describes the consequent feelings: "I was both angry
with life and afraid of it, because I told myself: 'This is the life I
will lead too; having many children, and having them die.' . . . I
was afraid of life and I'd ask myself: 'What will it be like when
I'm older'" (41, 88). Her most traumatic encounter with loss
came, of course, at the death of her father by fire during the
takeover of the Spanish embassy in Guatemala City in 1980 (ch.
25), and at the torture and execution of her mother as a "subver-
sive" by the army a few months later. Both these deaths led Rigoberta Menchú not into despair but into a hardening of her
resolve to resist. In fact, she had been prepared for these losses by
the kidnapping and slaughter of her sixteen-year-old brother by
the army in 1979, an event she describes in grotesquely realistic
detail (174).

The loss of these three—her brother, father, and mother—was
also the loss of Rigoberta's primary mediators in her spiritual and
political journey to consciousness. Her father had mediated her
knowledge of the world of political leadership and resistance in
the village; her mother had mediated her understanding of the
world of family, work, and native customs. Her brother was her
closest witness to the life of active resistance in her own age
group. Besides these family mediators, she refers to priests, sisters,
and village leaders (unnamed perhaps because of the political need
for secrecy) who taught her Christianity and mountain resistance.
The Christianity that she learned was a mixture of ancient piety
and an energetic form of Catholic teaching, worship, and practice
that transformed while inculturating their lives as native peoples.
Beneath her Catholic faith and work as a catechist, Menchú re-

veals some of the secrets of her native religion. But she gives only the vaguest description of the political movements that made up the heart of the Guatemalan resistance, leaving the reader with the impression that her brothers and sisters joined the guerrillas while she remained within a political but nonmilitary branch of the resistance movements.

One other trait of modern religious autobiography—its use of writing as a means of grace—was lacking to Menchú in her oral culture, but her desire to learn to speak and read Spanish turns out to be a recurring motif of her story, one that drives her to a higher level of social awareness and to independence from her father. Like Malcolm X, she is a person of the spoken word, a catechist and resistance instructor. Here the reader finds the same mixture of disclosure and secrecy concerning her steps in learning and using Spanish, the language of her people's oppressors (Sommer). As we shall see, her story is told in Spanish but contains far more gaps than are found in the other religious autobiographies of the century. These gaps arise not only from the native tradition of secrecy and the political desire to protect her fellow resisters, but also from the two extrinsic influences on her autobiography: its attempt to use anthropological models and its underlying doctrines from liberation theology.

I, Rigoberta Menchú: The Cultural Autobiography

As Alex Haley did with Malcolm X in the sections of his autobiography that explain the Nation of Islam, Burgos-Debray has Menchú weave into her personal story several chapters of "culture stories" to introduce the reader to the context of Quiché native customs. Since these are described in the mode of ideal models, these chapters not only slow up the story and break the authorial illusion, but also tend to romanticize village life (Stoll). After the personal story of her family and infancy in Chapter 1, Menchú breaks the autobiographical testimony to describe the birth and early childhood ceremonies of the native and Catholic traditions in Guatemala (ch. 2). For instance, she describes the typical responsibilities of family members: "The eldest son is responsible for the house. Whatever the father cannot correct is up to the eldest son to correct. . . . The mother is the one who is responsible for keeping an account of what the family eats, and what she has to buy. . . . And each one of us, as we grow up, has our own small area of responsibility" (16). She then explains the *nahual*, a sort of animal double for each person that is revealed to the individual only in adulthood (ch. 3). In chapter 4, she recounts the family work on the coastal plantations by giving a mixture of personal reminiscences and a description of typical work patterns. With most of chapters 2 through 5 as idealized background, Menchú returns to her personal story in Chapters 6 to 8, only to stop the narration for four chapters with idealized descriptions of planting and harvesting ceremonies, which show the communal solidarity of the villagers (ch. 9). This leads into a brief description of the nature-based ceremonies of the village:

> The prayers and ceremonies are for the whole community. We pray to our ancestors, reciting their prayers which have been known to us for a long time—a very, very long time. We evoke the representatives of the animal world; we say the names of dogs. We say the names of the earth, the God of the earth, and the God of water. Then we say the name of the heart of the sky—the Sun. . . . The sun, as the channel to the one God, receives the plea from his children that they should never violate the rights of all the other beings which surround them. (58)

This portrait of the village seen in a timeless anthropological model of peacetime is completed by a long exposition of the four stages of courtship and marriage (ch. 11). In one of the most important stages, in a ceremony similar to Black Muslim indoctrination tales, the Quiché couple learn the history of the oppression by the White Man. Here the elders say, " 'Who is to blame for all this? The White Man who came to our country. We must not trust them, white men are all thieves. We must keep our secrets from them' " (69). Chapter 12, although it begins with a personal narrative, soon lapses into a long description of the Catholic life of the village, the gender divisions in children's games, and the weekly rhythms of prayer, work, and village meetings. The use of these ideal models creates a tension in Menchú's story similar to that in Black Elk's—a tension between the static ideal forms of a traditional society and the changing realistic forms of her modern personal autobiography. In the traditional society, the form of a circle is relatively unchanging (an "eternal return," in Mircea Eliade's terms), whereas in her modern personal story, the circle becomes a moving spiral of individual conflict within a changing historical movement. When the personal autobiography returns as the dominant form in chapters 12 to 34, Menchú occasionally pauses in her accounts of her experience to give further contextual details or explanations. However, the contrast between the idealized form of village life given in her naïve anthropological descriptions and the brutally realistic accounts of her life as a maid in Guatemala City or as a farm worker in the *fincas* serves one of the ideological purposes behind the text. The tension betwen the idealized past native life and the actual present oppression by the government serves a further purpose, one more congenial to Menchú herself: to provide a concrete basis for the reflections of liberation theology.

I, RIGOBERTA MENCHÚ: ITS LIBERATION THEOLOGY SUBTEXT

Liberation theology is a mixture of social and theological movements that began in Latin America in the 1960s. What is distinctive about this socioreligious intellectual movement is its use of concrete social situations of oppression as the context for theological reflection by the local community. Unlike traditional theology, which began with reflection on Scripture, worship, tradition, or previous Christian experience, liberation theology takes its first step by describing the conflictual situation in the present day on the local level. In Rigoberta Menchú's case, the focus was on the unjust labor on the plantations, on the government takeover of the land, and on the aggression against the natives of the *Altiplano* in the 1970s. The second step for the liberation theologian is to find biblical and theological teachings that speak to these concrete situations, especially the doctrines of the social effects of sin, the ethical option for the poor by Christ and the Church, the presence of grace in the midst of secular needs, and a spirituality based on human solidarity (Boff, Gutiérrez, Segundo, Sobrino, Berryman, Haight). The main role of the Church for the liberation theologian is its mission to the world, especially the world of marginal people, and its responsibility to "build the kingdom of God" through calling for more just social and political structures. One of the most effective methods for liberation theology to inspire social change has been through the creation of "basic ecclesial communities," which consist of small groups of poor people who meet regularly for prayer, social analysis, Scripture reading and application. Liberation theology has extended itself beyond Latin America since the 1960s. Liberation theology, as one theologian describes it, "is an attempt to interpret Christian doctrine in a way that is responsible to the universal problem of human suffering, which is especially manifest in the social oppression of today's world. It draws together in a new way theology and the social teachings of the church by providing the social ethics with theology and doctrinal grounding. And by uniting theology, ethics, and spirituality, it provides answers to fundamental questions of why one chooses to be a Christian in the modern world" (Haight 276).

Even this brief overview of liberation theology suggests why it was important for Rigoberta Menchú when she "chooses to be a Christian in the modern world," and how essential it was to the narrative structure of her autobiography. When her long introductory descriptions of the ideal native village life contrast dramatically with the personal story of the pain of her work and family struggles, this conflict provides an opening for theological reflection. The liberation theologian sees these conflicts not merely as challenges to personal growth but also as rooted in unjust social structures (the division between the rich and the poor, the lack of land reform, racial conflicts, etc.). In response to the conflicts, the autobiographer of liberation theology applies theological and biblical teachings to illuminate the situation and motivate the reader. Both biblical passages and Church social teachings portray the kingdom of God as calling for a more just society on earth. The use of force as self-defense is given some legitimation from selective reading of the Old Testament (ch. 18). The concern of Jesus for the poor as lived out in his life serves as a model urging the villagers to take responsibility for their situation. Beneath all these doctrines is the belief that God's grace guides people in their struggles for justice in personal, family, and societal life. When people in Menchú's village reflect on the injustice of their situation, they are deeply moved and authorized by Scripture, Church teaching, and clerical and lay leadership to take a stand against the oppression.

For liberation thinkers, a central term and goal is consciencization—the development in awareness by oppressed peoples, first, of the injustice of their situation, and second, of the moral power and duty to work toward a more just society. My contention, as I have already noted in describing Menchú's self-image as witness to growth in awareness, is that the plot structure of her autobiography derives from liberation theology's pattern of consciencization.

The Circular Journey of Consciousness-Raising in *I, Rigoberta Menchú*

Consciencization normally takes two steps: the first, toward an awareness of the systemic problem; the second, toward strategies to change the system. Although these steps are seen by political theorists as stages on a linear path, I will show how they become parts of a circular journey upward. Menchú's first account of the childhood seeds of her consciousness-raising occurs when at age seven she gets lost in the mountains: ". . . they lost me for seven hours. I was crying, shouting, but no-one heard me. That was the first time I felt what it must be like to be an adult, I felt I had to be responsible, more like my brothers and sisters" (29). Here, at the age of reason, she first realizes that she must act for herself, but later acknowledges that her predicament of "being lost" was but a small symptom of the greater "lostness" arising from her family's poverty. Even when she is found again, she speaks primarily "of the anger I felt at the way we live" (29).

This minor episode prepares the reader for the many small steps in the circular movement upward into consciousness that Menchú takes from chapters 6 to 23 during the seven years leading up to the death of her parents. She recalls that at age five, "my consciousness was born" out of seeing her mother work herself to exhaustion on the plantations. However, Menchú herself could not earn money by picking coffee to help her family until she was eight years old. In the next chapter, Menchú grasps the full injustice of the plantation workers' situation when she and her family are fired without pay for taking time off to hold a small funeral for the youngest child who had died of inhaling pesticides on the *fincas*. Because the family cannot speak Spanish, they are cut off from asserting their rights to the plantation overseers. Menchu's reaction corresponds to her frustration: "From that moment, I was both angry with life and afraid of it. . . . I remember it with enormous hatred. That hatred has stayed with me until today" (41).

When she turns ten, she is formally initiated into the customs and responsibilities of adults in her village: "Suddenly they treated me like an adult. My father said, 'You have a lot of responsibility; you have many duties to fulfill in our community as an adult. From now on you must contribute to the common good' " (49). Here, for the first time, she consciously places the good of the village ahead of her own needs. Here, too, her early childhood consciencization ends, for her narrative pauses to recount her village's agricultural and social practices (chs. 9–12).

When Menchú is twelve, she begins to think, as she says, "like a responsible woman": "I joined the communal work; things like harvesting the maize. I worked together with the others. It was also then that I began making friends, closer friends, in the community. I began taking over my mother's role too" (79). At this point, she leaves behind her childhood faith to take on the task of spreading Catholic teaching as a catechist. In her description of this step, she emphasizes that her early Catholicism was an enrichment, not an abandonment of, her native culture: "By accepting the Catholic religion, we didn't accept a condition, or abandon our culture. It was more like another way of expressing ourselves. . . . We feel very Catholic because we believe in the Catholic religion but, at the same time, we feel very Indian, proud of our ancestors" (80–81). She also points out the social advantages of "the mixture of Catholicism and our own culture" (81) for the purpose of unifying the separated villages and tribes of the region (85). Because the priests visit the villages only every three months, Menchú as a catechist becomes a village leader. She teaches the doctrine, sets up various days of prayer and work, and establishes a rhythm to village life (86).

After Menchú has described her religious awakening, she gives an account of her first adult consciousness of the evil of the *finca* system. The catalyst that awakens her is the death from poisoning of her best friend. Her response, like Augustine's grief at the loss of his best friend and Day's anger at the injustice of the meatpacking plants in Chicago, leads to near despair: "I was afraid of life. . . . I was mad with grief" (88–89). Intuitively, however, she immediately leaps from this consciousness of evil to her first desire to learn Spanish, a skill that will help her learn more of liberation theology from the circuit-riding priests of the region and give her the skills needed to negotiate with the *ladinos* (89). Despite her father's objections that she may lose her culture, she persists in her longing for education and a second language. This struggle with her father is one of several interior conflicts within Menchú and within the resistance movement that make her autobiography more complex than some commentators have allowed (Beverley, "Real").

Menchú soon learns more than she anticipated. As she describes in chapter 14, she awakens to the racial prejudices and exploitation of Indian peoples in the cities. This awakening occurs when at age twelve she takes on a job as a housemaid to a rich *ladino* family in Guatemala City. Here, treated as "lower than the animals in the house" (92) by her mistress, Menchú learns how the rich look down on and degrade the Indians as quasi-slaves. Her narration of her abuse by the children and the mother of this family, of her future attempts to learn to satisfy their pleasures and flatter their whims, and of the excesses of the upper-class lifestyle in the city produces the most vivid storytelling of her autobiography. Here her consciencization expresses itself in pure narrative. She has moved from an early childhood circle of naïve village awareness to a later childhood circle of pain and death on the plantations to this early adolescent circle of social awareness of urban prejudice.

In chapter 15, Menchú abruptly interrupts her personal story of her growth in consciousness to recount the event that awakened her and her village to the systemic injustices of the land reform and the need for united resistance—the imprisonment of her father. Without mentioning any specific details (part of the secrecy of the resistance level of her story), she gives the reader a vague context for this imprisonment by telling of her father's "heroic struggle against the landowners," especially the Brol, the Martinez, and the Garcia families (103). Here also she recalls her earlier experience at age five of her father's resistance to being thrown out of the family house by agents of the landowners. At that earlier stage, she heard her father say, " 'We were the first families to come and cultivate this land and nobody can deceive us into thinking that this land is theirs. If they want to be the owners of more land, let them go and cultivate the mountain' " (106). Here her father had first planted the seeds of her political sensitivity to justice, but Rigoberta admits that "in those days we didn't have enough political clarity to unite with others and protest about our land" (107). It is only later, at the time of her father's imprisonment, that she and the village realize the need for unified regional resistence. When her father is arrested, the community learns not only how to work the system for a year to obtain his release, but also how to form an organization to resist the government—the Peasant Unity Committee (CUC). These efforts become more successful when her father is arrested a second time, held, and tortured. Here he learns from a fellow political prisoner how to organize against an entire system: "He said it wasn't our problem alone: our enemies weren't the landowners but the whole system" (115). These events also awaken Rigoberta herself to politics and to her need to learn the situations of Indian peoples throughout the *Altiplano*. She goes on to present what she learns at that time, a lesson phrased in liberation theology's language of class struggle and anthropological terms of cultural conflict:

> We began to understand that the root of all our problems was exploitation. . . . The fact that we were always waiting in offices, always bowing to the authorities, was part of the discrimination we Indians suffered. So was the cultural oppression which tries to divide us by taking away our traditions and prevents unity among our people. (118)

Menchú is shocked to learn of the degraded state of Indians in the minds of even the poorest *ladinos*, who tell her, " 'Yes, we're poor but we're not Indians' " (119).

Once Menchú and her village have reached this next circle of political consciousness, they face the choice of whether to use

force to resist the army sent by the government and the landowners. Although Menchú herself secretly becomes active in teaching
other children the need for political changes and in organizing
village groups of all sorts, she still feels herself only partially transformed: " 'I still hadn't reached the rewarding stage of participating fully, as an Indian first, then as a woman, a peasant, a
Christian, in the struggle of all my people' " (120). However, in
her desire for greater involvement in the revolutionary movements, she receives words of caution against the use of violence
from some of her religious teachers (121). Like Nelson Mandela,
she hesitates in her confusion but gradually makes use of the Bible
and her village's experience to justify the use of force in self-
defense. In fact, she spends two long chapters telling of this "painful change in herself and her village" (chs. 17–18). Supported by
her grandfather's story of their ancestors' resistance to the Spanish
conquerors and by the liberation theologians' methods of finding
biblical support for action, she describes the restructuring of the
village life to defend itself. Their biblical study included reading
the stories of Moses and Judith not as mere past events but, as
Menchú puts it, "to identify that reality with our own" (131). As
she sums up this new religious method of political discernment:

> We began studying more deeply and, well, we came to a conclu-
> sion. That being a Christian means thinking of our brothers around
> us, and that every one of our Indian race has the right to eat. This
> reflects what God himself said, that on this earth we have a right to
> what we need. . . . we realized that it is not God's will that we
> should live in suffering, that God did not give us that destiny, but
> that men on earth have imposed this suffering, poverty, misery and
> discrimination on us. We even got the idea of using our own every-
> day weapons, as the only solution left to us. (132)

Beneath this naïve summary of the method of reasoning within
liberation theological circles lay Menchú's faith in Christ as resur-
rected and present Liberator: "For me, as a Christian, there is one
important thing. That is the life of Christ . . . there was no other
way of defending himself or Christ would have used it against his
oppressors, against his enemies. He even gave his life. But Christ
did not die, because generations and generations have followed
him" (132–33). Although this simple testimony seems to over-

look the power of nonviolence that Gandhi found in Christ's
Sermon on the Mount and the power of Christ's death and resurrection, the testimony provides a justification for the use of some
degree of force in resistance to evil. Another conclusion Menchu
draws from her religious consciencization is also similar to that of
the liberation theologians—that "as Christians, we must create a
Church of the poor . . . as Christians, we have understood that
being a Christian means refusing to accept all the injustices which
are committed against our people." She concludes: " . . .we feel
it is the duty of Christians to create the kingdom of God on Earth
among our brothers" (133–34) With this new religious radicaliza-
tion, Menchú begins her dual role: to teach the methods of liberation theology in the base communities of the Indian village, and
to teach methods of physical self-defense (ch. 19). She describes
in great detail the capturing of soldiers and their reeducation by
the native peoples.

Menchú's consciousness-raising does not stop at political
awareness. After the brutal butchering of her friend Patrona
Chona at the hands of a lustful son of a landowner, Menchú becomes radicalized as a woman. When her father returns from
prison and a round of political activities in 1978, Rigoberta goes
with him to a farewell fiesta in which she is informally sent on a
mission to work throughout the *Altiplano* as a member of CUC.
In her travels, Menchú meets native peoples of various tribes and
languages, but also middle-class and poor *ladinos*. Like Malcolm
X learning to distinguish between a variety of characters in white
people, Menchú learns that many of the mixed-blood Guatemalans are poor and that some of the middle class sympathize and
work with the poor. She comes to admit her own prejudices
against *ladinos* and to open herself to persons of good will in all
classes and races (ch. 23).

As she enters into the mountain jungles to teach other villages,
Menchú's growth in consciousness becomes even more painful.
If chapters 1 to 12 are her account of her childhood "consciencization" within a relatively peaceful but unjust system, chapters 13
to 23 are her account of her adolescent awakening to a conflicted
situation of government war against its own people, especially the
native villages. Chapters 24 to 34, however, are her account of
the violent effects of class and cultural warfare by the government,

most directly on her own family and her villages, with particular vehemence against native women. Each of these sections is a circle within a spiral movement upward; each expands her consciousness and thus widens the circle; and each leads her from the static circle of a traditional village society to a spiraling movement of personal growth, historical change, and creation of new forms of social life.

In chapter 24, Menchú describes the torture of her activist brother in details traditionally reserved for the stories of Christian martyrs: "My brother was tortured for more than sixteen days. They cut off his fingernails, they cut off his fingers, they cut off his skin, they burned parts of his skin. Many of the wounds, the first ones, swelled and were infected. He stayed alive" (174). Finally, her brother and others are set on fire in front of their families. The burial only intensifies the desire of Rigoberta Menchú, her father, and her mother in their determination to resist. In chapter 25, she recounts the second martyrdom by fire in her family, that of her father during the occupation of the Spanish Embassy in Guatemala City in 1980. This public crushing of the largest protest by Indians and *ladinos* in Guatemalan history led to a major funeral and the further consciencization of Rigoberta. In chapter 26, she recalls her father's great influence on her and on the birth of native resistance in her country.

If these martyrdoms are not enough, the autobiography continues with a detailed sequence of the third and most painful atrocity, the slaughter of her mother. After a review of her mother's awakening to consciousness as a woman and as an Indian, Rigoberta tells how her mother was kidnapped, raped, tortured, and mutilated. After a brutally realistic account of her mother's death, Rigoberta reflects briefly on the meaning of death and dying for her culture. Traditionally, dying was a personal and communal event that everyone prepared for and participated in. The wake and burial ceremony united the entire village to assist the dying person on the final journey. Violent death at the hands of one's enemies, by contrast, shocks the native sensibility. As she says, "killing is something monstrous" (203). The killing of her brother, father, mother, and friend within a year angers Menchú but also radicalizes her determination to continue the resistance: "Our dedication to the struggle is a reaction against it [the killing], against all the suffering we endure" (203). She has learned to move from the circle of ritual to the circle of action for justice.

Menchú moves from reflection on her mother's death to three chapters on the status of women in Guatemala. She begins with an anthropological description of the fiesta, with particular emphasis on the annual selection of the town's Indian and *ladino* queens. She revolts against the commercialization of this event throughout Guatemala by the middle class and the government. In chapter 30, she elaborates on what her mother's lessons taught her about womanhood in Guatemala. As Rigoberta says, "My mother was a woman who already had a political vision and was already working in organizations before I knew anything" (218). This account of her mother leads Rigoberta to reflect on the ambiguous roles of women, not only in her native society, but within the resistance organizations themselves. She meets objections from macho village leaders and learns to use her personal power and authority to teach them respect for women. However, she rejects the notion of a separate women's resistance group which might only further split the already-fragmented revolutionaries (221–22). She then concludes her reflections by giving her reasons for living a celibate life for the cause of her people: "My idea is, though, that there will be time enough after our victory [for marriage]; but at the moment I wouldn't feel happy having a *compañero* and giving myself to him while so many of our people are not thinking of their own personal happiness and haven't a single moment to rest" (224–25).

Menchú concludes her autobiography as a "birth of conscience" with two major public events that lead to her status, at the time of the writing, as an exiled leader. The first event is the strike of 80,000 peasants in February 1980, and the second is the strike of the First of May, 1981. In these events, native peoples responded to an increase in repressions—more bombings, firing on houses, near-extermination of villages in the mountains. With support from the Catholic Church and from four guerrilla groups, the peasants' strike of 1980 leads to greater unity among the Indians and poor *ladinos*. On the First of May a year later, the resistance takes its demonstration to the cities:

> It was the most important action we've carried out in Guatemala.
> . . . Peasants, workers, and Christians undertook actions in the

capital and the interior . . . We set up barricades, threw 'propaganda bombs' and held lightning meetings . . . The First of May had arrived and we managed to do everything we wanted to do. The government and the factory owners had to give the workers the day off. . . . The important thing is that we were using all our resources. (232–33)

In these events, Ribogerta emphasizes the "incredible role of women." In recalling this first major political event which empowered women in Guatemala to participate in public protest, Menchú is telling the story of her own final stage of consciencization. As she concludes, "this gives us the courage to be steadfast in the struggle, in spite of the danger" (233). From these two successful events, Menchú and others form an organization in her father's memory: Vincente Menchú Revolutionary Christians. Despite her awareness of the split within the Church between what she calls the "Church of the rich" and the "Church of the poor," she is not discouraged, even by betrayals and weaknesses among the clergy. As a person of conscious political and religious faith, she is convinced of her vocation as a leader "practicing with the people the light of the Gospel" (246). As she concludes her story in exile, "I know that no-one can take my Christian faith away from me. . . . together we can build the people's Church, a true Church. . . . I chose this as my contribution to the people's war. . . . That is my cause" (246). After telling the story of her circular journey to full consciousness as a public witness for her people, Rigoberta Menchú reminds us at the end that she has kept the deep things secret—her native mysteries and the mystery of her religious faith.

REFERENCES

Berryman, Phillip. *Liberation Theology*. New York: Paulist, 1986.
Beverley, John. "The Margin at the Center: On *Testimonio* (Testimonial Narrative)." *De/Colonizing the Subject: The Politics of Gender in Women's Autobiography*. Minneapolis: U of Minnesota P, 1992. 91–114.
———. "The Real Thing (Our Rigoberta)." *Modern Language Quarterly* 57 (June 1996): 129–40.

Boff, Leonardo. *Jesus Christ Liberator: A Critical Christology for Our Time*. Trans. Patrick Hughes. Maryknoll, NY: Orbis, 1979.

Gutiérrez, Gustavo. *A Theology of Liberation*. Trans. Caridad Inda and John Eagleson. Maryknoll, NY: Orbis, 1973.

Haight, Roger. "Liberation Theology." *The New Dictionary of Theology*. Ed. Joseph Komanchak, Mary Collins, and Dermot A. Lane. Wilmington, DE: Glazier, 1987. 570–76.

Menchú, Rigoberta. *I, Rigoberta Menchú: An Indian Woman In Guatemala*. Trans. Ann Wright. Ed. Elizabeth Burgos-Debray. Verso, 1984.

Menchú, Rigoberta, with Dante Liano and Gianni Miará. *Crossing Borders*. New York: Verso, 1998.

Segundo, Juan Luis. *A Theology for Artisans of a New Humanity*. 5 vols. Trans. John Drury. Maryknoll, NY: Orbis, 1973–75.

Sobrino, Jon. *Christology at the Crossroads*. Trans. John Drury. Maryknoll, NY: Orbis, 1978.

Sommer, Doris. "No Secrets: Rigoberta's Guarded Truth," *Women's Studies* 20 (Oct. 1991): 51–72.

Stoll, David. "*I, Rigoberta Menchú* and Human Rights Reporting in Guatemala," a presentation at the Western Humanities Institute on "Political Correctness" and Cultural Studies. Berkeley, 20 Oct, 1990.

―――. *Rigoberta Menchú and the Story of All Poor Guatemalans*. Boulder, CO: Westview, 1999.

9
Dan Wakefield's *Returning*

ALTHOUGH PAUL COWAN'S AUTOBIOGRAPHY includes most of the patterns of twentieth-century spiritual autobiographies, his story has a distinctively different tone from that of Merton, Day, or Lewis. No longer dominated by the "Wasteland" and Depression periods between the world wars, Cowan's account takes for granted the post-1960s ruptures in Western society—the ongoing struggles for civil rights, the post-Vietnam distrust of military solutions, the alienation of youth, the exhaustion of the Cold War, the loosening of family ties and moral values, the assumptions of a large affluent middle class, and the pervasive reach of the media. Many of these traits are specific consequences of the religious alienation, political and social individualism, and personal need for self-appropriation and authenticity that I have noted as the context of modern religious autobiographies. In *An Orphan in History*, Cowan focuses less on the loss of God and more on the loss of traditional religious community. He assumes, rather than struggles for, a social consciousness and commitment to justice, needing primarily to learn how to integrate this public concern with his religious conversion. He ends his journey in a religious community compatible with his activist American values, for he fears severing himself from the political ideals of his mother's heritage. In the various levels of conversion, Cowan seems to follow no clear pattern, certainly not those stages apparent in Merton or Lewis. Finally, the end of Cowan's story leaves many strands— theological, practical, spiritual—to be tied together. How long will his loose confederation of conservative and reformed Jews last in their renovated temple? What sort of theology will he work out for himself? How will he relate his conversion to the Arab–Israeli struggles? What will he make of his wife's subsequent desire to study to become a rabbi?—these questions, like many in late twentieth-century religious lives, remain unresolved in his life story completed in 1982. Without being any less authentic, Cowan's conversion, along with many secular commitments of his generation, leaves itself open to unexpected developments. His death at forty-eight of leukemia within a decade of his recovery of Judaism cut short many of these potential developments.

Rigoberta Menchú's story also breaks the complacent reader out of too rigid an expectation of twentieth-century autobiography. Her situation as a native woman in Guatemala leads her to concentrate her story on the essentials of liberation—as a young person, an Indian, a woman, a victim, and a religious seeker. The violent deaths of her parents allowed her no time for a stage of wandering; her adolescence was a leap of faith into adulthood; her growth in consciousness was steadily toward liberation. In her conversion processes, the social and the political become intertwined with the psychological and the religious. Her position as a witness speaking "from below" to Europe and the United States from the jungles of Guatemala starkly challenges the privileges and power of her readers. With the success of peace talks in her country, Menchú's story now raises questions about the ability of liberation theology to move from resistance to reconstruction, from the use of force to the use of democratic procedures in an evolving post-colonial society. Written in her early twenties, *I, Rigoberta Menchú* calls, as Merton's *Seven Story Mountain* does, for a second volume to deal with her maturing inculturated faith as she and her people approach midlife in the mainstream (see Menchú, *Crossing*). To follow the path of an even more unexpected and open-ended convert, I turn to Dan Wakefield's *Returning: A Spiritual Journey*, published in its completed form in 1988, the year of Cowan's death and Menchú's fame. While manifesting the eight characteristics of other modern spiritual autobiographies, *Returning* holds these characteristics loosely within its structure. Its directional image is multiple rather than single. Its spiral journey begins at the moment of conversion, then circles back through the traditional three stages. Its portrayal of mediators and its autobiographical format indicate an explicit awareness of previous twentieth-century seekers of the ultimate (including mention of and influence from Merton, Day, and Cowan). Its psychological struggles are much more complex and self-conscious, painfully symptomatic of the therapeutic age. Its conversion sequence and confrontations with loss and death are surprisingly predictable. Its use of writing shows the mixed-media effects of the new journalism and the television and movie industries, thus making Wakefield's story seem livelier but more facile than those of his predecessors. The naïveté of the newly literate in Menchú gives way to the occasional slickness of the overly literate in Wakefield.

"Search for a Clean Well-lighted Place"

Unlike the other twentieth-century life stories, *Returning* opens in a cinematic fashion with a violent episode of stress that occurred just before Wakefield's year of conversion: "One balmy spring morning in Hollywood, a month or so before my forty-eighth birthday, I woke up screaming. I got out of bed, went into the next room, sat down on a couch, and screamed again" (3). Wakefield begins by mentioning a precise *place* of this low point in his life—Hollywood—and suggests the need for *light*: "This was not, in other words, one of those waking nightmares left over from sleep that is dispelled by the comforting light of day." These two images create the direction of his story: to find his *own place in the Light*. The rest of the opening chapter describes the two-year period from 1980 to 1982 during which he is transformed from alcoholic atheist in the darkness of exile in Hollywood to sober believer returning to the light of home in Boston. In the process of turning (and "returning"), he experiences moments of Lewis's "joy" as Wakefield "watched the sun go down and the lights come on in the towers downtown like golden signals" (9). His first tentative step back to religious practice occurs at Christmas in "candlelight service" at King's Chapel in downtown Boston (13). Even when his faith confronts darkness four years later, he learns about the deeper meaning of "light":

> Throughout all this [relapse into drugs] I never lost faith in God, never imagined He was not there, but only that His presence was obscured. Then the storm broke, like a fever, and I felt in touch again, and in the light. I was grateful, but I also knew that such storms of confusion and inner torment would come again, perhaps even more violently. (26)

At the time of this difficulty, Wakefield records a passage from an unlikely source that he came across in a chapel bookstore, Jean-

Pierre de Caussade, an eighteenth-century Jesuit spiritual writer:
" 'So we follow our wandering paths, and the very darkness acts
as our guide, and our doubts serve to reassure us' " (27). Wakefield's paradigm for this chapter on "returning" is that of the
Prodigal Son who finally "comes to himself" and seeks out the
place where he belongs—his home (18). Thus, both the image of
light and the meaning of place paradoxically reverse themselves
in the spiral of Wakefield's contemporary journey.

    This directional image of a *place of light* recurs throughout the
nine chapters of the second and third parts of his autobiography.
He titles the chapter on his childhood "The Light" in an effort
to recall the infancy memory of light from the Christmas lamp at
a moment when his family sings "In the dark streets shineth the
everlasting light" (31). Even more important, he centers this
chapter in the main religious experience of his childhood:

> On an ordinary school night I went to bed, turned out the light,
> said the Lord's prayer, as I always did and prepared to go to sleep. I
> lay there only a few moments, not long enough to go to sleep . . .
> when I had the sensation that my whole body was filled with light.
> It was a white light of such brightness and intensity that it seemed
> almost silver. It was neither hot nor cold, neither burning nor
> soothing, it was simply *there*, filling every part of my body from my
> head to my feet. . . . The light was the presence of Christ, and I
> was not simply in his presence, his presence was in me. (39–40)

Although this moment intensifies his childhood Protestant faith,
its effect fades along with his religious beliefs during late adolescence. At Columbia University in the 1950s (two decades after
Merton, but a student of some of Merton's teachers), Wakefield
uses William James's psychological theory of religion as an excuse
to "explain away," as he calls it, his youthful experience: "I had
simply experienced a hallucinatory or pseudo-hallucinatory experience called a photism" (118). But throughout his life, he continues to experience most of the *places* in his life story as either homes
of light or exiles of darkness—high school in Indianapolis, college
at Columbia, journalistic work in New York City, foreign correspondence in Israel, scriptwriting in Hollywood, an eventual
home in Boston. After his "returning" to faith, he finds that he
must make peace with his original place of searching, his hometown of Indianapolis. As he tells an audience there in 1985:

I was addressing my parents as well as the audience when I explained some of the deep feelings I had about this place and its people, feelings most brilliantly articulated by Eudora Welty in her essay, "Place in Fiction": "There may come to be new places in our lives that are second spiritual homes—closer to us in some ways, perhaps, than our original homes. But the home tie is the blood tie. And had it meant nothing to us, any other place thereafter would have meant less, and we would carry no compass inside ourselves to find home, ever, anywhere at all." (220)

As he matures after his conversion, Wakefield finds that he is at home not just in a physical place but in a home community, especially one that reaches out to make a place for others. In fact, he entitles his final full chapter "Family," even though it treats of both a community and a place. He also acknowledges the truth of Augustine's saying: " 'Do not plan long journeys because whatever you believe in you have already seen. When a thing is everywhere, the way to find it is not to travel but to love' " (245). Thus, he can finally acknowledge God's light in a multitude of persons and paths, but for Wakefield "the light is Christ, and it is not just a light as in 'sweetness and light' but an illumination of pain as well, and a force for understanding and bearing it. . . . The presence of Christ in pain as in joy reminded me again of the words of Psalm 139, 'the darkness and the light are both alike to thee' " (249).

THE ELLIPTICAL JOURNEY

Two brief sayings passed along by Wakefield's minister in Boston sum up the shape of the author's life story: "Faith is an elliptical journey" and "God is an earthquake, not an uncle" (241, 243). The image of an ellipse indicates the indirection of movement in his circular journey into the light. The image of an earthquake suggests the impact of religious experience in times of darkness. Wakefield's overall journey follows the four stages that he uses as titles of the sections of his book: Beginning (II, chs. 1–2); Wandering (II, chs. 3–7); Turning (Section I); Returning (II, chs. 8–9).

Beginning

The "beginning" of his religious journey includes his Protestant childhood in Indianapolis. Here the tensions of his first religious experience are embodied in the personalities of the local "stern imposing" Presbyterian minister who represents the "thunderous biblical God" and of his "warm and comforting" wife, who represents the "God of mercy" and who teaches divine universal love. After Wakefield's family move across town, he goes to a Baptist church, not because his own grandfather was a Baptist minister, but because a wealthy aunt of a childhood friend sends them both by taxi to Bible school. Here Wakefield experiences joy and excitement in the stories, hymns, and prayers, but the cost of travel forces him to join the Christian Church closer to home, a church with similar hymns but less exciting Sunday school. Despite the profound "light" experience of this period, he gradually drifts away from formal religion into a vague "spiritual refreshment out of doors" (40). Seeking his identity at the age of eleven, Wakefield asks for baptism by immersion, but, after a year and a half of preparation, experiences a dramatic letdown during the ceremony:

> This wasn't what I had in mind. I wanted to have the Lord on my side but I wanted to have *my own way*. I wanted God to be a kind of divine bodyguard and right-hand man in helping me achieve everything I wanted in life, defending me against my enemies and making me number one in whatever I chose. Now here I was about to be baptized while the opposite message was being played and sung, which I feared might make it come true! (49)

Preferring to run his life his own way, Wakefield rejects the notion of God as a "potter" shaping the "clay" of his life. He stops attending church and enters what he calls "the fury of adolescence."

The chapter on his adolescence generates enormous tensions—between his desire for the light and place of faith (found now in nature, the rituals of Scout camp, but rarely in church) and the fury of sports, Scouting activities, pimples, peers, dates, journalism, and speech contests. The greatest crisis of faith occurs in his battle with a severe case of *acne vulgaris*, which drives him to prayers, guilt, and occasional angry bouts with God. His brief encoun-

ter with the Moral Rearmament movement and its public
confessions gives him his "first bad taste about religion in general"
(58). Throughout this period, he finds mediators (his psychic
Aunt Ollie calls them " 'guardian angels' ") in his Scout leaders,
his boss in his job as high school sports "stringer" for a local
newspaper, and his high school friend Harpie. Frustrated by the
lack of response to his needs, Wakefield drifts into what he calls
"a high school version of agnosticism" but nevertheless continues
to pray. As he sums up his state of soul during the middle of his
first and disastrous year in college: "At the end of high school I
had thought I was one of the elect, one of the in-group of life
who was destined to look down benignly on the less fortunate as
I climbed my way to success. But something had gone wrong.
Instead of a bright collegiate future I saw only a blank wall. . . . I
prayed to God for help, but all I thought I could hear was mock-
ing silence" (75).

Wandering

The structure of Wakefield's years of wandering—from his college years at Columbia in 1950 until his return to faith in
1980—is both meandering and yet parallel to his childhood. The
titles of his chapters suggest both dimensions. At Columbia University (after failure at Northwestern to get into a fraternity and a
year at the University of Indiana), he experiences "another kind
of baptism"—into the secular sights, ideas, and culture of New
York City. Here he achieves a sort of intellectual transformation,
mediated, as with Merton, by Mark Van Doren. But Wakefield
becomes not the restless seeker after Christianity that Merton was,
but what he calls "an actively practicing intellectual agnostic"
(87), blaming his loss of Christian faith on the vapidity of Norman
Vincent Peale and the negative explanations of religion by Freud.
Van Doren, while not directly helping Wakefield with his faith
struggle, gives him, as "the most important thing" in college, "a
new, adult respect for Jesus" (94). After a severe back injury
(which occasions a sudden cure of his years of acne, an event
explained at the time in Freudian terms of repression), he struggles to find himself by a form of "substituting Freud for God"
(ch. 4). Yet, even in this period of agnosticism, when he writes

his first successful short story, he spontaneously kneels and gives thanks to God in prayer (121). In fact, it seems no coincidence that he mentions at this point his favorite Hemingway story, with its title reflective of Wakefield's own directional image and its inclusion of Christian form and agnostic despair: "A Clean, Well-lighted Place" (123).

In the traditional patterns of spiritual autobiography, Wakefield's wandering years include a mixture of the *battle* and the *journey* form. After the journey toward the light of faith in Childhood (ch. 1), he battles in "The Unknown Test" against the adolescent challenge to his faith (ch. 2). In chapter 3, he travels to New York City and begins an intellectual journey through secular authors who lead him to thirty years in the desert of agnosticism. In chapter 4, as a student and fledgling author, he battles depression and confronts a new idol—Freud—who provides him with a substitute for God. Then, in chapter 5, he embarks on "Pilgrimage" again, this time under the mentorship of journalist Murray Kempton and sociologist C. Wright Mills, to Mississippi and then to Israel to write a series of articles for *The Nation*. This journey (reversing the order of Cowan's journeys from Harvard) is taken by Wakefield because he wants to confront ultimate questions, to put his self in the face of death. As he dramatizes this period:

> I wanted to put myself at risk, to test my courage and integrity, to expose myself to the kind of life-or-death experience I could learn from in the Hemingway school of hard knocks journalism. I wanted to know what it felt like to face death, for I thought the experience would make me a better writer, and I jumped at the first opportunity to get myself shot at. (135)

Ironically, he never faces death but mysteriously relives events from the life of Jesus in the Gospels—fishing and eating breakfast on Lake Galilee (John 21), visiting Sodom by the Dead Sea, touring Jerusalem and the alleged room of the Last Supper—but rejects "any meaning beyond the strictly secular and journalistic" (140). Looking back on these events as they appear in letters to a friend, Wakefield later reflects on the inner battle on this journey: "I see now between the lines of my letters from Israel an almost constant, unconscious battle of a kind that must go on within many young people whose new intellectual faith in a Godless universe is at war with their earlier and sometimes deeper religious beliefs and impulses. . . . the old forms of thought and prayer kept breaking through my accounts of experience in Israel" (142). In order to visit Jordan, he has to pose as a Baptist pilgrim, but gets detained and barely escapes back to Jerusalem, from which he decides to work in a kibbutz in the Negev. Here he is given the job of shepherd, which once again turns him back to biblical themes. As he remembers later, "I went to the land I had heard and read and even sung about as a child in Sunday school and church, the land where Jesus had walked and preached to fishermen and shepherds, and I ended up working myself at those very jobs" (149). After breaking his arm—a second crucial injury just after a journey—he returns to New York thinking he has completed his journey.

Here Wakefield enters the central battle of his wandering life—a psychological battle on "The Couch" (ch. 6). The occasion is the most embarrassing situation in his life: the racy autobiographer who will tell the world most explicitly in his novels and life story about his teenage masturbation and petting, his collegiate girl friends, and his new theology of Freudian theory now meets the perfect woman—and experiences impotence and rejection. In despair, he fumbles with cutting his wrists, more a self-punishment than a suicide, but decides on Freudian psychoanalysis as his way to salvation:

> I entered psychoanalysis with the high seriousness of purpose and commitment of any acolyte taking his vows to a rigorous religious order. Like many in our generation, I had already made the intellectual substitution of Freud for God. . . . Now I was acting on my intellectual belief; I was setting out on a search for personal healing through a method that had in my culture replaced religion as the means of achieving salvation. As with many others like me, I had literally replaced religion with psychiatry, for I was seeking the long-lasting earthly kind of salvation I hadn't gotten from baptism and church and Jesus. (158)

What he thinks of as "a journey that would guide me to the truth" (158) turns out to be a five-year battle with two analysts whom he dislikes and who dislike him, even refusing to allow him to marry during this period. As Wakefield later says, his analyst "gave me a ticket to irresponsibility and made that non-involvement a way of life" (163). As a result, Wakefield cannot finish his writing projects, takes up heavy drinking, begins to have horrifying nightmares, and eventually undergoes a six-week-long hallucination. At the bottom of what he calls the "black hole" of psychoanalysis, he turns to praying the Twenty-third Psalm one day, a practice which marks the start of this "Turning" back to God, as recorded in the opening section of the autobiography.

In the last chapter of the "wandering" period of Part II of *Returning*, Wakefield sums up the numerous "Guides" (ch. 9) along the final stages of his journey toward the final "turn." As he begins this chapter, he tells us what we have seen in the lives of Day, Merton, Gandhi, and even Cowan: "I had gone into psychanalysis to save myself, and at about the same time I went to East Harlem in the hope of helping others . . . what I did to save myself nearly killed me . . . and what I did in the hope of helping others nourished and sustained me and maybe even saved my life" (178). He proceeds to introduce the mediators along this fifteen-year period of the 1960s and 1970s—Dorothy Day and the Catholic Worker community in the Bowery; Reverend Norm Eddy and the drug treatment center in East Harlem; even James Baldwin, Robert Phelps, May Swenson, and other writers he meets in New York City.

Two groups of mediators confront the lapsed Protestant Wakefield from unexpected directions—Catholics and Jews. In meeting Dorothy Day and especially one of her workers with whom he falls in love, he awakens to a deep desire for meaning. As he tells us much later, he identifies in himself the question a girl posed to him one night after a date: "What do you want?" In his 1992 memoir, *New York in the Fifties*, he sums up his lifelong quest: "I also wanted something else, something more, something I couldn't name but had instinctively come to this turbulent neighborhood to find—some connection beyond my ego-self . . . something all of us young seekers had sensed in the air of those Friday night meetings at the Catholic Worker, something Dorothy Day knew and possessed and somehow conveyed a sense of to others. . . . A chord struck and something opened: a flower, a door, a chapter" (*New York* 90).

In this quest for an opening, Wakefield found himself, like

Merton, journeying with secularized Jewish students and writers, with whom he later tells us that he identified: "I identified with Jews as outsiders, since part of me always felt that way myself, despite all my efforts to be In" (*New York* 46). Just as Cowan returned to his Jewish roots after confronting Berrigan and the Catholic left, so Wakefield returns to his Christian faith after traveling through the chaos of the New York of the 1950s and early 1960s with the Jewish founders of Cowan's own *Village Voice*. Among his favorites authors, he also found several mediators who lead him back toward faith, especially J. D. Salinger and Robert Coles. During this period, although he becomes successful as a novelist and journalist, his addictions grow worse and he suffers two broken marriages and eventually moves to Hollywood.

In the central chapter of "Turning" (placed first in the book), Wakefield continues the pattern we have followed in his religious childhood and anti-religious years of wandering. He finds a new place (Boston), he recovers a light, he replaces the psychiatrist and even the doctors with religious mediators, he replaces the rituals of addiction and sex with rituals of exercise and faith. But he also discovers new authors: Sagan on her alcoholism, Graham Greene's *The Power and the Glory* on the whiskey priest, Thomas Merton's *The Seven Storey Mountain*, Henri Nouwen on spirituality, de Caussaude on abandonment to God, and, of course, the Bible. It is from reading Merton's *He Is Risen* that Wakefield changes his life image:

> Merton . . . said in matter-of-fact prose that Christ "is in history with us, walking ahead of us to where we are going. . . ." I thought of those words while walking the brick sidewalks of Beacon Hill (in Boston), conceiving of my life for the first time as a "journey" rather than as a battle I was winning or losing at that moment. (23)

It is at this time that he moves from a naïve view of God and life in merely idealistic terms. He faces the problem of evil for the first time. He learns from Henry Nouwen that religious conversion does not necessarily bring emotional stability—"Christianity is not for getting your life together"—and, more important, that his way to God will not be a way to avoid difficulties. Rather, as he reads in Nouwen, " 'it would be just another illusion to believe that reaching out to God will free us from pain and suffering.

Often, indeed, it will take us where we rather would not go. But we know that without going there we will not find our life' " (24).

Returning

The second unusual structural shift in *Returning*—besides the proleptic placement of the conversion period at the beginning of the book—is the description in two supplementary chapters of the gradual integration of his rediscovered faith with his past. In particular, Wakefield comes to be reconciled with his parents (ch. 8) and becomes part of a new parish family (ch. 9). Despite his preoccupation with psychoanalysis at one stage of his life, he does not reveal enough of his father or mother's personalities to allow the reader to trace his psychological struggles back to either father or mother. Instead, Wakefield gives such a vivid picture of the "muted pitch of their battle" in the "fragile family" of his childhood that the reader can search out the underground forces within the family triangle (41–42). The inhibited tension between his father and his mother, which expressed itself in angry arguments over monthly bills or in the silence of supper time, was somewhat healed by the empathetic counseling provided by their Presbyterian minister's wife, Amy (who also embodied God's mercy for young Dan). Yet beneath Wakefield's adolescent religious battles lay what he describes as "some struggle of will between my parents that I felt caught in the center of" (44). This struggle of will leads to a divorce in 1957, the news of which drives their son to tears when he hears of it by letter in Israel. As he describes his feeling in a note to a friend at the time: "I am so sorry I couldn't have done anything to help it though I know there was nothing to be done. It was tragic because neither side was wrong, neither was bad, and essentially they destroyed each other not meaning to, only wanting to live, and they could not with any happiness live together. . . . I brought them some little happiness I think but much more pain I'm afraid" (150).

In chapter 8, "The Blood Tie," the forty-eight-year-old Wakefield, just starting his "turning" toward God, returns in 1980 to Indianapolis for the first time in decades. The occasion is the funeral of his father and mother, who had by then overcome their divorce and remarried. Although most of his emotional energy at that time was expended on grief and on reunion with his friends, he returns again in 1984 and visits his parents' graves once more, primarily to achieve "some kind of reconciliation with them" (214). Now fully returned to the practice of faith, he describes his private ritual at the graveside:

> I knelt in the snow beside my parents' graves, feeling cold and discomforted. I said the Twenty-third Psalm, going through it pretty briskly, muttered a request for forgiveness for not more freely expressing my love to them in their lifetime, then shifted on my knees. The layer of snow crunched beneath me. I wondered if the earth might open and swallow me, sucking me into a grave beside my parents. (214–15)

But he panics, as memories of being forced to accept a grave near his parents obsess his mind. Fearing a pull from them to drag him "home," he rushes off, hindered for a while by a pathetic scene when he cannot turn the key in the frozen lock of his car. A year later, during a visit to his hometown for a talk on "place" in fiction, Wakefield dedicates the evening to his parents and experiences himself as a prodigal son returning home for reconciliation—with himself, his home city, and his mother and father (221). Structurally, these scenes of attempted reconciliation with his parents provide a purgative extension of his recent reconciliation with God. Ironically, the entire chapter echoes in reverse one of two epigraphs which he borrowed from an article by George W. S. Trow in *Harper's* in 1987: "I believe that Humans are unable to live without some contact with what I call the third parent: God, or some culture growing up around a tradition of thinking about God or gods" (xiii).

In the final chapter of this autobiography, after finding his new home in a new place with a new light (Boston), Wakefield describes how he finds a new parish family at King's Chapel and how he becomes a mediator or "guardian angel" for others. These parallels to the events and persons of his childhood "beginnings" and antitheses of his early adult "wanderings" lead him to a final "turning"—a turning outward toward the poor, a movement that fulfills his earlier discovery (one night after a hangover) of the significance of an Albert Schweitzer poster message,

"Happy are those who have sought and found a way to serve." Like Cowan, Day, Gandhi, and others, he cannot undergo a religious conversion that does not eventually lead to a social–moral conversion. But, more like Cowan than the earlier autobiographers, he takes this final turn for granted.

Wakefield, again like his predecessors in this genre, ends his journey in journalistic fashion. Just as he had resolved the tensions of youth by his high school newspaper writing, and then the tension of his wandering years by his articles for *The Nation*, his short stories, and his novels, so now he tells us how he begins his account of his life story by first an essay on his return, and then, with help from a parish course on spiritual autobiographies, by creating his late twentieth-century *Returning*. In this belated story of the self, he self-consciously integrates references to previous stories we have examined—by Augustine, Merton, Day, Cowan—into his own circular journey. He uses a variation of the directional image in the final paragraph of his autobiography ("Light flooded in through the big windows of the chapel at Glastonbury Abbey"), but then records briefly the concluding topic of the book—"the sometimes conflicting images of God . . . found in the Bible" (250). Just as his directional images sometimes conflict but still drive him on his journey, so, too, the images of God in the scriptures conflict but only lead him, along with his final Benedictine mentor, to the ultimate referent of all images— for "we must take God as he comes to each of us."

Furthermore, in his variation of the circular journey, Wakefield adds his own post-1960s touch: much greater detail of his emotional and sexual wanderings, a stronger emphasis on the psychological patterns (usually in Freudian terms, while repudiating Freud), an acute awareness of the power of addiction, and a more explicit social consciousness. Writing after the "triumph of the therapeutic," the Vietnam era, the ecumenical religious age, and the "me" decade of the 1970s, he uses the novelistic devices of the new journalism and a cinematic prose to bring alive the hurly-burly life on the spiritual journey of a media-addicted urban writer. Although he provides only passing references to his failed marriages and near-marriages, he shows in the final chapter a new respect for women in his descriptions of the female minister and friends in his new parish family at King's Chapel. He also ends by alluding to evidence of the rise of prayer groups in American cities, part of a spiritual revival that crosses class lines and leads Wakefield, an unlikely convert, to return home to a new church. Yet his home is an open one—for he also studies, visits, and prays in Catholic and Jewish, as well as Protestant, "places." Thus, his returning is simultaneously a fusion of several levels of his conversion and a holistic recovery of health, family, and faith. Most profoundly, Wakefield comes to see and accept his journey to God as "real in times of anguish as it was in the fullness of joy" (249). Thus bringing together Lewis's orientation toward "joy" with Day's concern for the "harsh and dreadful love" of God, he concludes, like Augustine, with a line from the psalms—"the darkness and the light are both alike to thee."

REFERENCES

Wakefield, Dan. *New York in the Fifties*. Boston: Houghton Mifflin, 1992.
————. *Returning: A Spiritual Journey*. New York: Doubleday, 1988.

10

Retraveling the Century: Nelson Mandela's *Long Walk to Freedom*

THIS FINAL AUTOBIOGRAPHY of the century has puzzled its readers. Published in 1994 to great acclaim, it reads like a mid-century spiritual journey with a structure similar to those we have seen in Merton or Malcolm X. Yet it lacks the periods of wandering and dramatic conversion of its predecessors. Its style is quiet, full of understatement, with a mixture of idealizations and realistic admissions of faults. The autobiographer begins with a youth full of spiritual influences and convictions, but gradually mutes the religious dimension as he travels the long political road. This shift in tone has led some reviewers to read the book as a story of moral growth in dignity, not in religious faith (Sampson). Like Gandhi's autobiography, Mandela's story seems one of public successes but personal and family failures. Yet the *Long Walk to Freedom* ends in a triumphant emergence from jail into political victory, whereas Gandhi's final chapters are written while he is still in prison. The *Long Walk* has been condemned by conservative readers for its "ingenuous" pro-leftist comments but praised by liberal reviewers for its rejection of communism (Roberts). Mandela spends many years in prison with little contact with the outside world, but emerges stronger and more able to govern that world. The plot of the autobiography consists primarily in Mandela's struggles with his enemies, but he ends up working with them in a new government. A close study of the structure and images of Mandela's life story will give some answers to these puzzles.

The book was begun in prison two decades before it was completed with the assistance of Richard Stengel, a *Time* reporter, who helped Mandela retain the traditional language and tone of his original prison memoirs. Many of the tensions noted by reviewers will be seen as stages within the circular journey of the book's structure, and the changing religious tone indicates the gradual growth of the author's political awareness of the role of religion in South Africa. Finally, beneath the paradox of his final return to reconciliation and rule lurk the conflicting views of nonviolence and force that remained unresolved for so many years in the soul of Nelson Mandela.

SEARCH FOR THE VILLAGE OF HARMONY

Nelson Mandela begins his long walk by painting an ideal landscape of his childhood Xhosa village of Qunu in eastern South Africa. He looks back over seventy years and sees it as a "balanced and harmonious social order in which every individual knew his or her place" (4). This image of a rural tribal paradise reflects his young boy's "love of the veld, of open spaces, the simple beauties of nature, the clean lines of the horizon" (8). Within this peaceful circle of nature, he learns the "custom, ritual, and taboo" that promote the traditional values of respect for ancestors, proper gender roles, and the ritual of birth, rites of passage, and marriage (11). This village life is not without conflict, however, for the boys routinely play war games and learn to preserve honor even in defeat. The tribal religion of this idealized childhood consists of a belief in "cosmic wholeness" in which one discovers the sacred amid the profane of an agricultural cycle of life (11). After his father's death, the young Mandela repaints this picture of an harmonious society when he looks over his shoulder as he leaves the village to go with his mother to the family tribal center where he will attend school:

> I could see the simple huts and the people going about their chores; the stream where I had splashed and played with the other boys; the maize fields and green pastures where the herds and flocks were lazily grazing. I imagined my friends out hunting for small birds, drinking the sweet milk from the cow's udder, cavorting in the pond at the end of the stream. Above all else, my eyes rested on the three simple huts where I had enjoyed my mother's love and protection. (13)

This picture of an "harmonious social order" within a framework of "cosmic wholeness" becomes for Mandela the directional image of his long walk to freedom. As a son of a former chief who became an unordained priest and adviser to kings, Nelson is called by his family tradition to "settle royal disputes" (4) and live according to "a matter of principle" (7). Just as his father, at the cost of his leadership, had rejected British authority over tribal customs because of a "proud rebelliousness [and] a stubborn sense of fairness" (6), so Nelson will use the directional image of an harmonious order to reject the injustices he later discovers in the colonial history of his country and the Afrikaner system of apartheid. This image remains with him but becomes more nuanced when he experiences the council of chieftains' practices at Mqhekezweni, the provisional capital of Thembuland, where he spends his later childhood with his extended family. Here, he recounts, "My later notions of leadership were profoundly influenced by observing the regent and his court" at the Great Place. Here the regent and his councilors met from time to time to discuss urgent questions and practice "democracy in its purest form" where "all men were free to voice their opinions and equal in their value as citizens" (20–21).

Mandela's directional image is further clarified when he develops an interest in African history, which he first learns from the legends of Xhosa heroes recounted by chiefs and headmen who came to the Great Place to settle disputes. He learns also of the communal ownership of land, which Africans considered themselves as sharing with all peoples "as they shared the air and water" (24). Even when he is studying at Fort Hare University, Mandela joins other young men in hikes to surrounding farms and village "to recapture," as he says, "what was most homelike to us" (48).

This image of a tribal home—with its harmonious social order within a cosmic wholeness, its seeds of democracy, and its communal sharing of the environment—will remain for Mandela the guiding image of his journey. When he moves in 1941 to the chaotic urban life of Johannesburg, he will find the image recreated in the tribal solidarity he experiences among the Xhosa people working there in the mines or offices. He will find it expressed again in the harmony of tribes and groups dancing together in jail before his first trial in 1957: "Suddenly there were no Xhosas or Zulus, no Indians or Africans, no rightists or leftists, no religious or political leaders; we were all nationalists and patriots bound together by a love of our common history, our culture, our country, and our people" (202). Later, at his second trial in 1962, he will consciously re-create the tribal image for the court by wearing a traditional Xhosa leopardskin kaross, which he says is an expression of "the history, culture, and heritage" of his people (325). As he gives his political testament at that trial, he again re-creates his directional image for his listeners and for the whole world:

> Many years ago, when I was a boy brought up in my village in the Transkei, I listened to the elders of the tribe telling stories about the good old days before the arrival of the white man. Then our people lived peacefully, under the democratic rule of their kings and their *amapakati* . . . , and moved freely and confidently up and down the country without let or hindrance. The country was ours, in name and right. . . . The land . . . belonged to the whole tribe and there was no individual ownership whatsoever. There were no classes, no rich or poor, and no exploitation of man by man. (329–30)

Later in the same speech, Mandela explictly links the utopian image of his childhood society with his adult goal of a multiracial society—a "revolutionary democracy in which none will be held in slavery or servitude, and in which poverty, want and insecurity shall be no more" (330). Later in the same trial, in his final speech, he again cites the tales of "the elders of my tribe" as the motive for his current participation in his "freedom struggle" (364).

Mandela also keeps the directional image alive in his narrative by interspersing his political journey with stories of his infrequent but greatly treasured visits to his home villages. Just as he is becoming politically radicalized in 1942, he returns home after the death of his second father, the regent of Thembuland. At this time, however, he finds that he can no longer hope to follow the directional image backward in time or place. As he admits, "There is nothing like returning to a place that remains unchanged to find the ways in which you yourself have altered. The Great Place went on as before, no different from when I had grown up there. But I realized that my own outlook and world-views had evolved" (84–85). He must now seek to embody the image of the harmonious society where his people need it most—in Johannesburg and the whole of South Africa. In 1955, after the Congress of Peoples at which the Freedom Charter is first written, he returns again to the birthplace of the ideal expressed in that central document of the freedom movement. As he recalls, he has been longing for thirteen years "to visit the countryside again, to be in the open veld and rolling villages" and to see "the old friends and comrades" of his childhood (176–77). The effect of reentering the world of his directional image is invigorating:

> I ate the same foods I had eaten as a boy. I walked the same fields, and gazed at the same sky during the day, the same stars at night. It is important for a freedom fighter to remain in touch with his roots, and the hurly-burly of city life has a way of erasing the past. The visit restored me and revived my feelings for the place in which I grew up. (182)

At the same time, Mandela realizes that he has changed, has "moved on and seen new worlds and gained new ideas"—in short, has enlarged his horizon. In the story of his "political evolution," he says that the "magic world of my childhood had fled" (184), as he seeks to re-create it not merely on the tribal level but for "the entire nation" (183). Meanwhile, he keeps in touch with his origin by purchasing a plot of land near his home village. Like Black Elk and Rigoberta Menchú, Mandela comes from the static circle of a traditional society but faces the demands of oppression by forces within a modern society. Unlike Black Elk but like Menchú, Mandela will succeed in his struggle to retain the image of harmony from his childhood society but transform it on his upward circular journey into values that can bring harmony to an intercultural society.

During the twenty-seven years of his imprisonment, Mandela is hard pressed to keep his directional image alive on Robben Island and in a Capetown prison. However, he struggles to do so on the conscious level by embodying the image in the daily battle for *solidarity* among the political prisoners. More important, perhaps, on the unconscious level, he pursues the image in his dreams. As he writes of his "daydreams" to his wife in 1976 from Robben Island: "[T]he very first thing I would like to do on my return would be to take you away from that suffocating atmosphere, drive you along carefully, so that you could have the opportunity of breathing fresh and clean air, seeing the beauty spots of South Africa, its green grass and trees, colourful wild flowers, sparkling streams, animals grazing in the veld and be able to talk to the simple people we meet along the road" (498). When he hears in 1980 of tribal conflicts between his nephew and a Transkei king, Mandela admits that "as I grew older, my thoughts turned more and more often to the green hills of the Transkei" (507). A decade later, just as he is about to be released from prison, he confesses that his deepest desire is to return to the land of his youth: "My dream upon leaving prison was to take a leisurely drive down to the Transkei, and visit my birthplace, the hills and streams where I had played as a boy, and the burial ground of my mother, which I had never seen" (567). This dream is finally realized in April 1990 when he visits his mother's grave in Qunu. Here he finds that even his own village has joined him on the long walk to freedom. The children are singing political songs, the "warmth and simplicity" have endured, but the struggle with poverty is not being won and the traditional "[p]ride in the community seemed to have vanished" (581). Despite this setback, Mandela eventually, in 1993, builds a country house in Qunu. The directional image that has guided him on his journey—of a home in an harmonious society—becomes embodied in the final residence of his walk to freedom.

MEDIATORS OF HARMONY

As I have already noted, Mandela's mother and father were the first mediators in the traditional Xhosa village of his directional image of an harmonious society. From his father's life and stories about his heroic ancestors, Nelson learned a respect for both history and education, as well as a sense of justice as fairness and a passion for the primacy of ethical principles. More prophetically, he learned from his father's friendliness to other tribes the need to extend justice to all peoples, even beyond traditional or racial boundaries. Before his father's death when Nelson was nine years old, he learns to combine his father's belief in "cosmic wholeness" with his mother's Christianity (13). This union of the two religious traditions in Mandela's early life will prove to be a foreshadowing of his lifelong ecumenical struggle to unify, in the efforts for freedom, the range of sects and faiths that made up South Africa. His mother, who teaches him "virtue and generosity" through Xhosa fables, remains, despite her later reservations about his political party, his moral guidepost throughout his years of political struggle and imprisonment until her death in 1965.

Like Merton, Gandhi, and Malcolm X, Mandela lost his father at an early age, an experience that left him vulnerable to a need for substitute fathers throughout his youth. After his father's death, the primary mediator of Nelson's growth to cultural awarenss and student leadership was the regent of the area, Jongintaba, who taught him "democracy in its purest form" as found in the equality of all participants in tribal decision-making with its goal of consensus (21). From three Methodist ministers— Reverend Matyolo, Reverend Harris, and Reverend Mokitimi— the young Mandela learned of the importance of the Christian formation of leaders in his country. From an African teacher, Frank Lebentlele, who married outside his tribe, he learned of the need to "loosen the hold of the tribalism that still imprisoned" us (38). The final voice of inspiration during his formal education came from the poet Krune Mghayi, who visited Nelson's high school class and challenged them to be proud of their Xhosa culture and to resist the imposition of foreign values. The mediators of his political conversion are too many to numerate. Preeminent among those he mentions, however, are Gaur Radebe, who introduced him to the African National Congress (ANC), and Walter Sisulu, the self-educated leader in the Congress who instilled in Mandela his "wise tutelege" and led him by example to join that organization. More dramatic is the impact on Mandela of the "majestic" and "mystical" Anton Lembede, whom he met in 1943 and from whom he learned the "self-reliance and self-determination" of a proud Africanism. From those and other leaders, Mandela develops the political version of his directional image of an harmonious social order, a nonracial African nationalism. He describes the continuity of his goals in 1944 with the original goals of the ANC in 1912: "African nationalism was our battle cry, and our creed was the creation of one nation out of many tribes, the overthrow of white supremacy, and the establishment of a truly democratic form of government" (99).

Mandela's Circular Journey Toward Harmony

The chapter titles of Mandela's autobiography indicate that he imagined his long walk to freedom as an up-and-down linear journey from cultural imprisonment (pts. 1–2) through a long freedom-fighting struggle (pts. 3–7), into a second legal imprisonment (pts. 8–10), and, finally, a movement into personal and political freedom (pt. 11). A closer examination of the structure of the text, however, reveals that it can also be seen as a five-stage circular journey upward similar to those of other twentieth-century spiritual autobiographers. What is markedly different about the structure of Mandela's story is that, like Menchú, he lacks a period of wandering, and the four main stages of the "journey" surround the central "battles" of the autobiography, the public trials described in parts 5, 6, and 7. According to this format, the autobiography consists of:

1. an opening section which establishes his directional image and describes his education in the use of language and democratic negotiation (pt.1);
2. an upward spiral of struggle for political and social justice in South Africa through the African National Congress (pts. 2, 3, 4);
3. transitional middle section presenting the public trials in which Mandela is first exonerated and later convicted of treason (pts. 5, 6, 7);
4. a downward spiral of imprisonment on Robben Island which turns out to be a parallel struggle for political and social justice in a new context (pts. 8 and 9);
5. a concluding section in which his education in language bears fruit in negotiations with the Afrikaner government and, eventually, in his personal freedom, followed by the establishment of a nonracial democracy, the fulfillment of his directional image (pts. 10 and 11).

Thus, in a manner similar to that found in Augustine's *Confessions* and autobiographies by Merton, Day, Lewis, Malcolm X, and others, Mandela's *Long Walk to Freedom* contains a circular narrative with many parallels and interconnections between the earlier and later sections surrounding the central battle scene of the public trials.

Part One: Education in a Revolutionary Ideal and Method (1918–41)

As mentioned, Part One of *Long Walk to Freedom* consists of the planting of two seeds in the soil of Nelson Mandela's life, seeds that will later bear fruit in the final two parts of his journey. The first seed, of course, is the directional image he fashions from his country childhood into the ideal that will inspire his entire life: an harmonious social order. This ideal derives from his experience of tribal order, moral values, and cosmic wholeness passed on to him by his father, mother, and home villages of Gunu and the Great Place. The second seed consists of the methods he learns in his youth about how to attain and preserve this ideal of social harmony. He learns the complexities of these methods in various stages of his education: first, in the quasi-democratic procedures of the regent's Great Place, where tribal conflicts are settled by consultation and consensus; second, in the formal education in language, history, and religion which Nelson receives in the Methodist schools; third, in the procedures for obtaining justice (some of them successful, some frustrated) taught him by his white and African teachers in college and university, procedures that will be complemented later by his study of law in Johannesburg; fourth, in the models of religious and social commitment to lifelong struggle for a just society embodied in several mediators during his years of education. These cultural, ethical, and religious methods will serve him well, not only during his long years of struggle in the African National Congress (pts. 2–4) and in prison (pts. 8 and 9), but most notably in his final negotiations with the Nationalist government during the process of his release from prison (pts. 10). In these years of education, Mandela, like Gandhi, first learns the fundamental humanity of peoples of all cultures, a lesson that provides him with a ground for the ideal of a nonracial society. Furthermore, he learns the importance of truth-

ful communication and mutual trust in the lengthy struggle to
find a common ground for building an harmonious organization
within the liberation movement and later for building a social
order beyond cultural and ethnic conflicts.

*Parts Two, Three, Four: Coming to Political Consciousness and
Commitment (1941–56)*

The second stage of Mandela's spiral pilgrimage consists of the
years of political transformation and struggle that he calls the
"Birth of a Freedom Fighter" and "The Struggle Is My Life."
The plotting of these chapters of the ascending circular journey is
made up of multiple small steps that bring him to political awareness, commitment, involvement, and leadership in the ANC.
Driven by his youthful resistance to unjust control of the student
government at Fort Hare University, and then driven out of his
own region by an attempt to force him into an arranged marriage,
Nelson Mandela, like the young Malcolm X, flees to the big city.
Here in Johannesburg he encounters the second-class status of
blacks, coloreds, and Indians in the 1940s South African metropo-
lis. The result is similar to the gradual political awakening of Gandhi, an awakening that expands the scope of Mandela's youthful
directional image to include all of South Africa. As he searches
for work and a law degree, he recounts the step-by-step process
of becoming politically conscious and committed. He joins the
Youth League of the ANC, where he gradually works for inter-
tribal unity, multiracial cooperation, democracy, and resistance to
communist domination of the freedom movement. After 1948,
with the establishment of apartheid by the victorious Nationalist
Party, Mandela assists the ANC to take nonviolent action through
strikes, days of protest, and defiance compaigns for the next ten
years. Eventually, as he confesses, the struggle becomes his life, to
the detriment of his first marriage and his legal education. However, during this decade both Mandela and the ANC undergo a
radical transformation. They learn to struggle against the government's use of housing restrictions, of separation of neighborhoods, and of the takeover of education. Despite these setbacks,
the ANC manages to hold a Congress of the People in 1955 at
which Mandela's childhood ideal is embodied in the movement's

charter for a nonracial democracy. This climax of the first half of the circular journey is underscored, as we have noted, by Mandela's return to his Transkei village where he buys a plot of land for his future home.

Parts Five, Six, Seven: From Journey to Battles (1957–63)

The structure of this central section of the plot of *Long Walk to Freedom* consists in several battles—within his family, within the ANC, and within South African society. Here, in a format similar to that of Merton and Wakefield, Mandela shifts the shape of the central part of his life story from a circular journey to a battle. The most public of these battles is, of course, his two trials. Between the two trials, he is forced to work underground and is sent on a long trip throughout Africa in support of the ANC. Just as he is arrested in 1957 and charged with treason and the violent overthrow of the government, Mandela undergoes a severe family struggle with Evelyn, his first wife, who has become a Jehovah's Witness and consequently opposes Nelson's attempt to unite his own Methodist religious beliefs with his political activism. When her new faith, combined with Nelson's absorption in the political struggle, leads to a growing alienation from each other, his wife leaves him, and they are divorced soon after. While he is awaiting the trial, he meets Winnie Madikizela, who becomes his second wife in 1958 and later a coworker in the resistance movement. During the four years of preparation for and holding of the first trial, the ANC suffers several setbacks that discourage Mandela— the 1958 strike fails, the Pan African Congress is born as an all-black alternative to the ANC, the Bantu Self-Government Act is passed to establish separate homelands for natives, and the Sharpesville massacre outrages the world in 1960. However, the first trial itself concludes in 1961 with a verdict of not guilty. The government could not prove its contention that the ANC leaders had used violence or were planning the violent overthrow of the government.

Ironically, during the year after this first trial of vindication, Nelson Mandela and other ANC leaders begin a secret debate about the use of violence. For Mandela, unlike Gandhi, the use of nonviolence is primarily a question of tactics, not principle.

When this tactic begins to fail after 1960 to make significant changes in the apartheid system, he leads the ANC in a prolonged discussion and decision to make limited use of physical force against the government, primarily in the form of sabotage. This decision leads to the formation of a parallel oganization to the ANC, the "Spear of the People" (MK), which will attempt to sabotage government buildings and procedures. In 1961, when the MK goes public with its first bombing, Nelson Mandela is forced to work underground as the leader of the ANC. A year later, he leaves South Africa for a meeting of African leaders in Ethiopia, where he tries to gain international support for the ANC resistance movement and where he studies the use of guerrilla warfare. Upon his return to South Africa, he is soon captured and sentenced to five years in prison. However, in 1963, the ANC secret headquarters on the Rivonia farm near Johannesburg are discovered and Mandela joins the other leaders in a second major trial for treason and violence. At this trial, he proclaims to the whole world his vision of an harmonious society that he first saw in his childhood image of his Xhosa tribe. But the government now has witnesses and evidence of the use of violence, a fact that leads to the life sentences at the Robben Island prison for Mandela and the other leaders of the ANC.

Parts Eight and Nine: The Struggle Continues in Prison (1964–90)

What Mandela learns at the beginning of his twenty-seven years in prison is that the struggle for an harmonious society has not been defeated by imprisonment. The vision has merely been transposed to a new setting. As he acknowledges with irony, the government's greatest mistake in the prison was to put all the political prisoners together. In his words, "a new and different fight had begun" (387). Living and working together, they manage, despite severe restrictions and penalties, and even occasional solitary confinement, to keep alive the goals of the ANC struggle. They even learn how to apply the nonviolent methods and a sort of democratic process to their life in prison: "We regarded the struggle in prison as a microcosm of the struggle as a whole. We would fight inside as we had fought outside. The racism and repression were the same; I would simply have to fight on different terms" (390–91).

During the twenty-seven years, the objects of this struggle are various—the end of second-class food and garb for blacks; the mitigation of forced labor; the right to have study materials, books, and newspapers; and the punishment of prison guards for abuse. By keeping a solidarity among all prisoners, Mandela and the other political prisoners are able to organize themselves to resist and gradually improve prison conditions. Their tactics vary from work slow-ups to hunger strikes, but the philosophy beneath the struggle is quite similar to that of Gandhi—a belief in the common humanity of themselves and their enemies. In particular, Mandela believes in being "decent" to the prison guards for, as he says, "It was ANC policy to try to educate all people, even our enemies; we believed that all men, even prison service warders, were capable of change, and we did our utmost to try to sway them" (418). In some instances, Mandela is able to convert a guard to sympathy for the prisoners' cause, as one of them admitted about the ANC, "It makes more bloody sense than the Nats" (419).

By 1970, the six years of resistance on Robben Island begin to get results. The "host of small battles" begins to change what Mandela calls "the atmosphere of the island" (453). Each prisoner is allowed to keep his own uniform, the food is improving, recreational games are allowed, religious services are open to all. Along with these minor changes comes a sense that the prisoners, by influencing the life of the prison, are participating in a sort of self-government. Under these changing conditions, what Mandela calls the "dark years" of despair in Part Eight (1964–70) become the "beginning of hope" in Part Nine (1971–82). The prisoners succeed in getting a cruel commanding officer transferred, they organize a sort of "university" for the education of new prisoners, and in 1976–77 Mandela writes the first secret version of his memoirs. In 1977, the prison abolishes forced labor, and Mandela is able to study, write, and grow his garden. Through the admission of radio and movies, the prisoners begin to catch up on world news, including the "Free Mandela" movement which began in 1980. What is most important structurally within the autobiography, of course, is that the methods and goals of the liberation struggle described in Parts Two, Three, and Four are paralleled by the prison methods and goals of Parts Eight and Nine.

Part Ten: Negotiation Begins (1983–90)

Just as the long struggle of Mandela's prison years parallel in many ways the long struggle of his Johannesburg years, so Part Ten, which is entitled "Talking with the Enemy," parallels and brings to fulfillment many of the methods learned by Mandela in Part One, his years of education. His early skills in language, history, negotiation, and law, learned at Fort Hare University and in his legal internship, now assist him in using nonviolent methods in discussion with the South African government. As pressure mounts from the ANC tactics throughout the country and from international opinion and boycotts, the government moves Mandela back to Capetown in 1983, where he is gradually given the leisure and freedom to hold discussions with prison and political leaders. In 1987, two years after he decides to negotiate, the South African government finally agrees to talks. In three years of negotiations, Mandela compromises on minor points and procedures, but stands firm on the ANC goal of a nonracial, majority-rule democracy. After crossing the Rubicon of meeting with President Botha on July 4, 1989, Mandela continues the nonviolent process and eventually watches as apartheid is dismantled under F. W. de Klerk in 1990. Mandela's adolescent education at the Great Place in reconciliation and negotiation reaches it fulfillment at this major turning point in his nation's history.

Part Eleven: Release, Freedom, Elections (1990—)

The final section of Long Walk to Freedom brings Mandela full-circle to the leadership of an harmonious nonracial democracy in South Africa. The miracle of this transformation, in the midst of great conflict, fear, and violence, includes the miracle of his transposing the ordered village society of his youth into the electoral democracy of South Africa in the 1990s. His reception of the Nobel Prize with President de Klerk in 1993 and his later election as president in 1994 are the climax of the ascending circular journey begun within his family, village, and tribe in Gunu seventy years earlier. The son of a priestly counselor to tribal kings becomes president of a nonracial African democracy at the end of one of the longest walks to freedom in modern history.

CONVERSIONS ON THE JOURNEY TO HARMONY

The language Mandela uses to describe the major changes in his journey can be interpreted as signifying five radical conversions. The first is a youthful personal–social conversion from childhood to young adult responsibility; the second is a moral conversion to justice; the third is a political–moral transformation to make the struggle his whole life; the fourth and fifth conversions result from his experience with nonviolence and violence.

The first major change in Mandela's life occurs when he leaves his native village of Gunu and moves to the Great Place, where he is introduced to African tribal leadership.

> In that moment of beholding Jongintaba and his court I felt like a sapling pulled root and branch from the earth and flung into the center of a stream whose strong current I could not resist. . . . Suddenly a new world opened before me. . . . I felt many of my established beliefs and loyalties begin to ebb away. The slender foundation built by my parents began to shake. In that instant, I saw that life might hold more for me than being a champion stick-fighter. (16)

The uprooting leads immediately to a new planting, as he settles his roots into the "magical kingdom" of the Great Place. He is fascinated by his work on the farm, the games and dances of his friends, and the world of learning where he studies English, Xhosa history, and geography. He becomes entranced with the idealized past of the African history recounted in tales by the visiting chieftains. He falls in love for the first time. Most important of all, he learns of the worlds of what he calls the "chieftaincy and the Church" (19). Here he experiences the worldwide influence of Christianity and its permeation of the "fabric of life" in this tribal center. He also learns his first lessons in politics by observing the regent and his court where disputes are settled. This is the first transformation of young Nelson—from a village child to a curious teenager fascinated by the larger worlds of education, politics, and religion.

This movement out of boyhood into youthful responsibility is celebrated in 1934 when Nelson goes through the tribal ritual of circumcision, which he calls "a trial of bravery and stoicism" (27). Despite the pain of the ceremony, Mandela says that he recalls "walking differently on that day, straighter, taller, firmer" (29). Part of his transformation comes about from listening to the main speaker at the festival following the ritual, a chief who warns the young men that they are "slaves in [their] own country" who "have no power to govern themselves" (30). Although Nelson does not want to think about the power of colonialism when he first hears it, he admits that the chief "had planted a seed" which later begins to grow into political awareness. As he sneaks a look at the burning lodges where the circumcised youth had been secluded for the ritual, he sees that "In these ash heaps lay a lost and delightful world, the world of my childhood. . . . I was already in mourning for my own youth" (31).

The second major conversion in Mandela's journey takes place during his conflicts with authorities at Fort Hare University. When he arrives, he learns that no first-year students are allowed on the house committee for the freshman dormitory. Together with other new students, he protests and wins a first small victory for justice and harmony. As he describes this first action, "We had remained firm, and we had won. This was one of my first battles with authority, and I felt the sense of power that comes from having right and justice on one's side" (46). This moral conversion to concern for justice reaches its climax in his third year at the university when he and the majority of students decide to protest the lack of student power by boycotting the elections to the Student Representative Council. This decision, as he says, "would create difficulties that would change the course of my life" (51). Faced with an issue of principle, Mandela is threatened with explusion and decides not to return to the university. This confrontation with what he saw as the "absolute power" of school authorities over the students leads to a similar confrontation with the power of his family to provide him with an arranged marriage. Mandela rebels against the injustice of absolute power held by academic and tribal authorities by running away, "and the only place to run was Johannesburg" (55). This moral decision would lead to an even more radical political transformation.

This third major change in Mandela's life takes place in a series of dramatic steps when he tries to make his way in the big city. After some deceitful efforts with his cousin to try to get work, he eventually lands a job in a law firm and completes his studies for the B. A. degree in 1942. More significant, his moral horizon is expanded by the painful experiences of the treatment of blacks, coloreds, and Indians in Johannesburg. As he learns from his employers and friends that the injustices of the racial laws can be ignored, worked around, or protested, he gradually becomes politicized. When he returns to the Great Place for the funeral of the regent in 1942, Mandela realizes how much he has been transformed by his first years in the city: "My life in Johannesburg, my exposure to men like Gaur Radebe, my experiences at the law firm, had radically altered my beliefs. I looked back on that young man who had left Mqhekezweni as a naïve and parochial fellow who had seen very little of the world" (85). As he returns to Johannesburg, he looks back over his past eight years and realizes, in a term from Xhosa, that he is one "who has crossed famous rivers" but that he also "had many rivers yet to cross" (85). Although Mandela says that, unlike Gandhi and his ejection from the train car, he "cannot pinpoint a moment when I became politicized," the greatest river that he crosses, of course, is the decision to become an active member of the African National Congress. As he admits, "I had no epiphany, no singular revelation, no moment of truth, but a steady accumulation of a thousand slights, a thousand indignities, a thousand unremembered moments, produced in me an anger, a rebelliousness, a desire to fight the system that imprisoned my people" (95). This expression of his political conversion leads him to cross many subsequent rivers of political policy and practice. Never again could he keep his feet dry of political waters.

Mandela's fourth conversion comes from his confrontation with the use of nonviolence and violence in the pursuit of his directional image of an harmonious political society in the 1950s and 1960s. From his first mention of the discussions within the ANC about principles and methods, he admits that he "saw nonviolence in the Gandhian model not as an inviolable principle but as a tactic to be used as the situation demanded" (128). The ANC itself, however, remained committed to nonviolence as a principle from the inception of the party in 1912 until the discussions among its leaders, including Mandela, in the early 1960s. Although during the first trial Mandela had been exonerated of violent overthrow of the government and the ANC proclaimed its policy of principled nonviolence, in a meeting of June 1961 he and others proposed the use of a limited amount of force, primarily sabotage, to resist the stranglehold of the apartheid forces of the South African government. After a night of discussion, the ANC decided to form a parallel organization which would use limited amounts of force to reach the goals of the ANC. Mandela realizes the radical change in the moral code of the movement by this decision when he admits, "It was a fateful step. For fifty years, the ANC had treated nonviolence as a core principle, beyond question or debate. . . . We were embarking on a new and more dangerous path, a path of organized violence, the results of which we did not and could not know" (274). At his second trial, Mandela, in his famous statement from the dock, justifies the changes in his political struggle and that of the ANC, ". . . the hard facts were that fifty years of nonviolence had brought the African people nothing but more repressive legislation, and fewer and fewer rights. . . . our policy to achieve a nonracial state by nonviolence had achieved nothing" (365). But he is careful to point out in the trial that the ANC did not choose to use violence, but merely responded when provoked by the violence of the government used against the ANC's nonviolent protests (331). In this fateful change, it must be noted, for Mandela the transformation was primarily a change in tactics, whereas for the Gandhian members of the ANC, it was a fundamental change of moral principles.

    Although, after his years in prison, Mandela would still defend the use of limited force to achieve freedom as a right and a tactic consonant with his Christian beliefs, during his prison years he also advocated the principles which underlay Gandhian nonviolent methods to effect change in other persons and in society. As we have noted earlier, in his dealings with prison authorities and guards, he would always try to use persuasion to change the minds of his "enemies," for, like Gandhi, he believed that all people were capable of change. As he had said earlier during his trial about the symbolic power of justice to change the system: "I was the symbol of justice in the court of the oppressor, the representative of the great ideals of freedom, fairness, and democracy in a society that dishonored those virtues. I realized then and there that I could carry on the fight even within the fortress of the enemy" (317). This sounds very much like the Gandhian belief in the power of truth and justice within a system of law, as does Mandela's later belief that "all men, even the most seemingly cold-blooded, have a core of decency, and that if their heart is touched, they are capable of changing" (462). It was these beliefs that made it possible for him, in a sort of fifth conversion, to negotiate in good faith with his sworn enemies. Whether the change from fifty years of nonviolence was justified by the results—thirty more years of violence—is a question that Mandela does not attempt to answer.

MANDELA AND CHRISTIANITY: A MUTED CONVERSION?

In the first stage of his long walk, as I have noted, Mandela joins his mother in becoming a Christian when he is seven years old. This addition of Christian faith to his father's tribal beliefs in a "balanced and harmonious society" enhances his determination throughout his journey to personal and political freedom for himself, his tribe, and all South Africans. Since Western civilization had come to his people, as to most of South Africa, through Christian missionaries, Mandela ascribes much of his education to the Methodist teachers in his schooling in the Transkei. In such an education at the Great Place, "religion was a part of the fabric of life," in the form of daily family prayer and regular church attendance in the village and later at the university. He even teaches the Bible at Fort Hare University, along with Oliver Tambo, his lifelong friend who would become his main co-leader of the liberation movement.

In the second stage of his long walk, his years in Johannesburg, Mandela occasionally mentions his Christian beliefs and practices, but now they become a sort of transgression of the assumptions of the movement for policial change that he enters. His political conversion, however, merely mutes, but does not obliterate his earlier Christian conversion. As he mentions in the early days of his membership in the ANC, "I was also quite religious and the [communist] party's antipathy to religion put me off" (74). When in 1955 the apartheid government tries to take over all the mission schools, Mandela is disappointed that his Methodist teachers do not change their schools into private schools, as the Catholics, Jews, and Adventists did: "My own Church, the Wesleyan Church, handed over 200,000 African students to the government" (167–68). He then sends his own children to an Adventist School. Occasionally in his autobiography, Mandela mentions personal religious practices during the central political portion of the story, for example when he kneels in prayer for jailed resisters in 1956 or when he is married in church to Winnie in 1957. During his years underground before his final arrest and trial, Mandela first mentions the linkage between his faith and the resistance movement. He does so with humor by recounting a prayer made by an African minister in Cape Town who said "that if the Lord did not show a little more initiative in leading the black man to salvation, the black man would have to take matters into his own two hands. Amen" (265). In these same years of 1961–62, Mandela tells of attending "the old-fashioned Bible-thumping services of these Zionist Christian ministers" near Durban (278). In brief, during the active political years of his long walk, Mandela mutes his Christianity and only remotely relates it to his leadership in the liberation movement.

During the next stage of his autobiography, his prison years, he continues this muted religious undercurrent. He mentions being happy to serve as godfather for the child of a friend (359), he attends Christian services of all denominations in prison, and he begins the section entiled "Beginning to Hope" with the long account of his continuing but quiet practice as a Methodist (ch. 71). Later, in 1984, during the negotiations with the government for his release and for recognition of the ANC, Mandela describes himself to the press very openly: "I told them that I was a Christian and had always been a Christian" (521). He goes on to distinguish his advocacy of the limited use of force to end apartheid as a genuine Christian alternative to the total nonviolence of Martin Luther King.

Although no commentator has accounted for this process of

muting his Christianity, it may not be as strange as it might seem to readers outside South Africa. The role of Christian churches in South African history is very complex, both in the great number of sects and in the variety of responses to political issues and apartheid. Although some Christian churches were active in the anti-apartheid movement (Mandela himself mentions Bishop Tutu, the Catholic Church, and others), the Afrikaners themselves were a strong Christian Dutch Reform group who tried to use parts of the Bible to justify the system. The array of Christian churches did not always agree on the best methods for challenging and transforming apartheid (Bramwell, Shrivastava). Among African peoples themselves, there were many Christian denominations and tribal religions, some of which favored the separate homeland system. Furthermore, many secular groups, especially the Communist Party and the Liberal Party, were strong opponents of apartheid and supporters of many goals of the ANC. It is likely, therefore, that Mandela deliberately muted his Christianity, without abandoning or modifying it, for the purpose of social and political cooperation and change. As a private mover and shaker in a multiracial, multicultural, and multireligous society, he retained what he called his lifelong identity as a Christian, but did so in a manner that seemed to him socially and politically most effective.

The fruits of this effectiveness are still growing. On the very day of his inauguration in 1994 as president of South Africa, Mandela pointed out in his speech the religious and racial cooperation that had brought an end to division and the beginning of an harmonious society: "In honoring those who fought to see this day arrive, we honor the best sons and daughters of all our people. We can count amongst them Africans, coloreds, whites, Indians, Muslims, Christians, Hindus, Jews—all of them united by a common vision of a better life for the people of this country" (Nyberg 66). The common vision of harmony, which emerged from Mandela's childhood experience with the council of elders at the Great Place, became the vision enlightening the procedures of the Truth and Reconcilation Commission begun in 1995. Although modeled on similar amnesty courts in Latin America, this commission also embodies the "common view of a better life" that served as the directional image on Mandela's long circular journey in history (Boraine).

REFERENCES

Boraine, Alex, Janet Levy, and Ronel Scheffer, ed. *Dealing with the Past: Truth and Reconciliation in South Africa.* Capetown: Institute for Democracy in South Africa, 1995.
Bramwell, Bevil. "Christianity and Change in South Africa." *Providence: Studies in Western Civilization* 3 (Fall 1995): 94–109.
Chapman, Michael. "Mandela, Africanism and Modernity: A Consideration of *Long Walk to Freedom.*" *Current Writing* 7 (Oct. 1995): 49–54.
Chidester, David. *Religions of South Africa.* London: Routledge, 1992.
Mandela, Nelson. *Long Walk to Freedom: The Autobiography of Nelson Mandela.* Boston: Little, Brown, 1995.
Nyberg, Richard. "Church Eyes New Mandela Government with Caution." *Christianity Today* 38 (June 20, 1994): 66–67.
Roberts, David. Review of *Long Walk to Freedom. National Review* 47 (Jan. 23, 1995): 72.
Sampson, Anthony. "The True Secrets of Leadership: Review of *Long Walk to Freedom.*" *Times Literary Supplement* 30 Dec. 1994: 32.
Shrivastava, A. K. *Churches and Apartheid.* Delhi: P.B.D. Pub., 1989.
"South Africa's Liberator." Rev. of *Long Walk to Freedom,* by Nelson Mandela. *The Economist* 10 Dec. 1994: 97.

CONCLUSION

What will be the future direction of spiritual autobiography? If we look only at the kaleidoscopic style of Wakefield's new journalism, we realize that it reflects the loosely structured wanderings of Malcolm X, Paul Cowan, and other late twentieth-century seekers. The twists in the spiritual pilgrimage toward Mystery become for these writers so unpredictable as to raise questions about the future of religious autobiography. Is the era of classical spiritual journeys exhausted? Will future religious conversions be merely chapters in the plotting of a secular lifeline? Will the effects of the cultural fusions and confusions of the 1960s make the traditional religious conversion story, with its roots in Augustine's *Confessions*, obsolete? Will the unresolved aesthetic–religious search of books like Kazantzakis's *Report to Greco* (1965) become the life pattern of the future? Whatever the answer to these questions, readers may well look for a greater variety of twists in the spiral of conversions, as foreshadowed by the unpredictable patterns of Cowan and Wakefield's stories. Certainly, the author's voice in the future will become more self-conscious of speaking in an evolving language under the suspicion of hidden influence from social and other subliminal sources. Perhaps the voice may try to disappear entirely, fearful of deconstructive readers ready to unravel the loose threads of an inconsistent plot. The cultural shifts and pressures arising from ethnic and gender awareness will undoubtedly bring about the emergence of more religious autobiographies by women and minority writers. Along with these will appear, one can expect, a greater awareness of environmental concerns (as in Annie Dillard), of ecumenical sensitivity (as in Wakefield), and of world religions (as in Kazantzakis). Perhaps Nelson Mandela's *Long Walk to Freedom* gives us one example of the direction of future religious journeys. In his autobiography, as we have noted, he preserves the traditional spiral pilgrimage structure, but incorporates significant differences. Without a long period of wandering, his story lacks the radical religious conversion from sinner to saint as found in the Augustinian tradition. Although his narrative includes both the traditional structure of a journey (the "long walk") and a battle (the trials), his life is dominated by his central conversion to social commitment to "freedom." All his other conversions—imaginative, moral, or religious—are subordinated to this central transformation. As Michael Chapman has suggested, Mandela's African tribal roots in community may have been his greatest legacy to the world. As our study of his directional image has shown, this communal dimension is also his greatest legacy to the tradition of spiritual autobiography. For from his sense of cosmic harmony, enriched by his Christianity and political awareness, came his efforts at reconciliation of all races, classes, religions, and peoples. His journey in a country where a "third world" people gains freedom from domination by "first" and "second" world forces has something crucial to teach the world of the next century. For in this journey to freedom, he achieves not separation from but reconciliation with the very people who were his colonizers. In his personal journey, Mandela learns to harmonize the classless ideals of the "second" world with the democratic ideals of the "first" world, but in a manner that is consonant with the communal ideals of his own people and the ecumenical ideals of his own experience. Thus, Mandela has given the world not merely an heroic story of a courageous political leader but a moral exemplum of the need to transform all levels of the human condition and personality to achieve full freedom and harmony. He provides a new form of classic spiritual autobiography. Although we can learn much from these more recent autobiographies, what will be the influence on life stories of the three great religious shifts of the final decades of the twentieth century—the rise of fundamentalism, the opening of Eastern Christianity after the collapse of the Soviet Union, and the emergence of Third World majorities in the major religions? Some may see in these movements the arrival of the "end of history," with the disappearance of ideological clashes and the beginning of merely pragmatic or local political conflicts. But it seems unlikely that the individual life journey will relinquish the metaphysical quest. Although some recent autobiographies suggest the dominance of the psychological or other one-dimensional story of the self, the power of the giant religious autobiographers of the past centry still persists. With roots in Day's ability to find God in the Staten Island waters or Black Elk's vision of the circle of sacred nature, with echoes of Merton, Cowan, and Mandela in their concern for social transformation, with reflections of Gandhi, Malcolm X, Merton, or Mandela in their openness to religious experience in other religions, the spiritual journey of the next century will not be radically incomprehensible to the reader of these modern classics. Certainly, the next generation will, like Wakefield, write more explicitly of their struggles for affective conversion than the more circumspect writers of the earlier twentieth century did. Certainly, the next generation will search for a more nuanced notion of the Divine than that found in the unphilosophical searches of Cowan and Wakefield. But whether this notion will return to that of the early Merton or move toward the silence of his later contemplative journals, all one can trust is that the future journey of religious autobiographers will be at least as profoundly engaging and mysteriously circuitous as those I have examined.

REFERENCE

Kazantzakis, Nikos. *Report to Greco*. Trans. P. A. Bien. New York: Simon & Schuster, 1965.

INDEX

CPSIA information can be obtained
at www.ICGtesting.com
Printed in the USA
LVOW12s0012230317

528185LV00001B/2/P